ArcGIS® 9

Editing in ArcMap™

DATA CREDITS

Graphical Editing Map: Wilson, North Carolina

Universal Data Editor Map, Editing in data view and layout view map: Greeley, Colorado

Context menus and shortcut keys map: P.F.R.A., Regina, Saskatchewan, Canada

CONTRIBUTING WRITERS
Rhonda Pfaff, Bob Booth, Jeff Shaner, Scott Crosier, Phil Sanchez, Andy MacDonald

Contents

3 Creating new features   45

4 Editing topology 119

8 Spatial adjustment   245

Introduction

In addition to mapmaking and map-based analysis, ESRI® ArcGIS® ArcMap™ is the application for creating and editing geographic data and tabular data. With ArcMap, you can edit features in shapefiles and geodatabases with one common user interface. ArcMap contains sophisticated, computer-aided design (CAD)-like editing tools that help you construct features quickly and easily while maintaining the spatial integrity of your geographic information system (GIS) database. ArcView® seats of ArcMap can be used to edit simple features in shapefiles and geodatabases. ArcView seats also let you create a temporary map topology that can be used to edit simple features that share geometry. ArcEditor™ and ArcInfo™ seats of ArcMap can be used to edit geometric networks and geodatabase topologies as well as simple features.

Whether you use ArcView or ArcInfo, you use the same editing tools in ArcMap to work on your geographic data. In cases where your organization has multiple users simultaneously editing on a shared geodatabase, ArcMap, in concert with ArcSDE®, provides the tools necessary to manage long editing transactions as well as to manage versions and resolve potential conflicts. ArcEditor and ArcInfo seats of ArcMap can check out features from a master geodatabase to a checkout geodatabase for disconnected editing.

Whether you use ArcView, ArcEditor, or ArcInfo, the goal of this book is to help you learn and use the editing capabilities in ArcMap for any level of geographic database maintenance. The next few pages highlight some of the features you will find invaluable while editing in ArcMap.

Rich suite of graphical editing tools

ArcMap helps you create and edit geographic features quickly and easily by including many of the graphic editing functions popular with the latest CAD editing packages.

Sketch construction tools in ArcMap will allow you to quickly and accurately edit street rights-of-way.

ArcGIS data editor

ArcMap lets you edit shapefiles and geodatabases. Also, you can edit an entire folder of data at once. ArcEditor and ArcInfo seats can take advantage of a geodatabase's coded value and range domains and validation to make editing attributes quicker and maintain high data quality.

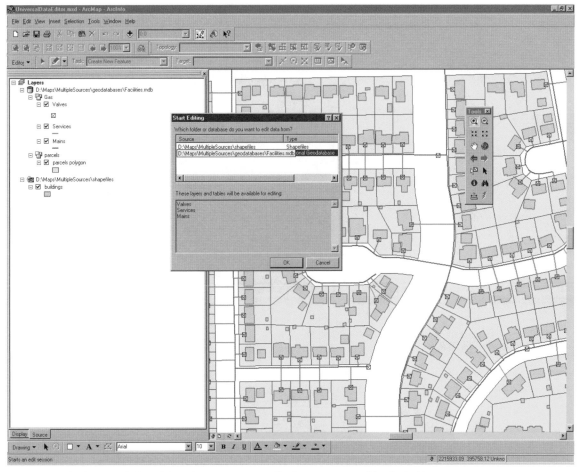

Pick the geodatabase or folder of data that you want to edit when you start editing in ArcMap.

Editing in data view and layout view

ArcMap provides two different ways to view a map: data view and layout view. Each view lets you look at and interact with the map in a different way. Data view hides all of the map elements on the layout such as titles, North arrows, and scalebars. In layout view, you'll see a virtual page upon which you can place and arrange map elements. You can edit your geographic data in either data view or layout view.

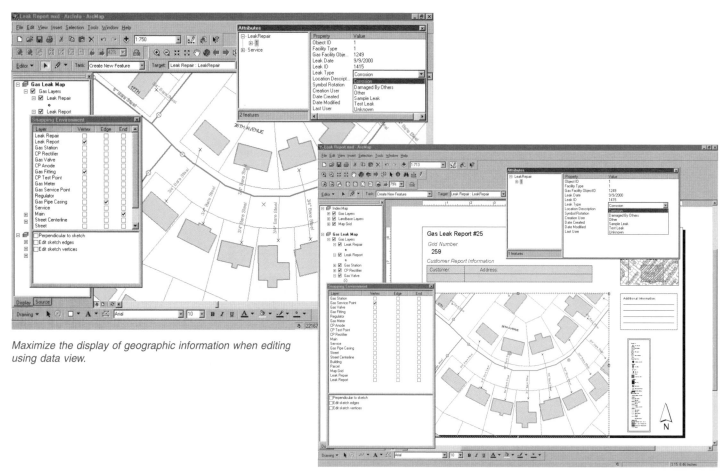

Maximize the display of geographic information when editing using data view.

When you are preparing a map, you can edit features directly using layout view.

Tools for editing and managing topologies

ArcMap provides tools to edit features that have topological relationships defined in a geodatabase or in a map topology. ArcView seats are limited to editing map topology, a simpler, temporary form of topology that allows shared parts of features to be simultaneously edited.

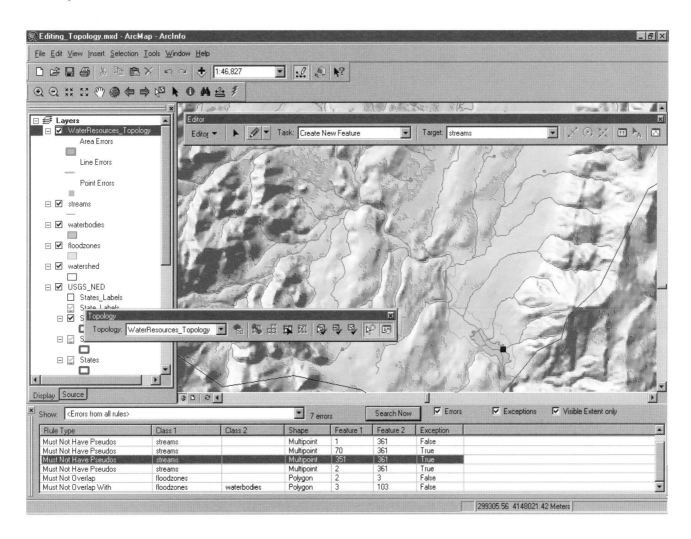

Tools for editing and managing networks in a geodatabase

ArcMap provides tools to edit geometric networks stored in a geodatabase.

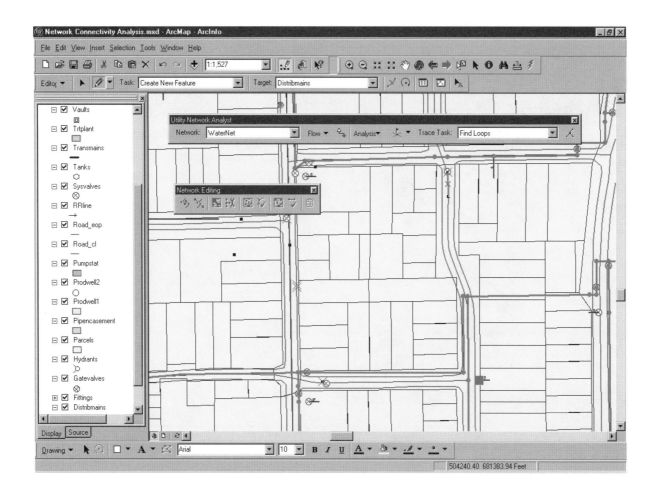

Context menus and shortcut keys for increased productivity

ArcMap contains numerous context menus and shortcut keys to help you create and edit features quickly.

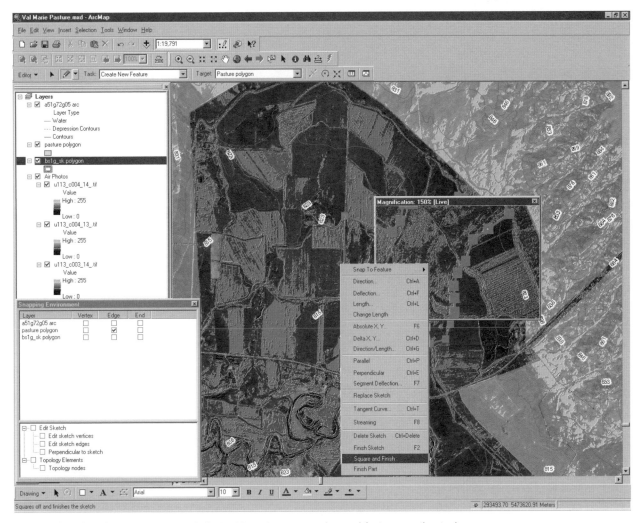

Use the Sketch tool context menu and shortcut keys to access advanced feature creation tools.

Tools for rubber sheeting, adjusting, and edgematching feature data

ArcMap provides tools to transform, adjust, rubber sheet, and edgematch feature data from different sources.

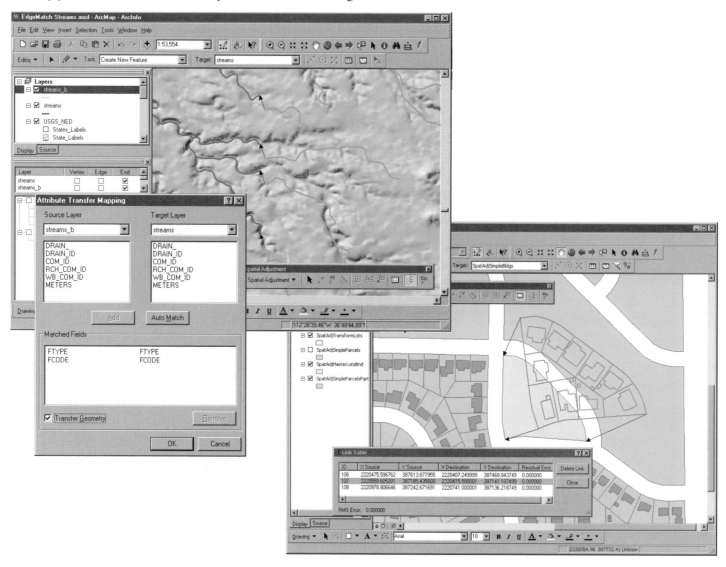

Multiuser editing with version management and conflict detection

If you have several users who need to edit the same data at the same time, ArcMap can help you manage versions of your ArcSDE geodatabase.

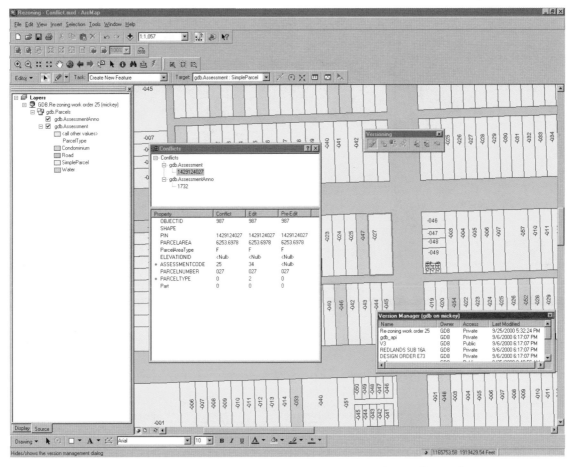

Sophisticated version management tools in ArcMap will help you maintain a multiuser editing environment.

Remote editing of data checked out from your versioned geodatabase

If you have people who need to work with part of your geodatabase away from your network, ArcEditor and ArcInfo seats allow you to check out features to a personal geodatabase, edit them in the field, and check them back into the master geodatabase upon their return.

Editing in projected space

If you've collected data from a variety of sources, chances are that not all layers contain the same coordinate system information. Using ArcMap, you can set the coordinate system for a data frame. As you add layers to your map, they are automatically transformed to that projection. That means that you can edit the shapes and attributes of a layer regardless of the coordinate system it was stored in.

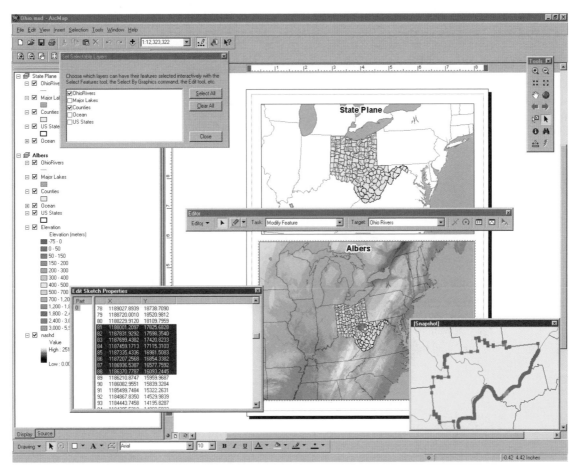

ArcMap has project on-the-fly capabilities that let you edit layers in the coordinate system that are most important to you without having to transform your data.

Tips on learning how to edit in ArcMap

If you're new to GIS, remember that you don't have to learn everything about editing in ArcMap to get immediate results. To learn how to edit your GIS data, see the *Geodatabase Workbook*. ArcMap comes with the data used in the tutorial, so you can follow along step by step at your computer. You can also read the tutorial without using your computer.

Finding answers to your questions

Like most people, your goal is to complete your tasks while investing a minimum amount of time and effort in learning how to use the software. You want intuitive, easy-to-use software that gives you immediate results, without having to read pages of documentation. However, when you do have a question, you want the answer quickly so you can complete your task. That's what this book is all about—getting you the answers you need, when you need them.

This book describes editing tasks—from basic to advanced—that you'll perform with ArcMap. Although you can read this book from start to finish, you'll likely use it more as a reference. When you want to know how to do a particular task, such as creating a new feature, just look it up in the table of contents or index. What you'll find is a concise, step-by-step description of how to complete the task. Some chapters also include detailed information that you can read if you want to learn more about the concepts behind the tasks. You may also refer to the glossary in this book if you come across any unfamiliar GIS terms or need to refresh your memory.

About this book

This book is designed to introduce editing in ArcMap and its capabilities. If you have never used a GIS before or feel you need to refresh your knowledge, please take some time to read *Getting Started with ArcGIS*, which you received in your ArcGIS package. It is not necessary to do so to continue with this book, but you should use it as a reference if you encounter tasks with which you are unfamiliar.

Getting help on your computer

In addition to this book, use the ArcGIS Desktop Help system to learn how to use ArcMap. To learn how to use the ArcGIS Desktop Help system, see *Using ArcMap*.

Contacting ESRI

If you need to contact ESRI for technical support, refer to 'Contacting Technical Support' in the 'Getting more help' section of the ArcGIS Desktop Help system. You can also visit ESRI on the Web at *www.esri.com* and *support.esri.com* for more information on ArcMap and ArcGIS.

ESRI education solutions

ESRI provides educational opportunities related to geographic information science, GIS applications, and technology. You can choose among instructor-led courses, Web-based courses, and self-study workbooks to find educational solutions that fit your learning style. For more information, go to *www.esri.com/ education*.

Editing basics

2

In addition to mapmaking and map analysis, ArcMap is also the application for creating and editing your spatial databases. ArcMap has tools to edit shapefiles and geodatabase feature datasets.

This chapter provides an introduction on how to edit in ArcMap and describes the basic tasks you need to know before you can start to create and edit spatial data. For instance, this chapter shows you how to perform such tasks as adding the Editor toolbar; adding other editing toolbars, such as the Map Cache, Advanced Editing, Spatial Adjustment, Topology, and Network Editing toolbars; starting and stopping an edit session; and selecting features.

An overview of the editing process

The following is a general overview of how to use ArcMap and the Editor toolbar to edit your data. Each of the following steps is outlined in detail in this chapter or other chapters in this book.

1. Start ArcMap.

2. Create a new map or open an existing one.

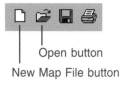

Open button

New Map File button

3. Add the data you want to edit to your map.

Add Data button

If there are no existing layers for the feature classes you want to edit, you can create them using ArcCatalog™. For more information on creating a feature layer, see *Using ArcCatalog*.

4. Add the Editor toolbar to ArcMap.

Editor Toolbar button

5. Click Start Editing from the Editor menu.

6. Create or modify features and/or their attributes.

7. Click Stop Editing from the Editor menu and click Yes when prompted to save your edits.

There is no need to save the map—all edits made to the database will automatically be reflected the next time you open the map.

The Editor toolbar

Edit tool:
Lets you select
features and
modify them.

Tool palette:
Use these
tools to create
a sketch.

Current Task
dropdown list:
The tasks in this list
work with a sketch
drawn with the
sketch construction
tools on the tool
palette.

Target layer
dropdown list:
Sets the layer to
which new
features will
belong.

Split tool:
Lets you
split a
segment at
a specific
location.

Attributes button:
Opens the
attributes dialog
box, which shows
attributes
for all selected
features.

Edit session
commands.

Rotate tool:
Lets you
rotate a
segment or
sketch to a
desired
orientation.

Sketch
Properties: Lets
you specify the
x,y locations of
the vertices in a
sketch.

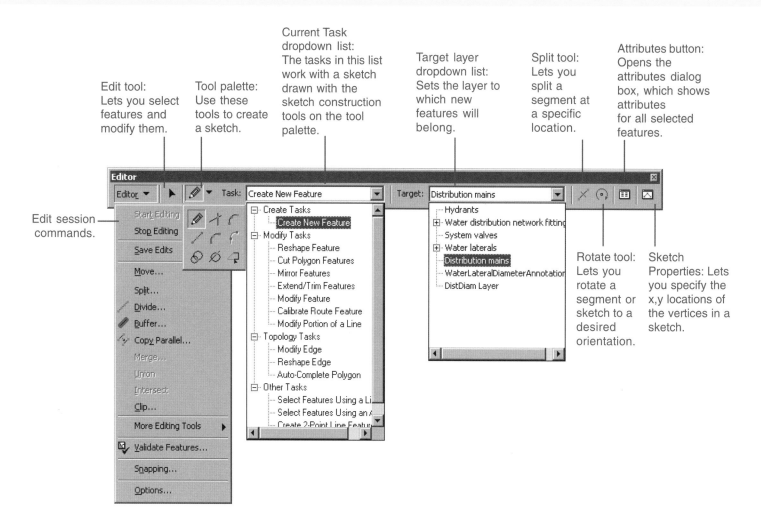

Exploring the Editor toolbar

This section shows you how editing in ArcMap helps you complete the tasks that you need to do. You'll learn about the types of data you can edit as well as the basics of creating and modifying features and their attributes.

The structure of vector datasets

ArcMap provides a common editing environment for features stored in geodatabase feature datasets and shapefiles.

When you edit data with ArcMap, you edit feature classes (collections of features) that the layers on your map represent.

Editing the feature classes lets you edit the actual data source, not just the representation on the map.

A feature class is a collection of the same type of features, for example, a collection of points or a collection of polygons.

A dataset is a collection of feature classes that share the same *spatial reference*. A dataset might be a collection of land base

---

Comparing the structure of vector datasets

	Geodatabase	Shapefile
Collections of datasets	A *geodatabase* is a collection of feature datasets.	A shapefile folder is a collection of shapefiles.
Datasets	A *feature dataset* is a collection of feature classes.	A *shapefile* has one shapefile feature class.
Collections of features	A *feature class* is a collection of features of the same type.	A shapefile feature class is a collection of shapefile features.
Features	Point, multipoint, polyline, polygon, annotation, dimension, and network.	Point, multipoint, line, and polygon.
Topology	Geodatabase datasets may contain topologies or a geometric network.	Map topology may be used to integrate and edit shapefile feature classes.

feature classes or a collection of utility feature classes. Shapefiles are an exception; they do not hold a collection of feature classes but only one shapefile feature class.

A collection of feature datasets is stored in a geodatabase. Shapefiles are stored in a shapefile folder. Although you may add multiple collections of datasets to your map, such as geodatabases, ArcInfo workspaces, and shapefile folders, you can only edit feature classes within one collection at a time. Coverage feature classes can't be edited with ArcMap.

What is a sketch and how does it work with a task?

A *sketch* is a shape you draw that performs various tasks when editing, such as adding new features, modifying features, and reshaping features. Tasks are listed in the Current Task dropdown list. You must create a sketch in order to complete a task.

For instance, the Create New Feature task uses a sketch you create to make the new feature.

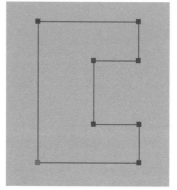

Building as sketch

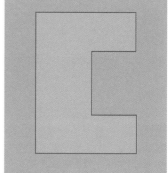

Building as feature

Current Task dropdown list

The Select Features Using a Line task uses a sketch you create to select features; the features the line intersects are selected.

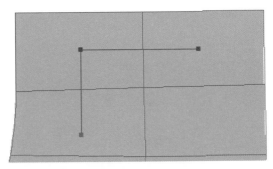

Sketch intersects parcels to be selected.

Parcels intersected by the sketch are now selected.

The Cut Polygon Features task uses a line sketch you draw to cut a polygon.

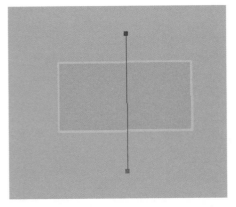

Sketch showing where the polygon is to be cut.

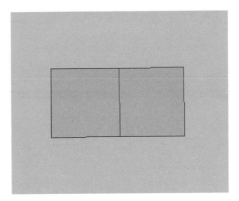

Polygon divided into two features where the sketch was drawn.

Creating new features

You can create three main types of features with the Editor toolbar: points, lines, and polygons.

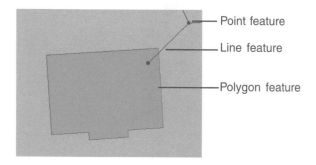

- Point feature
- Line feature
- Polygon feature

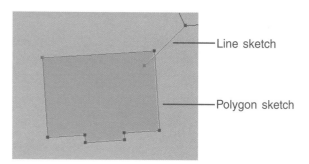

- Line sketch
- Polygon sketch

To create a line or polygon, you must first create a sketch. A sketch's shape is composed of all the vertices and segments of the feature. *Vertices* are the points at which the sketch changes direction, such as corners, and *segments* are the lines that connect the vertices.

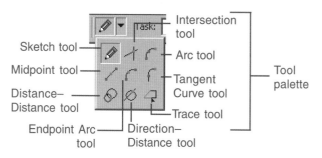

- Intersection tool
- Sketch tool
- Arc tool
- Midpoint tool
- Tangent Curve tool
- Distance–Distance tool
- Tool palette
- Endpoint Arc tool
- Direction–Distance tool
- Trace tool

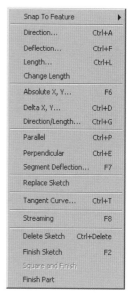

Snap To Feature	▶
Direction...	Ctrl+A
Deflection...	Ctrl+F
Length...	Ctrl+L
Change Length	
Absolute X, Y...	F6
Delta X, Y...	Ctrl+D
Direction/Length...	Ctrl+G
Parallel	Ctrl+P
Perpendicular	Ctrl+E
Segment Deflection...	F7
Replace Sketch	
Tangent Curve...	Ctrl+T
Streaming	F8
Delete Sketch	Ctrl+Delete
Finish Sketch	F2
Square and Finish	
Finish Part	

Sketch tool context menu

You can create a sketch by creating the vertices and segments that make up the features. Vertices are marked in green, with the last vertex added marked in red.

The Sketch tool is the tool you use most often to create a sketch. It has an accompanying context menu that helps you place vertices and segments more accurately. The Arc tool, the Distance–Distance tool, and the Intersection tool—located with the Sketch tool on the tool palette—also help you create vertices and segments using other construction methods.

When you're creating a new feature, the target layer determines in which layer a new feature will belong. After copying a feature, the target layer is also the layer you will be pasting into. When you're editing existing features, the target layer is the one you will be modifying or reshaping.

The Target layer dropdown list contains the names of all the layers in the datasets with which you're working. Subtypes are also listed, if applicable. For instance, if you set the target layer to Buildings: Commercial, any features you create will be part of the Commercial subtype of the Buildings layer.

Target layer dropdown list

You must set the target layer whenever you're creating new features—whether you're creating them with the Sketch tool, by copying and pasting, or by buffering another feature.

Modifying features

For every feature on the map, there is an alternate form, a sketch. In the same way that you must create a sketch to create a feature, to modify a feature you must modify its sketch. Because the vertices are visible in a sketch, you can edit the feature in detail; you can move the vertices, delete them, or add new ones using the Sketch context menu.

Besides editing a feature by working with its sketch, you can also use another sketch you create to modify the feature for certain tasks. An example of this type of task is Cut Polygon Features, where a sketch you construct is used to divide one polygon into two.

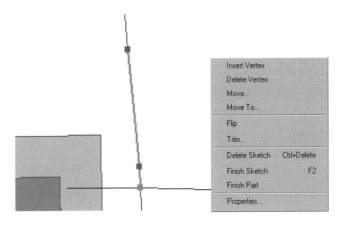

When you edit a feature's sketch, you edit its vertices using the Sketch context menu.

Simple modifications to features, such as moving, copying, or deleting, can be made by selecting the feature and choosing the appropriate tool or command.

Editing attributes

Attributes can be created or edited in the *Attributes dialog box.* After selecting the features whose attributes you want to edit, click the Attributes button on the Editor toolbar to see the dialog box.

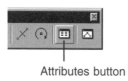

Attributes button

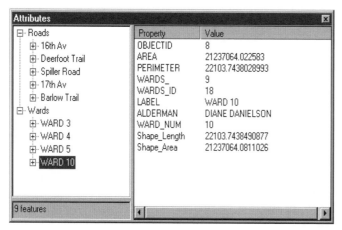

Attributes dialog box

Editing keyboard shortcuts

Keyboard *shortcuts* are associated with a number of the editing tools and commands. You can use keyboard shortcuts to make editing quicker and more efficient. Shortcuts common to all Editor tools can be used with any editing tool, while the shortcuts listed for a specific tool are only used with that tool.

Shortcuts common to all editing tools

Z	Zoom In
X	Zoom Out
C	Pan
V	Show vertices
Esc	Cancel
Ctrl + Z	Undo
Ctrl + Y	Redo
Spacebar	Suspend snapping

Edit tool

Shift	Add to/Remove from selection
Ctrl	Move the selection anchor
N	Next selected feature

Annotation-related shortcuts used with the Edit tool

E	Toggle between Sketch tool, Edit tool, and Edit Annotation tool

Edit Annotation tool

Shift	Add to/Remove from selection
Ctrl	Move the selection anchor
N	Next selected feature

R	Toggle to/from rotate mode
F	Toggle to/from follow feature mode
E	Toggle between Sketch tool, Edit tool, and Edit Annotation tool
L	Flip selected annotation features 180 degrees when in follow feature mode
O	Open Follow Feature Options dialog box when in follow feature mode
Tab	Toggle annotation placement between left side and right side when in follow feature mode
P	Toggle annotation placement angle between parallel and perpendicular when in follow feature mode

Sketch tool

Ctrl + A	Direction
Ctrl + F	Deflection
Ctrl + L	Length
F6	Absolute X,Y
Ctrl + D	Delta X,Y
Ctrl + G	Direction/Length
Ctrl + P	Parallel
Ctrl + E	Perpendicular
F7	Segment deflection
Ctrl + T	Tangent curve
F8	Streaming
Ctrl + Delete	Delete sketch
F2	Finish sketch
T	Show tolerance

Annotation-related shortcuts used with the Sketch tool

E   Toggle between Sketch tool, Edit tool, and Edit Annotation tool

A   Activate the Text box on the Annotation toolbar so you can change the text for constructing new annotation

S   Activate the Symbol box on the Annotation toolbar so you can toggle between defined annotation symbols

Ctrl + W Find Text: Populate the Text box on the Annotation toolbar with a text expression from a feature under the cursor position. If the target is a feature-linked annotation feature class, text is derived only from a feature in the origin feature class. With a standard annotation feature class as the target, the text is based on the label expression of the layer containing the first visible and selectable feature.

O   Open Follow Feature Options dialog box when creating new annotation in follow feature mode

L   Flip selected annotation features 180 degrees when creating new annotation in follow feature mode

P   Toggle annotation placement angle between parallel and perpendicular when creating new annotation in follow feature mode

Tab   Toggle annotation placement between left side and right side when creating new annotation in follow feature mode

Topology Edit tool

Shift   Add to/Remove from selection

Ctrl   Move the selection anchor

N   Select nodes

E   Select edges

S   Split and move node

Fix Topology Error tool

Shift   Add to/Remove from selection

Scale and Rotate tools

A   Set rotate angle

S   Toggle secondary anchor

Trace tool

Tab   Trace the other side of an edge

O   Open Trace Options dialog box

Endpoint Arc tool

R   Radius

Direction–Distance tool

D or A Direction

D or R Distance

Tab   Change location

Distance–Distance tool

D or R Distance

Tab   Change location

The Advanced Editing toolbar

Note: Some tools on the Advanced Editing toolbar are not available with ArcView.

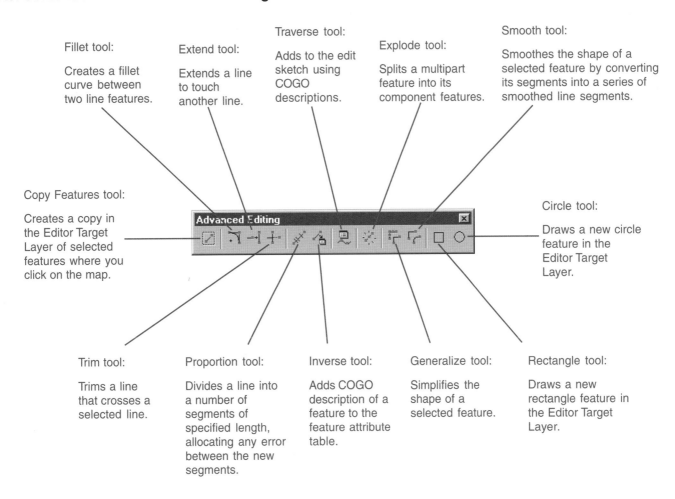

Fillet tool:

Creates a fillet curve between two line features.

Extend tool:

Extends a line to touch another line.

Traverse tool:

Adds to the edit sketch using COGO descriptions.

Explode tool:

Splits a multipart feature into its component features.

Smooth tool:

Smoothes the shape of a selected feature by converting its segments into a series of smoothed line segments.

Copy Features tool:

Creates a copy in the Editor Target Layer of selected features where you click on the map.

Circle tool:

Draws a new circle feature in the Editor Target Layer.

Trim tool:

Trims a line that crosses a selected line.

Proportion tool:

Divides a line into a number of segments of specified length, allocating any error between the new segments.

Inverse tool:

Adds COGO description of a feature to the feature attribute table.

Generalize tool:

Simplifies the shape of a selected feature.

Rectangle tool:

Draws a new rectangle feature in the Editor Target Layer.

Adding editing toolbars

Before editing geographic feature data within ArcMap, you must first add the Editor toolbar.

Tip

Adding the Editor toolbar from the Tools menu
You can also add the Editor toolbar from the Tools menu. Click Tools and click the Editor Toolbar button.

Tip

Adding the Editor toolbar from the View menu
You can also add the Editor toolbar by clicking the View menu, pointing to Toolbars, and checking Editor.

Tip

Adding the Editor toolbar using the Customize dialog box
Click the Tools menu and click Customize. Click the Toolbars tab and check Editor.

Adding the Editor toolbar

1. Start ArcMap.
2. Click the Editor Toolbar button to display the Editor toolbar.
3. Click the toolbar's title bar and drag it to the top of the ArcMap application window.

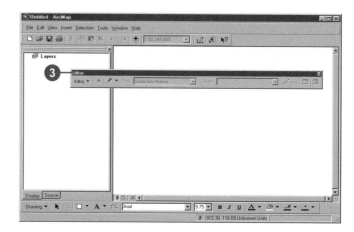

Adding other editing toolbars

1. Click Editor, point to More Editing Tools, and click the toolbar you want to add.

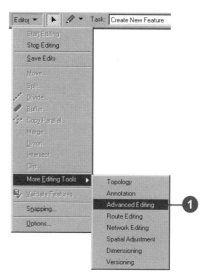

Upgrading a geodatabase

Geodatabases built using previous versions of ArcGIS do not support some of the newer functions of ArcGIS.

If your geodatabase was developed using a previous version of ArcGIS, you may wish to upgrade your geodatabase.

Tip

Creating a backup copy of your geodatabase

Bear in mind that once a geodatabase is upgraded, previous versions of ArcGIS can view, but cannot edit, the geodatabase. For this reason, you may wish to make a copy of the geodatabase and upgrade the copy, thus leaving you with both an original and an upgraded geodatabase.

1. Start ArcCatalog.
2. Right-click the geodatabase you want to upgrade and click Properties.
3. Click the General tab.
4. Click Upgrade Personal Geodatabase.
5. Click OK.

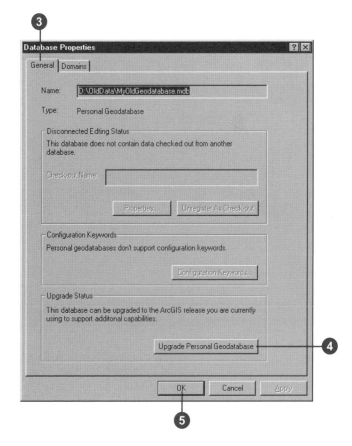

Adding the data you want to edit

Before you can start editing, you must add the data you want to edit to your map. In ArcMap, you can edit feature data in shapefiles or geodatabases.

Tip

Stopping the drawing of data
You can stop the drawing process without clearing the map by pressing the Esc key.

Tip

Loading data from a geodatabase
You can import features from a geodatabase into a layer on your map using the Load Objects command. For more information, see Building a Geodatabase.

1. Start ArcMap.

2. Click the Add Data button.

3. Navigate to the location of your data and click Add.

   The data is added to your map.

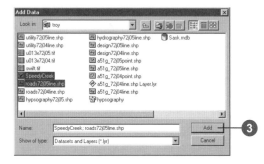

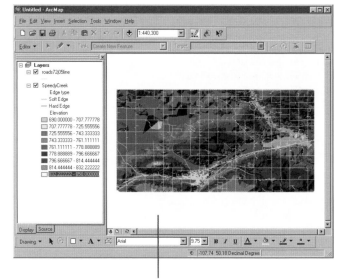

Data is added to the map.

Starting and stopping an edit session

All editing takes place within an *edit session*. To begin, click Start Editing on the Editor menu. The edits you make are immediately visible on your map but are not saved to the database until you choose to do so.

If you're working with large amounts of data, you can speed up the editing and selection of features by creating a map cache. To learn more, see 'Managing the map cache' in this chapter.

When you're finished editing, you can save any changes you've made or quit editing without saving. You can also save the edits you've made at any time by clicking Save Edits on the Editor menu.

Tip

Editing a map with more than one collection of datasets

You can only edit one collection of datasets at a time. These can be geodatabases or folders containing a collection of shapefiles. If your map contains more than one collection, when you choose Start Editing you will be prompted to choose which one you want to edit.

Starting an edit session

1. Start ArcMap and add the Editor toolbar.

2. Click Editor and click Start Editing.

   The Editor toolbar is now active.

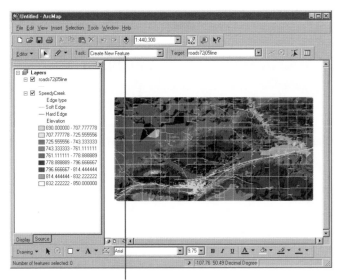

The Editor toolbar is now active.

Tip

Editing a map with more than one data frame

If your map contains more than one data frame, you will be editing the data frame that is active when you choose Start Editing. To edit a different data frame, you must choose Stop Editing, then choose Start Editing with the desired data frame active.

For a discussion of data frames, see Using ArcMap.

Tip

Editing in layout view

You can also edit data in a map that you're preparing. Click the View menu and click Layout View. For more information about working in layout view, see Using ArcMap.

Saving your edits in the middle of an edit session

1. Click Editor.

2. Click Save Edits.

   Any edits you have made are saved to the database.

Stopping an edit session

1. Click Editor and click Stop Editing.

2. To save changes, click Yes. To quit without saving, click No.

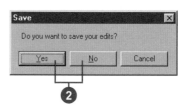

Managing the map cache

If you're working with data stored in a personal or ArcSDE geodatabase, building a *map cache* can often speed up editing as well as selecting, labeling, and drawing features. The map cache improves the performance of your edit session and also reduces the load on the server itself in a multiuser environment.

In general, when editing data in a geodatabase, especially network data, you should use the map cache. The map cache places features in the current display extent into memory on your local machine. The features can be accessed much faster from memory than from the server.

The auto-cache can be useful if you are going to be working in a series of different geographic areas and you don't want to rebuild the cache for each area. It is also convenient when you don't know the exact bounds of the area you want to cache. Since auto-caching may hinder performance, you should set an auto-cache minimum scale.

Adding the Map Cache toolbar

1. Click View and point to Toolbars.

2. Click Map Cache.

   The Map Cache toolbar appears.

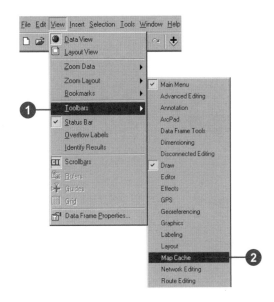

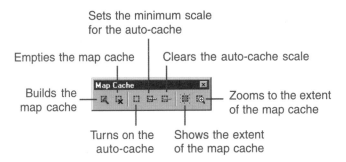

Sets the minimum scale for the auto-cache

Empties the map cache

Clears the auto-cache scale

Builds the map cache

Zooms to the extent of the map cache

Turns on the auto-cache

Shows the extent of the map cache

Building a map cache

1. Add data stored in a geodatabase to your map.

2. Pan or zoom to the area on the map that you want to work with.

3. Click the Build Map Cache button on the Map Cache toolbar.

   The features in the current extent are held in memory locally.

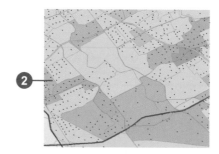

Setting the auto-cache minimum scale

1. Zoom out just beyond the scale at which you'll be working.

2. Click the Set Auto-Cache Scale button on the Map Cache toolbar.

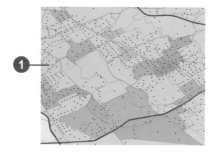

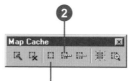

You can click the Auto-Cache button to turn auto-caching on or off.

Changing the options of the Task menu

Many times your project may call for specific editing tasks to be used more than others. Task options can be added to or removed from the Task dropdown menu. This will simplify your editing interface and facilitate your selection process.

Modifying the Task dropdown menu

1. Click Editor and click Options.

2. Click the Edit Tasks tab.

3. To remove tasks, select the task to be removed and click Remove.

4. To add tasks, click Add.

5. On the Add Tasks dialog box, select the tasks to add and click OK.

   The Task dropdown menu will be modified according to the changes made.

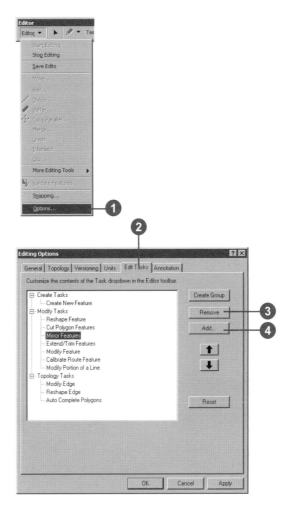

Selecting features

Selecting features identifies the features on which you want to perform certain operations. For example, before you move, delete, or copy a feature, you must select it. You must also select features before you can view their attributes.

You can select features in several different ways, either by clicking them with the Edit tool or by creating a line or a polygon that intersects the features you want to select. The number of features selected is shown immediately after you make the selection, in the lower-left corner of the ArcMap window. ▶

Tip
Selecting more than one feature
To select more than one feature, hold down the Shift key while you click the features. You can also use the Edit tool to draw a box around a group of features.

Tip
Removing features from the selection
To remove features from the selection set, hold down the Shift key while you click the features.

Selecting features using the Edit tool

1. Click the Edit tool.

2. Move the pointer over a feature and click.

   The selected feature is highlighted.

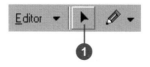

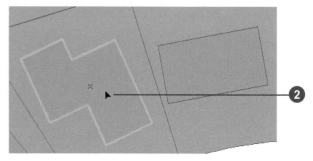

The selected building is highlighted.

The small "x" located in the center of the selected features is the *selection anchor*. The selection anchor is used when rotating features, moving features using snapping, and scaling features.

You can choose which layers you can select by choosing Set Selectable Layers from the Selection menu and using the *Selectable Layers list*.

For example, suppose you wanted to select a large number of buildings by drawing a box around them but selected a parcel by mistake as you drew the selection box. To avoid this, you might uncheck the Parcels layer in the Selectable Layers list so that parcels cannot be selected.

Tip

Adding options to the Task dropdown menu

Tasks on the Task dropdown menu can be added or removed from the selection on the Edit Options dialog box under the Edit Tasks tab. For further details, see 'Modifying the Task dropdown menu' in this chapter.

See Also

For more information on creating a line, see Chapter 3, 'Creating new features'.

Selecting features using a line

1. Click the Task dropdown arrow and click Select Features Using a Line.

2. Click the tool palette dropdown arrow and click the Sketch tool or any of the other construction tools in the tool palette.

3. Construct a line that intersects the features you want to select.

   The features that the line intersects are now selected.

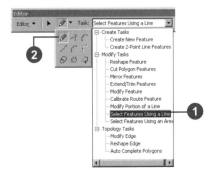

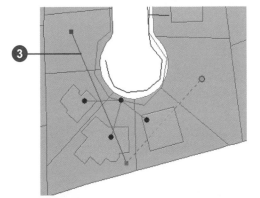

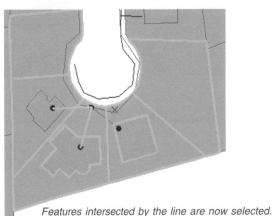

Features intersected by the line are now selected.

Selecting features using a polygon

1. Click the Task dropdown arrow and click Select Features Using an Area.

2. Click the tool palette dropdown arrow and click the Sketch tool or any of the other construction tools in the tool palette.

3. Construct a polygon that intersects the features you want to select.

   The features that intersect with the polygon you created are now selected.

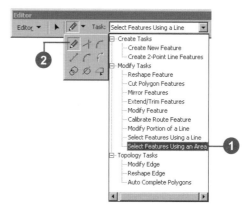

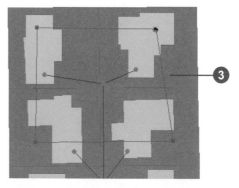

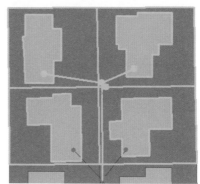

Features that intersect with the area are now selected.

Adding the Selection tab to the ArcMap table of contents

You can quickly change the selectable layers from the ArcMap table of contents if you add the Selection tab. You can add the Selection tab to the table of contents from the Table of Contents tab of the Tools > Options dialog box.

Making a layer selectable

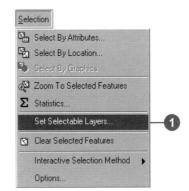

1. Click Selection and click Set Selectable Layers.

2. Click the check boxes next to the layer names you want to be able to select. Uncheck the boxes next to the names you don't want to be able to select.

   Layers whose names are unchecked are still visible in your map but cannot be selected.

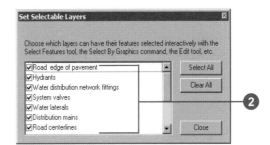

Moving features

You can move features in three different ways: by dragging; by specifying delta x,y coordinates; or by rotating.

Dragging is the easiest way to move a feature. Use this method when you have a general idea of where you want to move the feature.

Specify delta x,y coordinates when you want to move a feature to a precise location. ArcMap uses the current location of the selected feature or features as the origin (0,0) and moves them from that location according to the coordinates you specify. ▶

Tip

Avoiding accidental moves
The sticky move tolerance allows you to set a minimum number of pixels your pointer must move on the screen before a selected feature is moved. This can be a useful way to prevent features from being accidentally moved small distances when they are clicked with the Edit tool. You can set the sticky move tolerance on the General tab of the Editing Options dialog box.

Dragging a feature

1. Click the Edit tool.
2. Click the feature or features you want to move.
3. Click and drag the feature or features to the desired location.

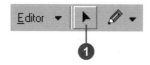

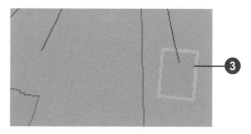

The selected building is dragged to a new location.

The coordinates are measured in map units. The graphic below illustrates the change in location when delta x,y coordinates of 2,3 are specified for a building.

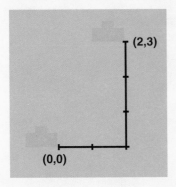

In the example above, the building is moved up and to the right, as positive coordinate values are specified. To move the building left or down, you would specify negative values.

You can rotate features in ArcMap using the Rotate tool. After selecting the features, drag the mouse pointer so that the features rotate to the desired position. Features rotate around the selection anchor, the small x located in the center of selected features.

If you want to move a feature to a precise location in relation to another feature, you can use the snapping environment. For example, you can move a ▶

Moving a feature relative to its current location

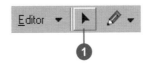

1. Click the Edit tool.

2. Click the feature or features you want to move.

3. Click Editor and click Move. ▶

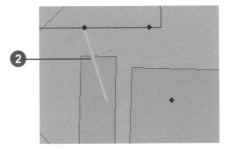

parcel and have one of its corners jump, or snap, precisely to a corner of another parcel. Simply move the parcel's selection anchor to its corner vertex after setting the appropriate snapping properties. Then move the parcel toward its new location until the selection anchor snaps to the corner vertex of the other parcel. Snapping is discussed in Chapter 3, 'Creating new features'.

Tip

Moving the selection anchor

To move the selection anchor, move the pointer over it, press the Ctrl key, and drag the selection anchor to the desired location.

Tip

Undoing a move

You can undo any edit you make to a feature by clicking the Undo button on the ArcMap Standard toolbar.

4. Type the desired coordinates and press Enter.

   The feature is moved according to the specified coordinates.

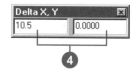

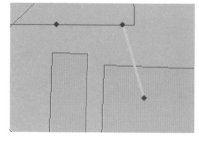

The feature is moved 10.5 map units to the right.

Rotating by degree

To specify the exact amount of rotation, click the Rotate tool, press A, and type the number of degrees. A positive number rotates the feature in the clockwise direction, a negative number in the counter-clockwise direction.

Rotating with snapping

If you want to rotate a feature until a point on it snaps to a feature specified in the current snapping environment, add a secondary selection anchor and drag it to the part of the feature that you want snapped to another feature. You can add a secondary selection anchor by pressing the S key when using the Rotate tool. The secondary selection anchor also works with the Scale tool.

Rotating a point's symbology

If your data already has a field that contains the rotation angle for each point symbol, you can use ArcMap to rotate the symbology.

Right-click the point layer name in the map's table of contents and click Properties. Click the Symbology tab. Click the Advanced button, then click Rotation. From the dropdown list, choose the field that contains the rotation angle. Click the option that describes how you want that angle calculated.

Rotating a feature

1. Click the Edit tool.

2. Click the feature or features you want to rotate.

3. Click the Rotate tool.

4. Click anywhere on the map and drag the pointer to rotate the feature to the desired position.

   The feature or features rotate around the selection anchor. You can drag the selection anchor to a new location to change the center of rotation.

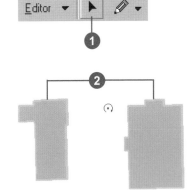

The selected features are rotated.

Copying and pasting features

To copy an existing feature, use the tools on the ArcMap Standard toolbar. From the Target layer dropdown list, choose the layer containing the type of features you want the new feature to be—for example, a building.

You can copy a feature and paste it as part of another layer, but it must be the same type of layer—point, line, or polygon—as the one from which you copied. There is one exception to this rule—you can copy polygons into a line layer.

Attributes from the original feature are only copied to the new feature if you are copying and pasting within the same layer.

See Also

For more information on attributes, see Chapter 9, 'Editing attributes'. You can also see Using ArcMap.

1. Click the Target layer dropdown arrow and click the layer containing the type of features you want the new features to be.

2. Click the Edit tool.

3. Click the feature or features you want to copy.

4. Click the Copy button.

5. Click the Paste button.

   The feature is pasted on top of the original feature.

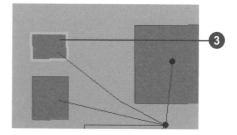

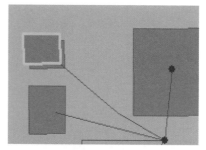

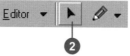

The selected feature is pasted on top of the original feature.

Deleting features

To delete a feature from the map and from the database, use the Delete button on the ArcMap Standard toolbar.

Tip

Deleting features using the Delete key

You can also press the Delete key on the keyboard to remove selected features.

1. Click the Edit tool.
2. Click the feature or features you want to delete.
3. Click the Delete button.

    The selected features are deleted.

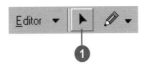

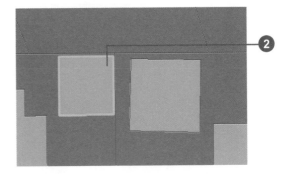

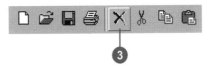

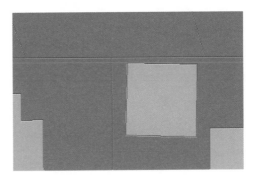

The selected building is deleted.

Setting the number of decimal places used for reporting measurements

When creating or editing a feature with the Sketch tool, you can use the Sketch tool context menu to view such measurements as the distance between two vertices, the angle between two segments, or the current coordinate location of the pointer.

By default, ArcMap displays these measurements using three decimal places. However, you can easily change the number of decimal places displayed. After you set the number of decimal places, ArcMap will report all measurements using that number of decimal places.

1. Click Editor and click Options.
2. Click the General tab.
3. Type the number of decimal places you want to use.
4. Click OK.

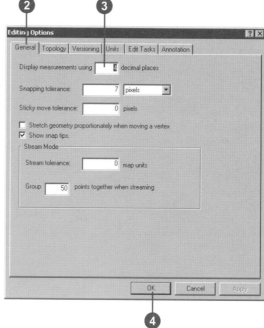

Creating new features

3

It's easy to create a wide array of new features using the editing sketch construction tools. To begin, simply specify the layer in which you want to create the new feature. Then, use the appropriate tool to digitize the vertices of the feature.

With the editing tools, you can create new point, line, or polygon features for many practical purposes. Using the Sketch tool and its accompanying context menu, you can add a water main perpendicular to an existing water main in a subdivision. The Distance–Distance tool lets you create a land parcel that begins 55 meters from one corner of an existing lot and ends 40 meters from another lot corner. Creating a cul-de-sac is simplified using the Arc tool to create a circular arc curve. With the Intersection tool, you can add a parcel to a subdivision by establishing a corner vertex using segments of an adjoining parcel.

Using the editing tools, you can create a variety of features by constructing segments at specific angles and of specific lengths. You can create features that are parallel or perpendicular to other features. You can also create multipoint features, such as a system of oil wells, and multipart features, such as a group of islands that forms a country or state.

These are just a few examples of how you can use ArcMap to easily and accurately create new features for your database.

How to create a new feature

To create a new feature using ArcMap, you create an edit sketch. A *sketch* is a shape that you draw by digitizing vertices. You can use a sketch to complete various tasks; these tasks are listed in the Task dropdown list shown below.

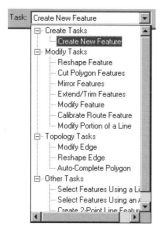

Task dropdown list

Tasks you can complete with a sketch include creating new features, modifying features, extending or trimming features, and reshaping features.

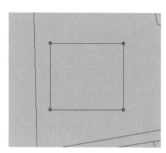

Building as sketch

Building as feature

This chapter focuses on using sketches to create new features. When the current task setting is Create New Feature, the shape you create becomes the new feature.

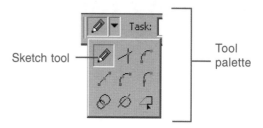

A sketch is composed of *vertices*—the points at which the sketch changes direction, such as corners—and *segments*—the lines that connect the vertices. You create a sketch using the Sketch tool located on the tool palette.

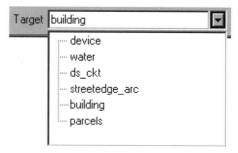

Target layer dropdown list

The type of feature you create is determined by the setting of the Target layer dropdown list. This list contains the names of all the layers in the datasets with which you're working.

Choose the layer to which you want to add new features before you start to create them.

To create point features, click once on the map. To create line or polygon features (see the example below), use the Sketch tool to click on the map to digitize the vertices that make up that feature.

To create the last vertex and finish the sketch, double-click with the mouse. After you finish the sketch, ArcMap adds the final segment of the sketch, and the sketch turns into a feature.

Of course, you won't always be able to place vertices or segments interactively. When you're using the Sketch tool, you can see the Sketch tool's *context menu*. You can access this menu when you right-click the mouse away from the sketch you're creating. The menu has choices to help you place the

1. Click here to place the first vertex.

2. Click here to place the second vertex.

3. Click here to place the third vertex.

4. Double-click here to place the last vertex and finish the sketch.

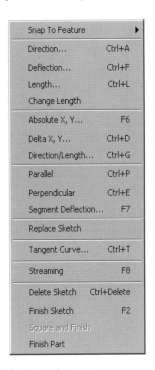

Sketch tool context menu

vertices and segments exactly where you want them. For example, you can set a segment to be a certain length or angle, or create a vertex at a specific x,y coordinate location.

All the tools on the tool palette help you create a sketch. Three tools use more specific construction methods to create either points or vertices: the Distance–Distance tool, Direction–Distance tool, and the Intersection tool.

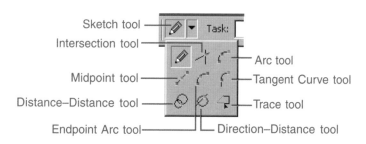

The Distance–Distance tool lets you create a point or vertex at the intersection of two distances from two other points. You

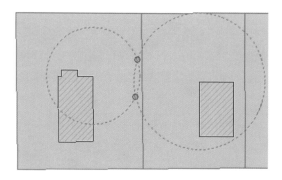

The Distance–Distance tool allows you to choose one of two intersection points of two circles; the size of the circles is determined by the radius you set.

might use this tool to place a new electrical primary based on field measurements. Suppose you know that the next point for the primary is 50 feet from one building corner and 75 feet from another.

The Distance–Distance tool creates two circles based on these distances and finds two possible intersection points where the primary can be placed.

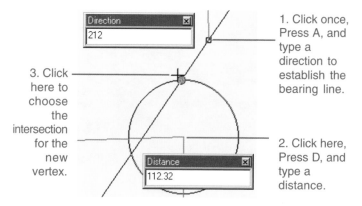

The Direction–Distance tool, like the Distance–Distance tool, allows you to create a vertex using a distance from a known point, plus information from another point. Instead of using a distance from the second point, the Direction–Distance tool uses a direction from a known point to define a bearing line. You can choose which of the intersection points will be the new vertex.

You could use the Direction–Distance tool to place a tree location point based on field notes stating that the tree is on a bearing of 212 degrees from a fence corner and 112 feet from the northeast corner of a building.

The Intersection tool creates a point or vertex at the place where two segments would intersect if extended far enough.

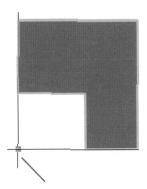

The Intersection tool creates a vertex here— at the place where the two segments would intersect.

Suppose you want to create a parking lot adjoining an L-shaped building. The outer corner of the lot should be located at the point where the two outermost walls of the building would intersect if they were extended. You could use the Intersection tool to find this implied intersection point and create the corner vertex of the lot.

The Midpoint tool lets you define the location of the next vertex by clicking two points—the new vertex is placed at the midpoint of the line between these points.

1. Click once to establish the first point.

2. Click here to establish the second point.

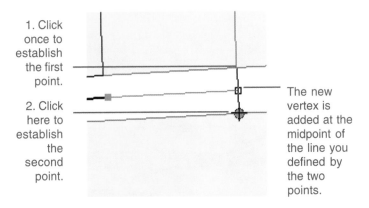

The new vertex is added at the midpoint of the line you defined by the two points.

You might use the Midpoint tool to place the next vertex of a street centerline midway between the parcels on either side of the street.

The Arc tool helps you create a segment that is a circular arc.

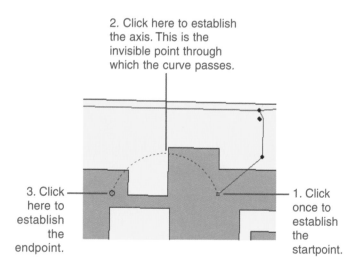

2. Click here to establish the axis. This is the invisible point through which the curve passes.

3. Click here to establish the endpoint.

1. Click once to establish the startpoint.

The Endpoint Arc tool, like the Arc tool, helps you create a segment that is a circular arc. The Endpoint Arc tool allows you to specify the start and endpoints of the curve, then define a radius for the curve.

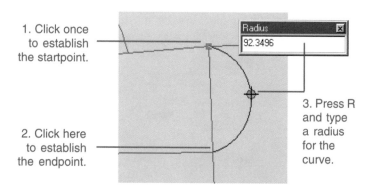

1. Click once to establish the startpoint.

2. Click here to establish the endpoint.

Radius
92.3496

3. Press R and type a radius for the curve.

The Tangent Curve tool helps you create a segment that is a circular arc. This tool adds a segment that is tangential to the previously sketched segment. The Tangent Curve tool can only be used if you have already sketched a segment using one of the other sketch tools.

Once a line segment has been sketched, the Tangent Curve tool will draw a circular arc off of the previous line segment.

The Trace tool helps you create segments that follow along existing segments. Suppose you want to add a new road casing feature that is offset 15 feet from the front of a parcel subdivision.

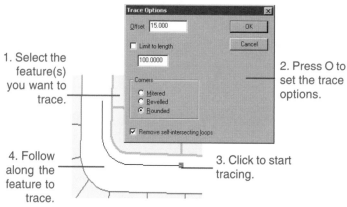

1. Select the feature(s) you want to trace.

Trace Options
Offset 15.000
OK
Cancel
☐ Limit to length
100.0000
Corners
○ Mitered
○ Bevelled
⦿ Rounded
☑ Remove self-intersecting loops

2. Press O to set the trace options.

3. Click to start tracing.

4. Follow along the feature to trace.

You could use the Trace tool to trace along the existing line features instead of typing the angle and length of each segment.

You can use any combination of the following methods for creating vertices or segments to create a new line or polygon feature:

- Sketch tool
- Sketch context menu
- Distance–Distance tool
- Direction–Distance tool
- Intersection tool
- Midpoint tool
- Arc tool
- Endpoint Arc tool
- Tangent Curve tool
- Trace tool

ArcMap has another context menu—the Sketch context menu—that works more directly with the sketch as a whole. With this menu, you can add, move, or delete vertices; switch the direction of the sketch; reduce its length; or display the properties of the sketch shape.

From the properties dialog box, you can remove parts from a multipart feature, remove many vertices in one operation, add points, and/or modify x,y values as well as m- and z-values. The Sketch context menu is available when you right-click while the pointer is positioned over any part of the sketch using any tool. It differs from the Sketch tool context menu, which you can access only when working with the Sketch tool and when you right-click away from your sketch.

Sketch context menu

Creating point features and vertices

You can think of vertices as being much the same as point features, except that vertices are connected by segments and make up line or polygon features.

Point features and vertices are created using the same methods. The Target layer setting determines whether you're creating a point feature or a vertex that is part of a line or polygon sketch.

You can create point features or vertices of a sketch in several different ways:

- By digitizing freehand with the Sketch tool (you can also use the snapping environment to help)

- By using Absolute X, Y or Delta X, Y on the Sketch tool context menu ▶

Tip

The snapping environment can help you create points and vertices

The snapping environment can help you create points or vertices at more exact locations relative to other features. For more information, see 'Using the snapping environment' in this chapter.

Creating a point or vertex by digitizing

1. Click the Task dropdown arrow and click Create New Feature.

2. Click the Target layer dropdown arrow and click a point layer.

3. Click the tool palette dropdown arrow and click the Sketch tool.

4. Click on the map to create the point.

   The point is created on your map and marked as selected.

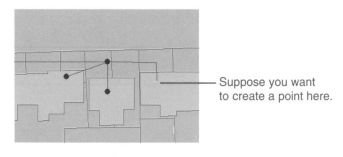

Suppose you want to create a point here.

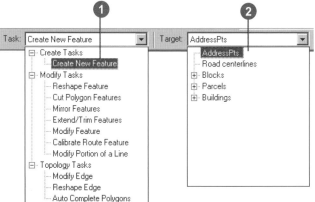

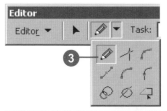

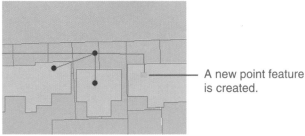

A new point feature is created.

- By using the Distance–Distance, Direction–Distance, Midpoint, or Intersection tools

To create new features, you must have an existing layer to which you want to add them. If you do not, you can create one using ArcCatalog. For more information on creating a feature layer, see *Using ArcCatalog*.

To digitize freehand, simply click the Sketch tool and click on the map.

Absolute X, Y on the Sketch tool context menu lets you create a point or vertex at a specific location using the map's coordinate system. You might use Absolute X, Y to create a pole in a utility database if you have the x,y coordinates of a pole from using a global positioning system (GPS) unit. ▶

Tip

Shortcut for Absolute X, Y
After clicking the Sketch tool, you can press F6 to set the x,y coordinates.

Tip

Closing the Sketch tool context menu
You can close the Sketch tool context menu by pressing the Esc key.

Creating a point or vertex using the coordinate system of the map (Absolute X, Y)

1. Click the tool palette dropdown arrow and click the Sketch tool.

2. Right-click anywhere on the map and click Absolute X, Y.

3. Type the coordinates and press Enter.

   A vertex or point is created at the specified coordinates.

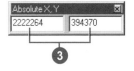

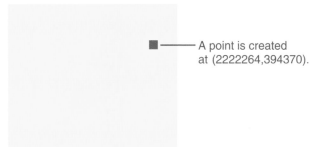

A point is created at (2222264,394370).

Delta X, Y on the Sketch tool context menu lets you create a vertex using the last vertex in the sketch as the origin. You can think of it as another way of measuring angle and length from a point already on the map.

For example, just as the red point in the diagram below can be measured at a distance of 20 feet from the last point at an angle of 53 degrees, it can also be measured in coordinates measured from the last point. ▶

20 ft.

53°

Point measured using an angle and length

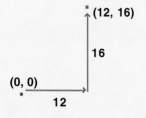

(12, 16)

16

(0, 0)

12

Same point measured using delta x,y coordinates

Creating a vertex relative to the location of the last vertex (Delta X,Y)

1. Click the tool palette dropdown arrow and click the Sketch tool after creating at least one vertex.

2. Right-click away from the vertex or sketch and click Delta X, Y.

3. Type the coordinates and press Enter.

   A vertex is created at the specified coordinates.

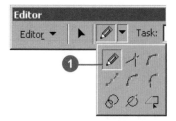

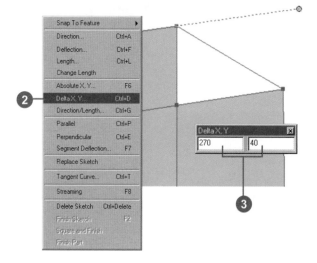

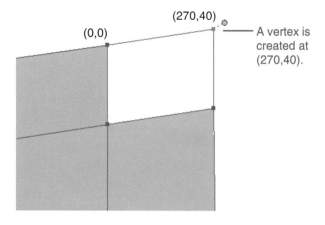

(270,40)

(0,0)

A vertex is created at (270,40).

The Distance–Distance tool offers another way to create a point or vertex at a specific location. Suppose you want to create a pole feature. If you don't have the exact coordinate location but know that it is at the intersection of 50 map units from the corner of one building and 70 map units from the corner of another, you can use the Distance–Distance tool to place the point. The Distance–Distance tool lets you create a point or vertex at the intersection of two distances from two other points. ▶

Tip

Undoing and redoing a vertex

You can undo any vertex you create by clicking the Undo button on the ArcMap Standard toolbar. Click the Redo button if you want to re-add the vertex.

Creating a point or vertex using the Distance–Distance tool

1. Click the tool palette dropdown arrow and click the Distance–Distance tool.

2. Click once to establish the centerpoint of the first circle and press the D key on the keyboard.

3. Type the radius length for the first circle and press Enter.

   A circle is created with the specified radius. ▶

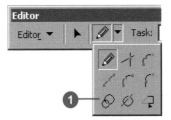

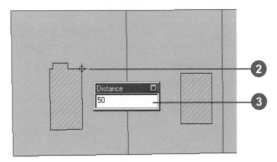

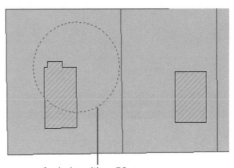

A circle with a 50-map unit radius is created.

As shown in the example, you'd create one circle with the centerpoint on the corner of the first building and a radius of 50 map units. You'd create another circle with the centerpoint on the corner of the other building and a radius of 70 map units. The Distance–Distance tool calculates the two locations where the radii of the circles intersect. ▶

Tip

Choosing an intersection point

Press Tab to alternate between the two points of intersection and press Enter to create the point.

4. Click once to establish the centerpoint of the second circle and press the D key on the keyboard.

5. Type the radius length for the second circle and press Enter.

   A second circle is created with the specified radius. The two locations where the radii of the circles intersect are highlighted when you move the pointer over them.

6. Position the pointer over the location you want and click.

   A vertex or point is added to your map.

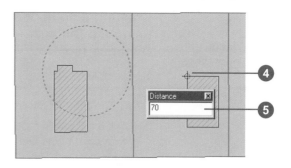

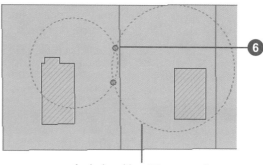

A circle with a 70-map unit radius is created.

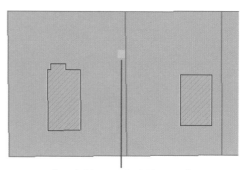

A point is created at one of two places where the radii of the circles intersect.

The Midpoint tool is ideal for placing a vertex directly between two known features. For example, you may want to place the road center line directly between two parcels or place an additional power pole directly between two preexisting power poles. ▸

Pan and zoom while adding points

Hold down the Control key and press Z to zoom out, X to zoom in, or C to pan the display when using any sketch tool.

Creating a point or vertex using the Midpoint tool

1. Click the tool palette dropdown arrow and click the Midpoint tool.

2. Click once to establish the first of two points. The new vertex will be created between this point and the next point you click.

3. Click the second point.

   A vertex or point is placed at the midpoint of the line between the two points you clicked.

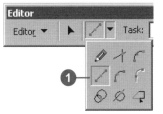

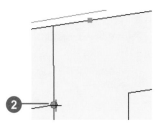

A point is created at the midpoint along the line defined by the two points you clicked.

The Intersection tool creates a point, or vertex, at the implied intersection of two segments. Implied means that the segments don't have to actually intersect on the map. In the example, suppose you want to create a new parcel. One corner of the parcel must be placed at the implied intersection of two segments of an adjoining parcel. You can use the Intersection tool to find this implied intersection point and create the corner vertex of the new parcel. ▶

Creating a point or vertex using the Intersection tool

1. Click the tool palette dropdown arrow and click the Intersection tool.

   The pointer turns into crosshairs.

2. Position the crosshairs over the first segment and click.

3. Position the crosshairs over the second segment and click.

   A vertex or point is added at the implied intersection of the two segments.

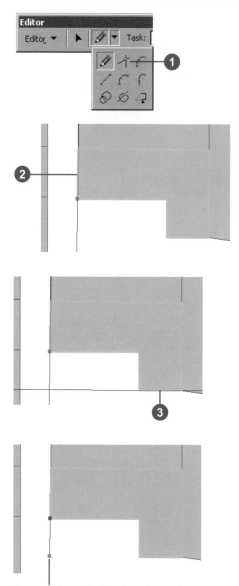

A vertex is added at the place where the two segments would intersect if extended.

Often a vertex location is only known according to the direction and the distance from two known features. For example, the location of a tree on a lot could be located at a particular direction from the corner of the lot and a given number of feet from another corner. In this situation, the Direction–Distance tool will place a vertex at the specified location.

As illustrated in this example, the direction is specified from one corner of the parcel. ▶

Creating a point or vertex using the Direction–Distance tool

1. Click the tool palette dropdown arrow and click the Direction–Distance tool.

2. Click a point to specify from where the direction to the next vertex was measured.

3. Move the pointer to get the approximate direction toward the next vertex.

   As you move the pointer the direction from the point you clicked to, the pointer is displayed in the lower-left corner of the ArcMap window.

   Press the D key and type the direction to the vertex from the point you clicked, then press Enter.

   You can also click again on the map to set the direction.

4. Click a point to specify from where the distance to the next vertex was measured. ▶

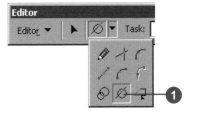

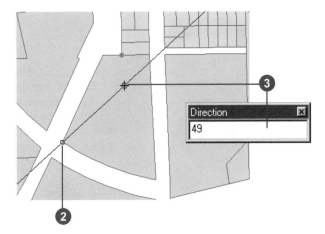

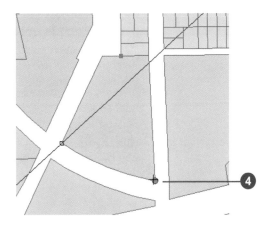

The distance is specified from another corner of the parcel, and the locations where both the direction and distance criteria are met, a potential vertex is placed. By clicking one of the two vertices, the new vertex is placed. ▶

Tip

Determining map units
With many of these sketch tools you must specify a distance in map units. The map units are specified under the General tab of the Data Frame Properties dialog box. This is found by clicking View on the Main menu, then clicking Data Frame Properties.

5. Move the pointer to get the approximate distance from the point you clicked to the next vertex.

   As the cursor is moved, a circle, centered at the second point you clicked, is dragged out to intersect the direction line you just defined. The radius of the circle is displayed in the lower-left corner.

   Optionally, you can press the D key and type a distance, in map units, to the next vertex from the point you specified. Pressing the Enter key will set the size of the circle.

   The new vertex will be at one of the intersection points of this circle and the direction line.

6. Click the intersection of the circle and the direction line which corresponds to the position of the new vertex.

   The intersection point nearest the cursor will be highlighted and, once clicked, the new vertex is placed.

   Optionally, you can use the Tab key to switch between the two intersection points and press Enter to select one of them.

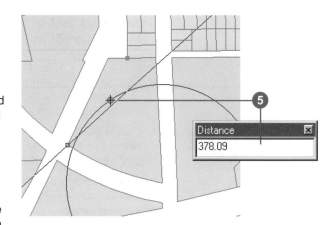

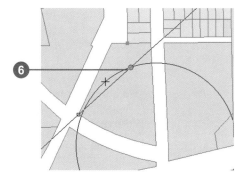

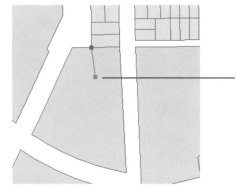

A vertex is added at the intersection you chose. It is at the angle you specified from the first point and the distance you specified from the second point.

You can also create a *multipoint feature*, a feature that consists of more than one point but only references one set of attributes in the database. For example, a system of oil wells could be created as a multipoint feature; the database references a single set of attributes for the main well and the multiple well holes in the system.

Tip

Creating multipoint layers

When creating multipoint features, your target layer must also be a multipoint feature class.

Creating a multipoint feature

1. Click the Task dropdown arrow and click Create New Feature.

2. Click the Target layer dropdown arrow and click a multipoint layer.

3. Click the tool palette dropdown arrow and click the Sketch tool.

4. Click the map to create parts of the multipoint feature.

5. Right-click anywhere on the map when you have created the last point of the multipoint feature and click Finish Sketch. ▶

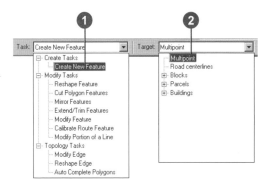

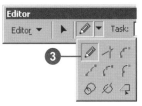

Modifying existing features

Double-click a feature or select single features and change the task in the Editor toolbar to Modify Feature. Use the Sketch Properties dialog box to edit vertices. You can open the sketch properties by clicking the Sketch Properties button on the Editor toolbar.

Now when you click one part of the multipoint feature to select it, all points are automatically selected because they all belong to one multipoint feature.

All points of the feature are selected.

Creating lines and polygons

You can create lines or polygons by digitizing the vertices that make up the feature. For example, to create a square building, you would digitize the four corners, using any combination of methods for creating vertices or segments.

By selecting in the target list a feature class that is represented by lines or polygons, the editor tools will create the corresponding feature type.

Shortcuts for finishing the sketch

You can double-click the last vertex of the feature to finish the sketch. Or, press F2 when you've finished creating the sketch.

Creating circles and rectangles with the Advanced Editing toolbar

You can use the Circle and Rectangle tools on the Advanced Editing toolbar to create lines and polygons of these shapes in the Target layer.

Creating a line or polygon feature by digitizing

1. Click the Task dropdown arrow and click Create New Feature.

2. Click the Target layer dropdown arrow and click a line or polygon layer.

3. Click the tool palette dropdown arrow and click the Sketch tool.

4. Click the map to digitize the feature's vertices.

5. Right-click anywhere on the map when finished and click Finish Sketch. ▶

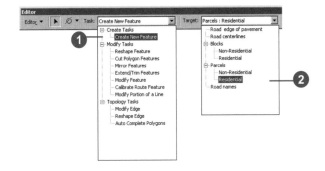

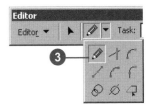

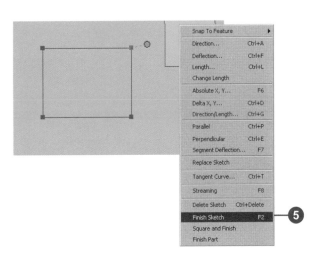

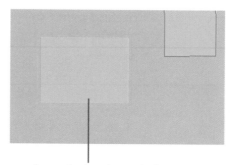

Tip

Deleting a vertex

To delete a single vertex from a sketch, center the pointer over the vertex, right-click, then click Delete Vertex.

Tip

Deleting the sketch

To delete the entire sketch of the feature you are creating, position the pointer over any part of the map, right-click, and click Delete Sketch. You can also delete a sketch by pressing Ctrl + Delete.

If the sketch has already been finished, select the feature with the Edit tool, right-click, and click Delete Sketch.

The line or polygon is created on your map.

A new feature is created on your map.

ArcMap also provides a way to create a *multipart feature*, a feature that is composed of more than one physical part but only references one set of attributes in the database. For example, the State of Hawaii could be considered a multipart feature. Although composed of many islands, it would be recorded as one feature. A multipart feature can only share vertices, not edges.

Replace sketch

You can add the shape of a line or polygon feature to the sketch by right-clicking over the feature with the Sketch tool and clicking Replace Sketch. The sketch will contain the shape of the feature you clicked over. Using the Edit tool, the sketch can be dragged and dropped anywhere on the map.

Undoing and redoing a vertex

You can undo the last vertex you created by clicking the Undo button on the ArcMap Standard toolbar. Click the button again to undo the second-to-last vertex you created, and so on. Click the Redo button if you want to re-add the vertex.

Creating a multipart line or polygon

1. Create a line or polygon feature.

2. Right-click anywhere on the map when you have finished creating the first part of the feature and click Finish Part.

3. Create the next part of the feature.

4. Right-click anywhere on the map when you have finished the last part of the feature and click Finish Sketch. ►

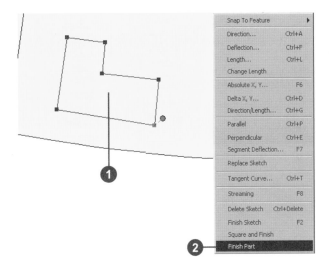

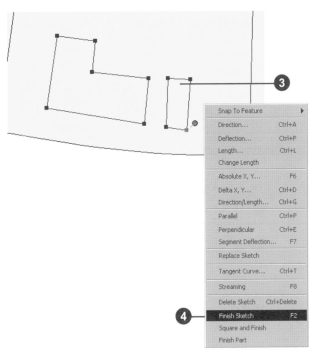

Tip

Shortcut for finishing the sketch

You can double-click the last vertex of the new feature to finish the sketch.

Tip

Shortcut for finishing a part

When creating a multipart sketch, you can hold down the Shift key and double-click the last vertex of a part to finish it.

Now when you click one part of the feature to select it, all parts are automatically selected because they all belong to one multipart feature.

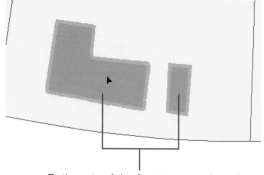

Both parts of the feature are selected.

The Square and Finish command on the Sketch tool context menu is a way of completing a polygon. It finishes a polygon by adding two new segments at 90-degree angles. Square and Finish saves you time and ensures precision when creating square-cornered buildings.

Squaring a polygon or polyline

1. Click the Current Task dropdown arrow and click Create New Feature.

2. Click the Target layer dropdown arrow and click a polygon or polyline layer.

3. Click the tool palette dropdown arrow and click the Sketch tool.

4. Digitize at least two segments.

5. Right-click anywhere away from the sketch and click Square and Finish. ▶

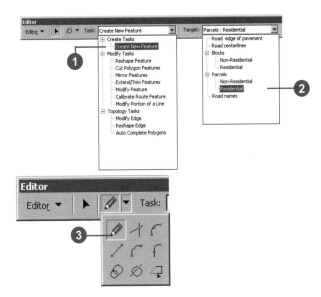

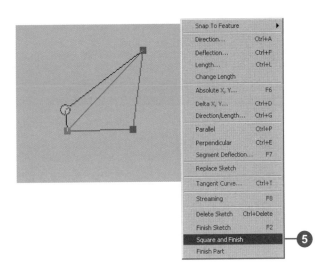

The angles from the first
vertex and the last vertex are
squared. A new vertex is
added, and the sketch is
finished where the resulting
segments intersect.

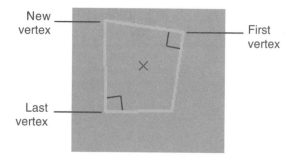

Creating segments using directions and lengths

The edit tools help you create segments in specific directions, measured either using the map coordinate system (Direction) or from the last segment (Deflection).

The Direction command uses east as 0 degrees and measures positive angles counterclockwise by default. For example, a 90-degree angle represents north and a 180-degree angle represents west. You can change the direction measuring system and angular units on the Units tab of the Editing Options dialog box.

The Deflection command uses the last segment as 0 degrees and calculates the angle you specify from there. Positive values are calculated in a counterclockwise direction from the existing segment, while negative values are calculated clockwise. ▶

Tip

Shortcut for direction angle
After clicking the Sketch tool and creating at least one vertex, you can press Ctrl + A to set the direction angle.

Creating a segment using an angle and a length

1. Click the tool palette dropdown arrow and click the Sketch tool after creating at least one vertex.

2. Right-click away from the sketch and click Direction.

3. Type the direction and press Enter.

   The segment is constrained to the specified direction. ▶

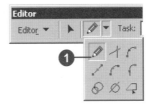

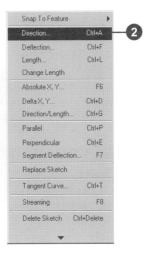

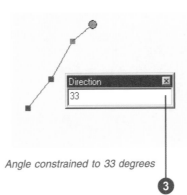

Angle constrained to 33 degrees

You might use Deflection to create the bent end of a water or gas line at a 33-degree angle to a house.

Both the Direction and Deflection commands constrain the angle of the segment. For example, if you type 45 as the Direction, the segment will be constrained to a 45-degree angle one way and a 225-degree angle the other.

Use the Length command to specify the length of a segment you're creating.

4. Right-click anywhere on the map and click Length.

5. Type the length and press Enter.

   The vertex that makes the segment the desired angle and length is created.

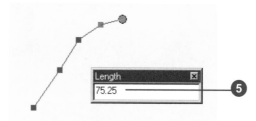

The vertex that makes the segment the desired angle and length is created.

Shortcut for deflection

After clicking the Sketch tool and creating at least one vertex, you can press Ctrl + F to set the deflection angle.

Creating a segment at an angle from the last segment (deflection)

1. Click the tool palette dropdown arrow and click the Sketch tool after creating at least one vertex for the new segment.

2. Right-click away from the sketch.

3. Click Deflection.

4. Type the desired angle from the last segment and press Enter.

   The segment is constrained to the specified angle.

5. Click once to digitize the endpoint of the segment or choose Length from the Sketch tool context menu.

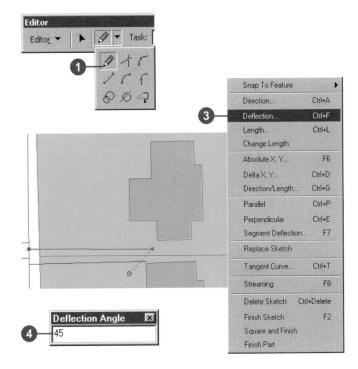

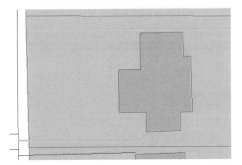

Creating segments using angles from existing segments

Three commands on the Sketch tool context menu—Segment Deflection, Parallel, and Perpendicular—help create segments with angles relative to segments that already exist.

The Segment Deflection command lets you create a segment at an angle relative to any existing segment. While Deflection creates a segment at a specific angle from the last segment in the sketch you're creating, Segment Deflection lets you choose a segment in an existing feature.

As with the Deflection command, the segment you work from with Segment Deflection is 0 degrees, and the deflection ▶

Tip

Shortcut for segment deflection

After clicking the Sketch tool, creating at least one vertex, and positioning the pointer over the segment from which you want the specific angle to be drawn, you can press F7 to set the angle.

Creating a segment at an angle from any other segment

1. Click the tool palette dropdown arrow and click the Sketch tool after creating at least one vertex.

2. Position the pointer over the segment of a feature class from which you want to create a segment and right-click with the mouse.

3. Click Segment Deflection.

4. Type the desired angle from the segment you chose and press Enter. ▶

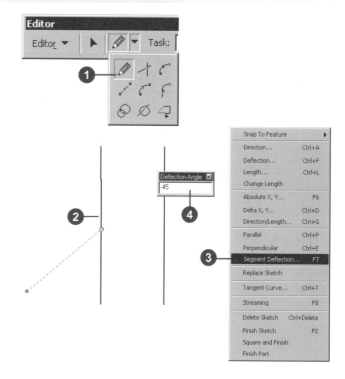

angle you specify for the new segment is calculated from there. Positive values are calculated in a counterclockwise direction from the existing segment, while negative values are calculated clockwise. The example given shows a cross street created at a -45-degree angle to the existing streets. ▶

Tip

Using only positive values with segment deflection

If you wish to work only with positive angle values, convert negative angles to positive angles by adding 180 to the negative value. For example, a -45-degree angle, measured clockwise, becomes a 135-degree angle, measured counterclockwise.

The segment is constrained to the specified angle.

5. Click once to digitize the endpoint of the segment or choose Length from the Sketch tool context menu.

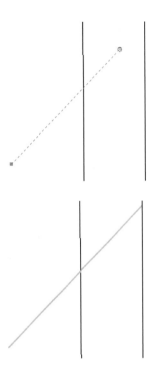

The Parallel command on the Sketch tool context menu constrains a segment to be parallel to any segment you choose. For instance, you might use this command to create a gas main line parallel to the street.

The Perpendicular command on the Sketch tool context menu constrains a segment to be perpendicular to an existing segment. You might use this command to place a service line perpendicular to the main line.

Tip

Shortcut for parallel

After clicking the Sketch tool, creating at least one vertex, and positioning the pointer over the segment to which the new segment will be parallel, you can press Ctrl + P to make the segment parallel.

Creating a segment parallel to another segment

1. Click the tool palette dropdown arrow and click the Sketch tool after creating at least one vertex.

2. Position the pointer over the segment to which the new segment will be parallel and right-click.

3. Click Parallel.

   The segment is constrained to be parallel to the specified segment.

4. Click once to digitize the endpoint of the segment or choose Length from the Sketch tool context menu.

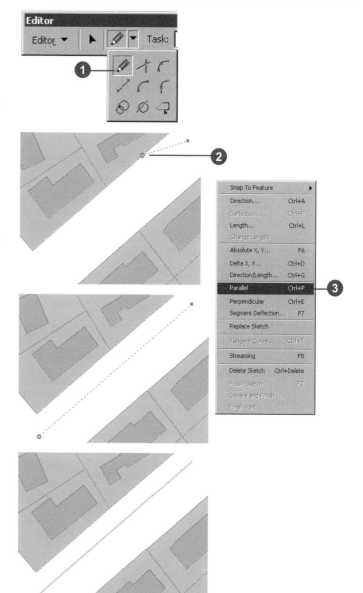

Creating a segment perpendicular to another segment

1. Click the tool palette dropdown arrow and click the Sketch tool after creating at least one vertex.

2. Position the pointer over the segment to which the new segment will be perpendicular and right-click with the mouse.

3. Click Perpendicular.

   The segment is constrained to be perpendicular to the specified segment.

4. Click once to digitize the endpoint of the segment or choose Length from the Sketch tool context menu.

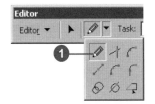

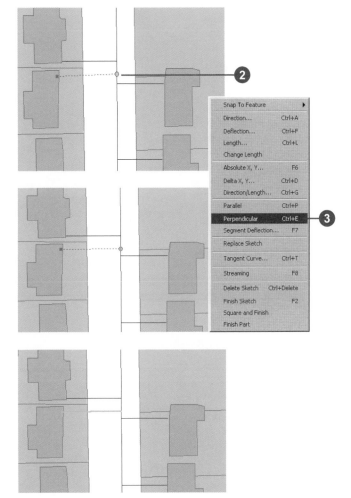

Creating segments that are circular arc curves

When creating features, it is often necessary to create a circular arc. Instead of being made of numerous vertices, a circular arc has only two vertices as endpoints. ArcMap offers four ways to create a segment that is a circular arc. These include the Arc tool, the Endpoint Arc tool, the Tangent Curve tool, and the Tangent Curve command.

First, you can create a circular arc using the Arc tool. You might use the Arc tool to digitize a cul-de-sac using an aerial photo image as a backdrop.

A circular arc can also be created using the Endpoint Arc tool. This tool allows you to place the vertices for both ends of the arc and adjust the radius.

The Tangent Arc tool creates a circular arc based on the previously sketched segment.

You can also create a circular arc using the Tangent Curve command on the Sketch tool context menu. You can use the Tangent Curve command to ▶

Creating a segment that is a circular arc using the Arc tool

1. Click the tool palette dropdown arrow and click the Arc tool.

2. Click to establish the starting point of the arc.

   A vertex is created.

3. Click to establish the axis of the arc.

   This is the invisible point through which the curve passes.

4. Click again to establish the endpoint of the arc.

   A segment that is a true curve is created.

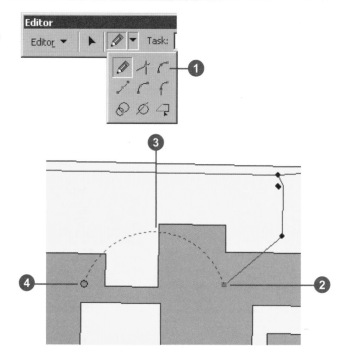

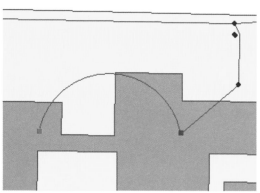

A segment that is a true curve is created.

add a circular arc to an existing segment. For example, you might use this command to add a curved segment to extend a centerline along a curved road.

When you create a tangent curve, you must specify two parameters for the curve from the following options: arc length, chord, radius, or delta angle. You must also specify whether you want to create the curve to the right of the line or to the left of the line, according to the direction in which the line was drawn. The curve is created from the last vertex of the existing segment based on the parameters you defined.

If you choose chord length and radius to construct the curve, there are two possible solutions: the major and minor portions of the circle. ▶

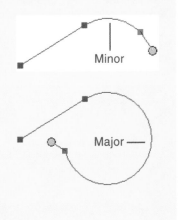

Creating a segment that is a circular arc using the Endpoint Arc sketch tool

1. Click the tool palette dropdown arrow and click the Endpoint Arc tool.

2. Click the starting point of the arc.

3. Click the endpoint of the arc.

4. Move the pointer to get the approximate radius for the curve.

   Press the R key and type the radius for the curve.

   You can also click again on the map to set the radius.

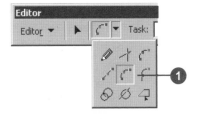

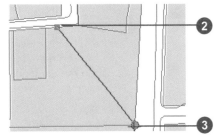

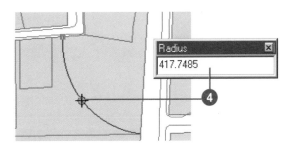

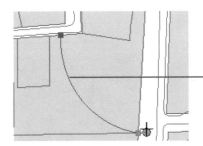

A circular arc with the radius you specified is created between the two points you clicked.

The Minor check box will appear at the bottom of the Tangent Curve dialog box. Check it to construct the minor portion of the circle.

Creating a segment that is a circular arc using the Tangent Curve tool

1. Click the tool palette dropdown arrow and click the Tangent Curve tool once a segment has been created using one of the other sketch tools.

   As the cursor is moved, the arc will bend and change length to remain tangent to the previous segment.

2. Click again to place the endpoint of the arc.

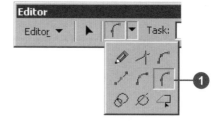

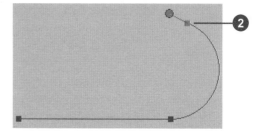

Creating a segment that is a circular arc using the Tangent Curve command

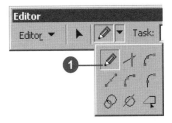

1. Click the tool palette dropdown arrow and click the Sketch tool after creating at least one segment.

2. Right-click anywhere on the map and click Tangent Curve.

3. Click the dropdown arrows and click two parameters by which you want to define the curve.

4. Type the appropriate values for the parameters—distance in map units for arc length, chord, and radius; degrees for delta angle.

5. Click Left to create the tangent curve to the left of the segment. Click Right to create the curve to the right.

6. Press Enter. ▶

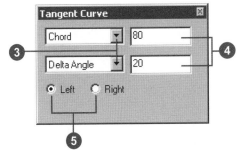

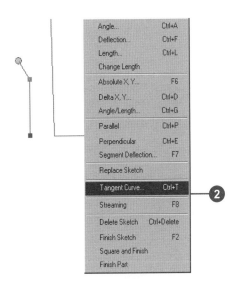

A segment that is a true curve is created from the last vertex of the segment according to the parameters you specified.

A circular arc curve with a chord length of 80 map units and a delta angle of 20 degrees is created to the left of the last vertex.

Creating segments by tracing features

You can create segments by tracing over the segments of selected features using the Trace tool.

Suppose you want to create a new water main that is offset seven meters from the parcel boundaries. Using the Trace tool, you can create new segments in the sketch that are at the same angle as the selected parcel boundaries yet constructed at an offset value of seven meters.

Tip

Backing up a trace
If you traced too far or have traced the wrong direction, move the mouse backwards over what you have traced. If you have clicked to stop the trace, click Undo to remove all vertices added during the trace.

Tip

Canceling a trace
Press Esc to quickly cancel a trace.

Tip

Finishing the sketch
When you're finished tracing, double-click to finish the sketch.

Creating segments by tracing features

1. Click the Edit tool.

2. Select the feature or features you want to trace.

3. Click the tool palette dropdown arrow and click the Trace tool.

4. Press O to open the Trace Properties dialog box.

   The Trace Properties dialog box lets you specify many of the properties of the trace segment.

5. Type an offset value. If you want to trace directly on top of existing features, enter a value of 0.

6. Optionally, you can limit the length of the trace segment.

7. Click the corresponding radio button to specify the type of corners.

   Close the Trace Options dialog box by clicking OK.

8. Click to start tracing.

9. Click to stop tracing.

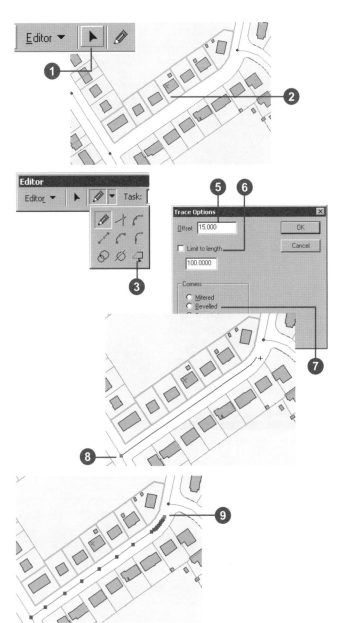

Duplicating features with the Copy Features tool

You can quickly create a duplicate of a selected feature or features by using the Copy Features tool. The Copy Features tool is located on the Advanced Editing toolbar. Only the geometry, not the attributes, of the selected feature are copied to the Target layer.

If the Target feature class or subtype has default values, feature-linked annotation, or connectivity rules defined in a geodatabase, the copy will have the default values and behavior appropriate for the Target layer. Attributes without default values will have a null value.

Tip

Using the Advanced Editing toolbar
The Advanced Editing toolbar has a more complex set of editing tools. Some tools on this toolbar are not available with ArcView licenses.

Tip

Opening the Advanced Editing toolbar
The Advanced Editing toolbar is found on the Editor context menu under More Editing Tools.

1. Click the Edit tool.
2. Select the features that you want to copy.
3. Click the Copy Features Tool.
4. Click the place where you want a copy of the feature to be placed.

   A copy of the geometry of the selected feature is created at the location you clicked. The feature is created in the Editor's current Target layer.

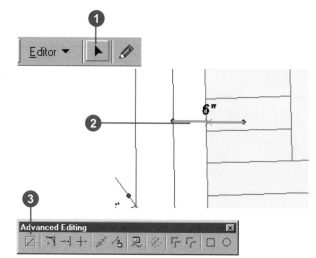

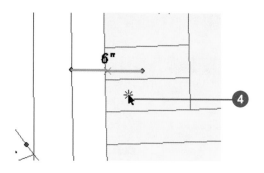

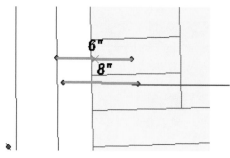

The duplicate feature has the default values and behavior that are defined for the Target feature class in the geodatabase.

Creating a fillet curve between two lines

Fillets are segments of a circular arc that are often used to connect two intersecting lines. Fillets are used to create smoothly curving connections between lines, such as edge of pavement lines at street intersections or rounded corners on parcel features.

Tip

Shortcut for fillet radius
After clicking the Fillet tool, you can set a default fillet radius on the Fillet Options dialog box by pressing the R key. If a default radius is set, the fillet curve will be constructed immediately with that radius when you click the second line of those you want to fillet.

Tip

Radius units
The Fillet Options will use current data frame coordinate system units for the fillet radius, unless you specify another unit of measure when you type the fillet radius.

Tip

Placement of the fillet
If you specify a fixed radius, the fillet curve is created on the side of the second line where the pointer was when you clicked.

1. Click the Fillet tool.

2. Click first one line then the other to specify which lines you want to construct the fillet between.

   The radius of the fillet curve will change as you drag the pointer away from the first line you clicked.

   When the curve looks like it has the right radius, you can click to finish the curve. If you want the curve to have a specific radius, you can set the radius from the Fillet Options window.

3. Press the R key to set the Fillet Options.

4. Optionally, check Trim existing segments if you want to remove the segments outside the curve's radius.

5. Optionally, check Fixed radius if you want to specify a radius for the curve.

6. Type a radius for the curve and press Enter, or click OK.

7. Click the map to indicate the quadrant of the intersection of the lines where the fillet will be created.

   A new fillet curve joins the two selected lines. The extra line segments outside the curve are trimmed off, if you checked Trim existing segments.

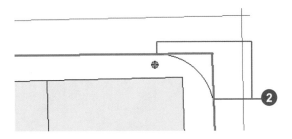

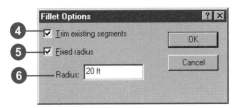

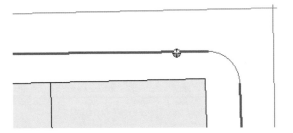

Extending a line

You can extend a line segment that's a little too short so that it touches another line segment. The Extend tool on the Advanced Editing toolbar lets you click a line feature and extend it to another selected line feature.

1. Click the Edit tool.

2. Select the line segment to which you want to extend a line.

3. Click the Extend tool.

4. Click the end of the feature that you want to extend.

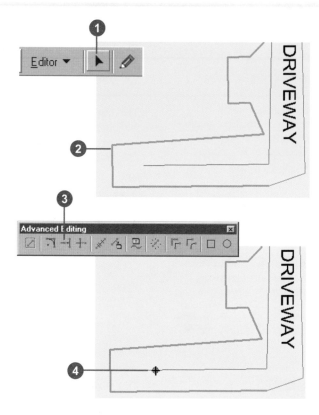

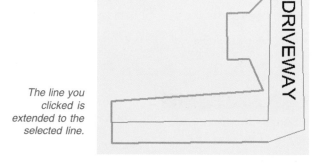

The line you clicked is extended to the selected line.

Trimming a line

You can trim off the part of a line that crosses another line segment. The Trim tool on the Advanced Editing toolbar lets you click one side of a line feature that crosses a selected line in order to trim it off.

1. Click the Edit tool.
2. Select the line segment at which you want to trim a line.
3. Click the Trim tool.
4. Click the end of the feature that you want to trim.

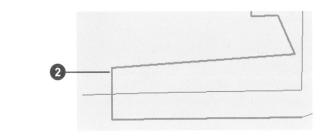

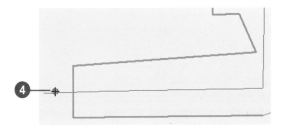

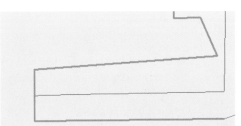

The line you clicked is trimmed at the selected line.

ArcInfo and ArcEditor

Proportionally dividing a line

One common coordinate geometry editing task is to divide an existing line feature into a number of segments of a specified length.

Sometimes the task can be complicated by measuring errors. For example, the length of the line in the GIS might not be exactly equal to the total length of the segments, as measured in the field. The Proportion tool allows you to divide a selected line into a number of segments and allocate the difference between the length of the line feature and the total length of the segments between all of the new segments.

Suppose you have a line that you want to divide into segments that you can snap to when creating new parcel corners. The length of the line feature in the GIS is 320.38 ft. The lot plan you've been given shows that the lot corners are at 111.78 ft, 70.43 ft, and 138.65 ft along this line. Unfortunately, there is a difference of 0.48 ft between the measurements and the feature length.

The Proportion dialog box lets you enter the lengths of the ▶

1. Click the Edit tool.
2. Select the line that you want to proportionally divide.
3. Click the Proportion tool. ▶

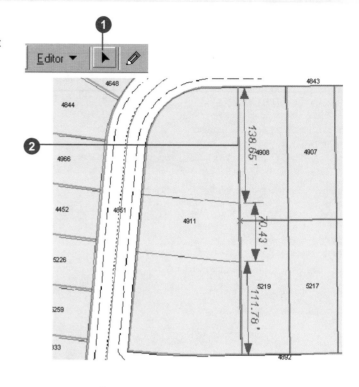

segments. As you do, it reports the length of the selected feature, the sum of the lengths of the segments, the amount that is left over, and the relative error, expressed as the ratio between the leftover and the original feature length.

The Proportion tool creates new proportioned features of 111.61 ft, 70.32 ft, and 138.44 ft, dividing the difference between the features.

If the line feature that you are splitting has an attribute named Distance, the new line features will have the values that you typed as the attributed length, and the Shape_length field will show the true length.

4. Type the lengths of the segments into which to divide the line.

5. Optionally, click Reverse to switch the orientation of the line if the arrows indicating the orientation of the feature on the map are the reverse of the order in which you entered the segments.

6. Click OK.

The line is split proportionally to the length of the measured segments. Any difference between the line length and the sum of the length of the segments is allocated proportionately to the new lines' lengths.

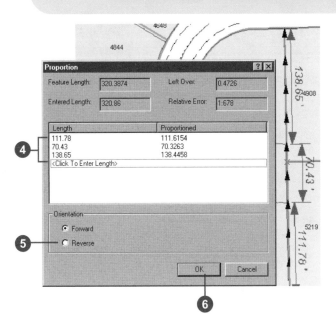

New lines ——

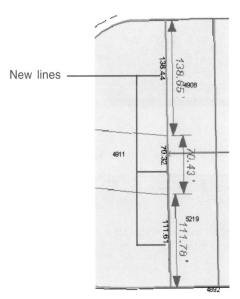

ArcInfo and ArcEditor

Getting a COGO description of a feature with the Inverse tool

You can get the *COGO* description of a feature using the Inverse tool. The Inverse tool will calculate the direction and length of the feature as well as curve parameters, if required, and populate appropriate attributes on the feature.

In order to use the Inverse tool, the feature must have the following attributes as text fields: Direction, Distance, Radius, Delta, Tangent, Arclength, and Side.

The feature must be either a straight line or circular arc. It typically only has two vertices but more are allowed as long as the feature is consistently straight or consistently curved. The current direction type and angular units are used when populating the attributes.

Tip

Changing the COGO attribute names

The names of the COGO attributes can be changed by using the Advanced ArcMap settings utility.

1. Click the Edit tool.
2. Select the feature that you want to generate a COGO description for.
3. Click the Inverse tool.

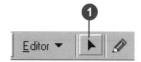

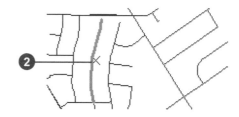

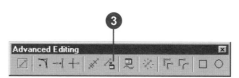

Creating edit sketch geometry with the Traverse tool

Another common coordinate geometry editing task is to create a line or polygon edge using a set of survey measurements collected in the field. The data may be in the form of directions and distances, angles and distances, curves, or tangent curves, measured from a known point. These are collectively known as a *traverse*.

The Traverse tool lets you create edit sketch geometry from a wide variety of traverse measurements. ▶

Interactive start point
You can click the Interactive Start Point Selection tool to set a start point by clicking on the map.

Starting from a sketch
If you have already started an edit sketch when you click the Traverse tool, the start point will be the last vertex of the edit sketch.

Starting a traverse from a known coordinate

1. Click the Traverse tool.

2. Click Edit, to the right of the Start box.

3. Type X and Y values for the starting coordinate.

4. Click OK.

   The start point of the traverse is set in the Start Point text box. The next vertex of the edit sketch will be placed on the measurements you specify from this location.

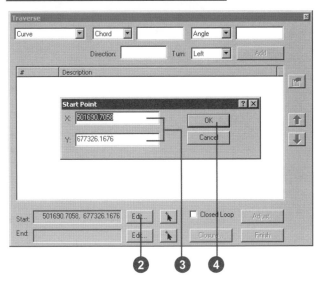

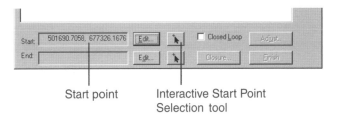

Start point   Interactive Start Point
                     Selection tool

Once you've started a traverse you can add segments or curves to the edit sketch using Direction–Distance, Angle–Distance, Curve, and Tangent Curve methods.

The Traverse tool adds each segment as a line in the Traverse course table and to the edit sketch. You can select each course segment by clicking it in the table—the corresponding segment will flash on the map.

Tip

Duplicating segments
You can insert a duplicate of a segment by right-clicking it in the table and clicking Insert.

Tip

Reordering segments
You can reorder a segment by selecting it in the table and clicking the up and down arrows.

Tip

Removing segments
You can remove a segment by selecting it in the table and clicking Remove.

Adding a segment to a traverse using a Direction–Distance course

1. Click the course type dropdown arrow and click Direction–Distance.

2. Type a direction.

   The Traverse tool uses degrees measured counter-clockwise from east by default. You can change the angular measuring system and units on the Editing Options dialog box, Units tab.

3. Type a distance.

   The Traverse tool uses the data frame's coordinate system units of measurement by default. You can change these units by modifying the coordinate system description, but not during an edit session.

4. Click Add.

   The course is added to the course table, and the segment is added to the edit sketch.

   You can continue to add segments using any of the traverse methods.

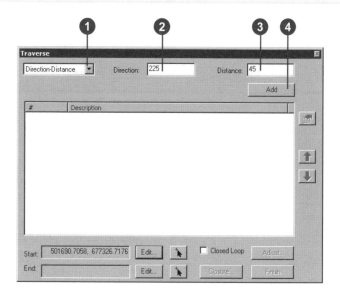

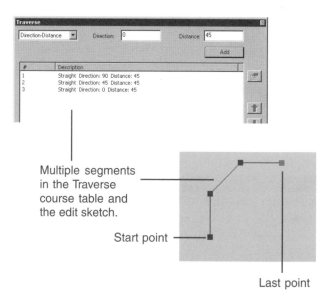

Multiple segments in the Traverse course table and the edit sketch.

Start point

Last point

Limitations to first course

The first course in your traverse table cannot be based on an Angle–Distance or Tangent Curve because these techniques are calculated from the direction of the previous course.

Adding a segment to a traverse using an Angle–Distance course

1. Click the course type dropdown arrow and click Angle–Distance.

2. Type an angle.

   The Traverse tool uses degrees measured counter-clockwise from the previous course of the traverse. You can change the angular measuring system and units on the Editing Options dialog box, Units tab.

3. Type a distance.

   The Traverse tool uses the data frame's coordinate system units of measurement by default. You can change these units by modifying the coordinate system description, but not during an edit session.

4. Click Add.

   The course is added to the course table, and the segment is added to the edit sketch.

   You can continue to add segments using any of the traverse methods.

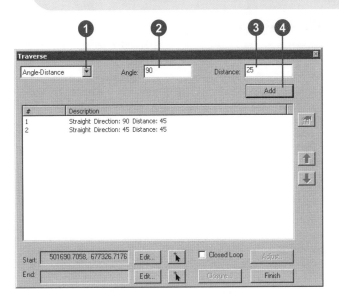

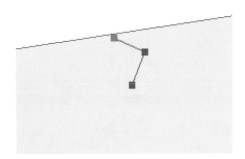

ArcInfo and ArcEditor

Tip

Productivity with the Traverse tool

You can use the keyboard to enter and manage courses in the traverse. Enter can be pressed whenever there is enough information to add a course. The Tab key and Shift + Tab can be used to navigate between the fields. For dropdown lists, the first letter of the choice can be used as a shortcut or you can use the Up/Down Arrow keys to make your selection.

Adding a segment to a traverse using a Curve course

1. Click the course type dropdown arrow and click Curve.

2. Click the dropdown arrows and choose two parameters to use in determining the curve.

3. Type the appropriate values for the parameters. Distance values will use map units.

4. Type a chord direction for the curve.

5. Click the dropdown arrow to choose whether the curve will be to the right or left.

6. Click Add.

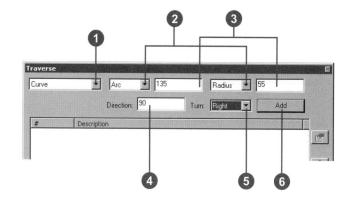

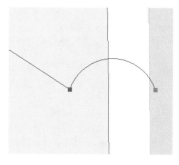

Adding a segment to a traverse using a Tangent Curve course

1. Click the course type dropdown arrow and click Tangent Curve.

2. Click the dropdown arrows and choose two parameters to use in determining the curve.

3. Type the appropriate values for the parameters. Distance values will use map units.

4. Click the dropdown arrow to choose whether the curve will be to the right or left.

5. Click Add.

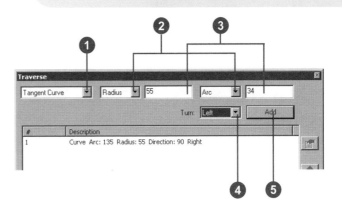

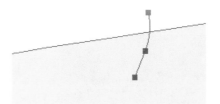

Creating two-point line features to populate COGO attributes

You can easily create features using the Traverse tool to populate COGO attributes in a feature class. Using the Create 2-Point Line Features task allows you to not only create the feature geometry with the Traverse tool, it also allows you to save each course in the traverse as a COGO two-point line feature.

To create two-point line features using this process, the target layer must have the following attributes as text fields: Direction, Distance, Radius, Delta, Tangent, Arclength, and Side.

1. On the Task dropdown menu, click Create 2-Point Line Features.

2. On the Editor toolbar, set your target layer to a layer that contains COGO attributes.

3. Using the Traverse tool, specify the courses of the traverse.

4. When you finish the traverse, click Finish.

   The new line features will be saved as COGO two-point line features.

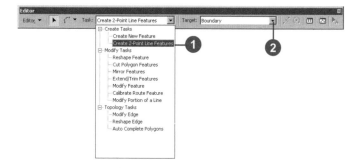

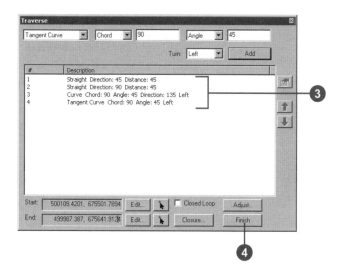

Tip

Opening the Course properties dialog box

You can open the properties for the Course dialog box using three different methods. You can double-click the segment in the course list, click the segment and click Properties on the Traverse dialog box, or right-click the course and click Properties.

Modifying a segment in a traverse

2. Click the Properties button.

3. In the Course properties, adjust the values as required.

The traverse and the sketch are updated.

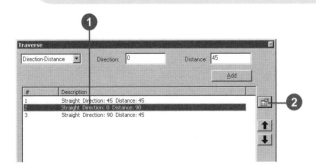

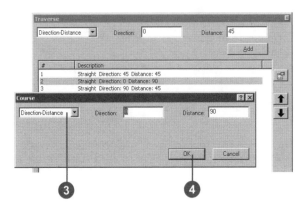

ArcInfo and ArcEditor

Obtaining a closure report

A traverse must always start from a known coordinate. It can also end at a known coordinate. When this occurs, a difference can be calculated between the specified endpoint and the traversed endpoint.

A *closure report* is a summary of the difference between the endpoint coordinate of a traverse and the calculated endpoint.

Tip

Interactive endpoint
Click on the Endpoint Selection tool to set the endpoint by clicking on the map.

Tip

Starting and ending at the same point
Checking the Closed Loop check box sets the beginning and ending points the same.

1. Click Edit to the right of the End box.

2. Type the x,y coordinates for the ending point.

3. Click OK.

4. Click Closure.

   The closure report lists the following:

   • Number of courses

   • Total length of the traverse

   • The specified and calculated endpoints

   • The difference of misclosure in both x,y and direction/ distance values

   • Relative error that is a ratio of the distance misclosure over the total length

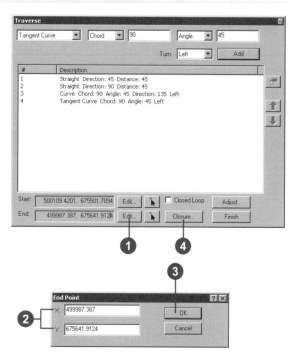

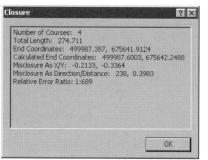

Techniques for adjusting a traverse

Often when generating a traverse, the coordinates of an ending destination are known. You have already discovered that ArcMap provides a method to specify this endpoint and determine the difference between the traverse endpoint and the desired ending point. This difference is known as the misclosure.

ArcMap also provides three different techniques for adjusting the traverse to eliminate misclosure. Each of these adjusting techniques vary in the amount of adjustment of the direction and distance of the individual courses of the traverse. These techniques include *compass* correction, *transit* correction, and *Crandall* correction.

The compass correction technique specifies that the misclosure, or difference in x and y between the resulting endpoint and the desired endpoint, are equally distributed among the individual two-point arcs and curves that make up the traverse. This is done by adjusting the location and distance of each arc proportional to the difference in closure. The compass correction technique is the most often used to resolve errors in misclosure. It assumes that the errors are related to both errors in the direction measurements as well as the distance measurements. Thus, the corrections are reflected in each distance and direction value. This technique is also known as the Bowditch rule.

Much like the compass correction technique, the transit correction method specifies that the misclosure is equally distributed among the individual two-point arcs and curves that make up the traverse. However, this technique favors the direction measurements over the distance measurements. In determining the location change required of each arc, the proportion assigned to each arc is proportional to the total x or y values of all the arcs. This results in changes that will affect both the direction and the distance of each arc, but will alter the distance to a greater extent.

The Crandall correction technique is used when the direction values are assumed to be precise and accurate and that any misclosure is due solely to errors in distance measurements. This adjustment will preserve all of the direction measurements and will alter only the distance measurements to eliminate the closure error.

With this array of correction techniques, you will be able to not only correct the errors in the traverse, but you will also be able to place greater or lesser value on specific characteristics of the traverse data.

Adjusting a traverse

1. Ensure that an endpoint is set.

2. Click Adjust.

3. Choose an adjustment method from the dropdown menu.

4. Optionally, you can save the adjusted values in a text file by clicking Save Report.

5. Click Accept.

    The traverse will be adjusted based on the adjustment method chosen and feature created.

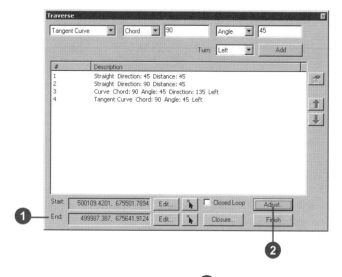

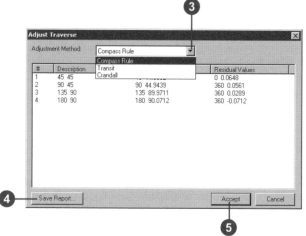

Saving a traverse

You can save a traverse to a text file to share with others or for your own use later.

1. Right-click the Traverse dialog box and click Save Traverse.

2. Navigate to the place where you want to save the traverse.

3. Type a name for the traverse.

4. Click Save.

   The traverse information is saved to the text file.

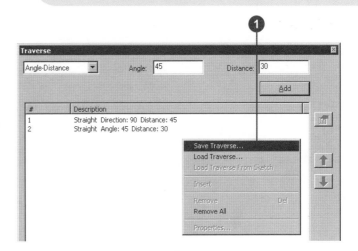

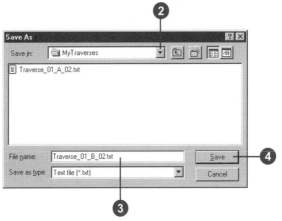

ArcInfo and ArcEditor

Loading a traverse

You can load a traverse that has been saved to a text file.

1. Right-click the Traverse dialog box and click Load Traverse.

2. Navigate to the traverse text file.

3. Click the traverse you want to open.

4. Click Open.

   The traverse information is loaded from the text file.

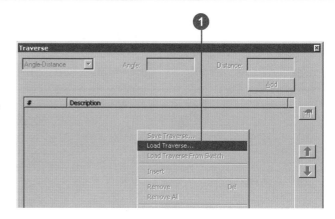

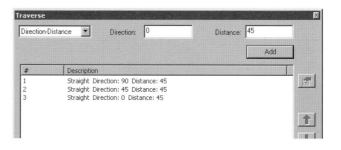

Exploding a multipart feature

You can use the Explode tool to separate a multipart feature into its component features.

1. Click the Edit tool.

2. Select the multipart feature that you want to Explode.

3. Click the Explode tool.

   The parts of the multipart feature become independent features.

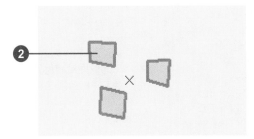

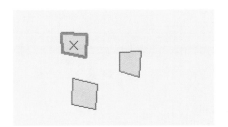

ArcInfo and ArcEditor

Generalizing a feature

You can use the Generalize tool to simplify the shape of features. The Generalize tool uses the Douglas–Poiker algorithm to simplify the input geometry of the selected feature.

The degree to which the geometry is simplified depends on the Maximum allowable offset, which limits how far the output geometry can be from the input geometry.

For features composed of linear segments, the output vertices will be a subset of the original feature vertices.

If you use the Generalize tool on a true curve, the output will be a series of straight line segments. The vertices may fall on all parts of the original curve, not just the vertices. The output of the Generalize tool on lines with nonlinear curves may have more vertices than the original curve, but all of the segments will be straight.

1. Click the Edit tool.

2. Select the feature that you want to Generalize.

3. Click the Generalize tool.

4. Type the Maximum allowable offset.

   The Maximum allowable offset is the maximum distance any part of the output geometry can be from the input geometry, in map units.

5. Click OK.

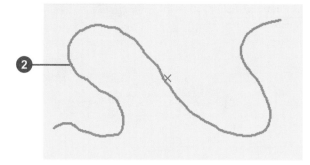

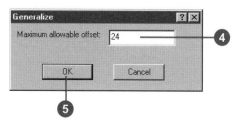

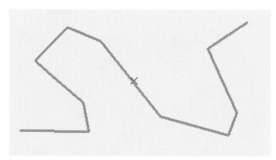

Smoothing a feature

You can use the Smooth tool to smooth the straight edges and angular corners of a feature. The feature geometry is replaced by a series of smoothed line segments.

The degree to which the geometry is smoothed depends on the Maximum allowable offset, which limits how far the output geometry can be from the input geometry.

1. Click the Edit tool.

2. Select the feature that you want to Smooth.

3. Click the Smooth tool.

4. Type the Maximum allowable offset.

   The Maximum allowable offset is the maximum distance any part of the output geometry can be from the input geometry, in map units.

5. Click OK.

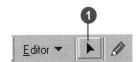

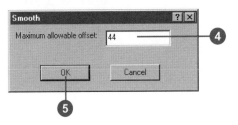

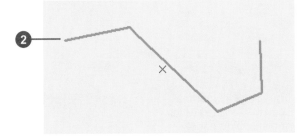

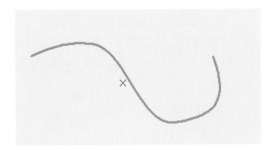

The Snapping Environment window

You can keep the window open as you work— any changes in settings are effective immediately. Click the Close button when you are finished.

The layers in your map document are listed here. Set the snapping priority— the order in which snapping will occur by layer—by dragging the layer names to new locations.

Check the type of snapping properties you want for each layer.

The bottom portion of the window shows snapping properties that work with a sketch or with elements of a topology.

Snapping Environment ☒

Layer	Vertex	Edge	End
Water distribution r	☐	☐	☐
System valves	☐	☐	☐
Distribution mains	☐	☐	☐
Blocks	☐	☐	☐
Parcels	☑	☑	☐
Water laterals	☐	☐	☐
DistDiam Layer	☐	☐	☐
WaterLateralDiame	☐	☐	☐
Hydrants	☐	☐	☐
Road edge of pav	☑	☐	☐
Road names	☐	☐	☐
Road centerlines	☐	☐	☐

⊟ ☐ Edit Sketch
 ☐ Edit sketch vertices
 ☑ Edit sketch edges
 ☐ Perpendicular to sketch
⊟ ☐ Topology Elements
 ☑ Topology nodes

Types of snapping properties

When you use the snapping environment to create or place a new feature in an exact location relative to other features, you must choose to which part of existing features—vertex, edge, or endpoint—you want your feature to snap. These choices are called layer *snapping properties*. You can also specify snapping properties for the edit sketch and for topology elements; these are called sketch and topology snapping properties. You can set all three types of snapping properties using the Snapping Environment window. The following table briefly explains each of the layer snapping and sketch snapping properties.

Layer snapping properties	Sketch snapping properties	Topology snapping properties
Vertex — Snaps to each vertex of the features in that layer.	**Perpendicular to sketch** — Lets you create a segment that will be perpendicular to the previous.	**Topology nodes** — Snaps to the nodes in the topology.
Edge — Snaps to the entire outline—both segments and vertices—of each feature in that layer.	**Edit sketch edges** — Snaps to the entire outline—both segments and vertices—of the sketch.	
Midpoint — Snaps to the midpoint between the two end vertices of the segment.	**Edit sketch vertices** — Snaps to the vertices of the sketch.	
Endpoint — Snaps to the first vertex and the last vertex in a line feature.		

Using the snapping environment

The *snapping environment* can help you establish exact locations in relation to other features. Suppose you're creating a new segment of primary that begins from an existing transformer; you want to ensure that the vertex of the primary connects precisely to the transformer.

The snapping environment makes this type of task accurate and easy. Setting the snapping environment involves setting a snapping tolerance, snapping properties, and a snapping priority. ▶

Tip

Showing snap tips

You can choose to display the layer name or target being snapped to. Check Show snap tips on the General tab of the Editing Options dialog box. A small text box will appear when snapping, which identifies the layer you have snapped to.

Tip

Viewing the snapping tolerance

To see the current snapping tolerance area, hold down the T key while using the Sketch tool.

Setting the snapping tolerance

1. Click Editor and click Options.

2. Click the General tab.

3. Click the Snapping tolerance dropdown arrow and click the type of measurement unit you want to use for the snapping tolerance—pixels or map units.

4. Type the desired number of measurement units in the Snapping tolerance text box.

5. Click OK.

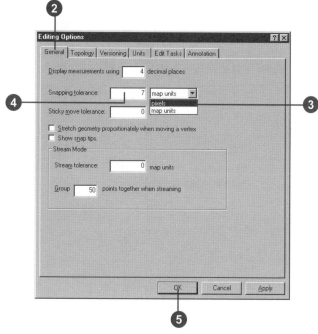

The *snapping tolerance* is the distance within which the pointer or a feature is snapped to another location. If the location being snapped to—vertex, edge, or endpoint—is within the distance you set, the pointer automatically snaps (jumps) to the location.

The circle around the pointer in the graphics below represents the snapping tolerance. When the location being snapped to (orange point) is outside the

snapping tolerance, the snapping location (blue dot) stays with the pointer (top graphic). When the location being snapped to is inside the snapping tolerance, the snapping location moves away from the pointer and snaps to the target location (bottom graphic).

You can choose the part of the feature—vertex, edge, or endpoint—to which you want your new feature to snap by ▶

Setting snapping properties

1. Click Editor and click Snapping.

   The Snapping Environment window appears.

2. Check the snapping properties you want.

   The snapping properties are effective as soon as they are checked or unchecked.

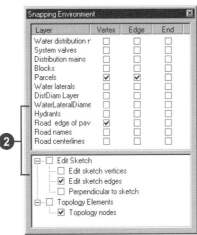

setting the layer snapping properties. For example, if you want your new feature—a segment of primary—to snap to the vertex of an existing transformer in the transformers layer, you would check the box under Vertex and next to the transformers layer in the Snapping Environment window. When the pointer comes within the snapping tolerance of the transformer, the first vertex of the primary snaps to the vertex of the transformer.

You can also set the *snapping priority* for layers on your map. The order of layers listed in the Snapping Environment window determines the order in which snapping will occur. Snapping occurs first in the layer at the top of the list, then in each consecutive layer down the list. You can easily change the snapping priority by dragging the layer names to new locations.

Tip

Sketch and topology snapping properties

You can set snapping properties that apply specifically to the edit sketch and to topology elements in the Snapping Environment dialog box; these are located at the bottom of the Snapping Environment window. For more information, see 'Types of snapping properties' in this chapter.

Setting the snapping priority

1. Click Editor and click Snapping.

   The Snapping Environment window appears.

2. Click and drag the layer names to arrange them in the order in which you want snapping to occur. The first layer in the list will be snapped to first.

   The snapping priorities you set are effective immediately.

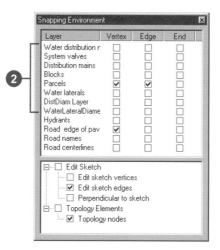

The Snap to Feature command

Apart from the rules set in the Snapping Environment, you can also snap on the fly to specific features. This is done through the Snap to Feature command of the sketch context menu.

By specifying a feature and the part of the feature to which you wish to snap, your next vertex will automatically be placed regardless of the Snapping Environment settings.

Snapping to a specific feature

1. Click the tool palette dropdown arrow and click the Sketch tool.

2. Right-click the feature to which you want to snap your next vertex.

3. On the dropdown menu, choose Snap to Feature.

4. Click the part of the feature to which you want to snap the next vertex.

   The vertex will be placed at the nearest location that matches your selection.

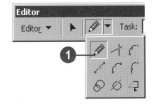

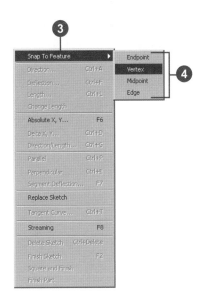

Setting the direction measuring system and units for editing tools

Some of the ArcMap editing tools allow you to enter an angle, direction, or deflection when constructing an edit sketch. These include the Direction–Distance tool and Traverse tool as well as several of the commands on the sketch context menu. You can change the direction measuring system and units these tools use on the Units tab of the Editing Options dialog box. When you change the direction measuring system and units, the editing tools will all recognize inputs in the new system and units.

Direction measuring systems

You can choose from the following direction measuring systems: North Azimuth, South Azimuth, Quadrant Bearing, and Polar. By default, the tools accept angular measurements in the Polar direction measuring system.

Polar angles are measured counterclockwise from the positive x-axis.

In the North Azimuth system the azimuth of a line is the horizontal angle measured from a meridian to the line, measured in the clockwise direction from north.

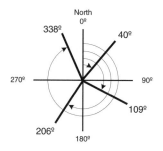

In the South Azimuth system the angles are measured clockwise from south.

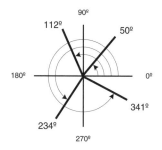

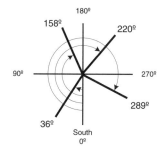

In the Quadrant Bearing system the bearing of a line is measured as an angle from the reference meridian, either the north or the south, and measured toward the east or the west. Bearings in the Quadrant Bearing system are written as a meridian, an angle, and a direction. For example, a bearing of N 25 W defines an angle 25 degrees west measured from north. A bearing S 18 E defines an angle 18 degrees east measured from the south.

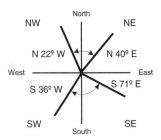

Valid input formats for Quadrant Bearing measurements include:

- [NS] dd.dddd [EW] where the first letter is an N or S, indicating the meridian of origin, and the last letter is an E or W, indicating which direction the angle is toward.

- dd.dddd-[1234] where the second to last character is a - (dash) and the last digit indicates the quadrant that the bearing is in. The quadrants are numbered 1—NE, 2—SE, 3—SW, 4—NW

Direction measuring units

The editing tools use decimal degrees as their default units of angular measure. You can choose from the following direction measurement units: decimal degrees, degrees/minutes/seconds, radians, gradians, and gons.

Degrees are the standard unit of angular measurement, where one degree represents 1/360 of a circle, and fractions of a degree are represented as decimal values.

Degrees Minutes Seconds also uses the degree, but fractions of a degree are represented in minutes and seconds, where one minute equals 1/60 of a degree, and one second equals 1/60 of a minute.

Valid input formats for degrees/minutes/seconds values include:

- dd-mm-ss.ss
- dd.mmssss
- dd^mm'ss.ss"

Radians are the Standard International (SI) unit of plane angular measure. There are 2 pi, approximately 6.28318, radians in a circle. One radian is equivalent to about 57.296 degrees. The length of a circular arc with an angle of one radian is equal to the radius of the arc.

Gradians are a unit of angular measure where the right angle is divided into 100 parts. One gradian equals 1/400 of a circle.

Gons are the same as gradians. One gon equals 1/400 of a circle. The term gon is primarily used in German, Swedish, and other northern European languages where the word grad means degree.

Setting the direction type and angular units

You can set the direction measurement system and the units with which you measure angles from the Units tab of the Editing Options dialog box. All of the editing tools that accept angular measurements will interpret angular measurements using the direction type and units that you specify here.

Setting the direction type

1. Click Editor and click Options.

2. Click the Units tab.

3. Click the Direction Type dropdown list and choose a direction measuring system.

4. Click OK.

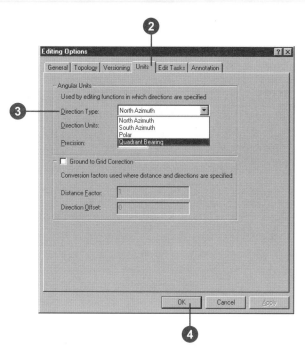

Setting the direction units

1. Click Editor and click Options.

2. Click the Units tab.

3. Click the Direction Units dropdown list and click the type of direction measurement unit you want to use.

4. Set Precision to specify the number of decimal places used when displaying angles and directions.

5. Click OK.

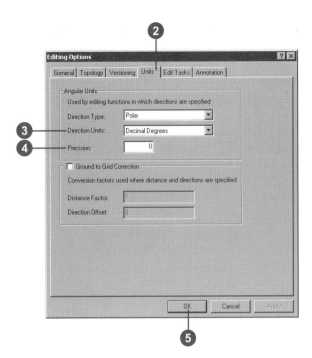

Setting the ground to grid conversion

Sometimes when creating features using the coordinate geometry tools in ArcMap, you need to convert angles and distances measured in the field so they match the coordinate system of your data. For example, if you are given distances measured in ground units at a high elevation, the distances will need to be adjusted slightly to fit your GIS dataset's coordinate system, in which distances are assumed to have been measured at a given ellipsoid—or sea level—surface. The distance conversion is applied as a scale factor to distances you type into the coordinate geometry editing tools.

Sometimes you need to correct angular measurements taken in the field as you enter them in your GIS. For example, suppose you are creating features using coordinate geometry from a set of measurements on a surveyor's field notes. The surveyor's angular measurements were based on True North—defined using the astronomical meridian. Your GIS dataset has a coordinate system where north differs by 0 degrees, 2 minutes, and 3 seconds from true north. Instead of going through the field notes and manually converting the measurements, you can set a direction offset to automatically correct the angles as you type them.

Direction and distance corrections can be calculated by measuring directions and distances between control points in the GIS and comparing them to directions and distances measured on the ground, as shown on a survey plan.

Using a ground to grid correction

You can set distance and direction conversion factors to allow you to correct for differences between your GIS coordinate system and the angles and distances a surveyor may have measured in the field.

Setting a ground to grid distance conversion factor

1. Click Editor and click Options.

2. Click the Units tab.

3. Check Ground to Grid Correction.

4. Type a conversion factor to convert distances measured in the field (ground distance) to distances in the GIS (grid distance).

5. Click OK.

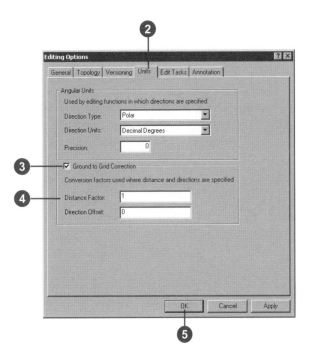

Setting a ground to grid direction offset

1. Click Editor and click Options.

2. Click the Units tab.

3. Check Ground to Grid Correction.

4. Type the desired number of measurement units in the Direction Offset text box.

5. Click OK.

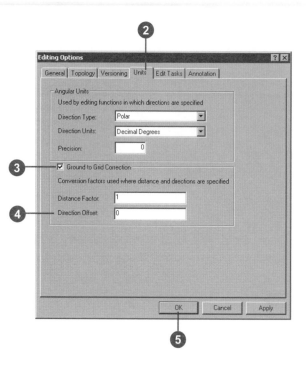

Setting the distance units for tools

Sometimes when creating features using the editing tools in ArcMap, you need to enter data that was recorded in different distance units than the coordinate system of your data.

For example, suppose your data is in a State Plane coordinate system and the linear units are U.S. Survey Foot (1 Foot_US = 0.3048006096 m). You are given measurements in International Feet (1 Foot = 0.3048 m). Rather than convert all of the measurements, you can type the abbreviation for International Foot, ft, after the measurements and the tools will convert the distance correctly. You could also change the dataset coordinate system definition to use International Feet, and type the distances without a unit suffix.

Whenever you are typing a distance into one of the editing tools, you have the option to specify the linear units to use or to simply type a number, which the tool will interpret as being in the dataset's coordinate system units.

Distance Units	Abbrev.	Meters per Unit	Description
Metric Units			
Kilometer	km	1,000	1,000 meters exactly
Meter	m	1	International meter
Centimeter	cm	0.01	1/100 meter exactly
Millimeter	mm	0.001	1/1000 meter exactly
Imperial or international units			
Foot	ft	0.3048	Standard foot used in the United States. Also known as international foot or imperial foot that was used in most non-U.S. countries before the metric system.

Distance Units	Abbrev.	Meters per Unit	Description
Imperial or international units (Cont'd)			
Mile	mi	1,609.344	Also referred to as a statute mile, equal to 5,280 international feet.
Nautical mile	nm	1,852	The nautical mile is a unit of distance used primarily in sea and air navigation. The nautical mile is defined to be the average distance on the earth's surface represented by one minute of latitude. In 1929, the nautical mile was defined to be exactly 1,852 meters or 6,076.11549 feet, a distance known as the international nautical mile.
Chain	ch	20.1168	66 international feet
Yard	yd	0.9144	Three international feet
Rod	rd	5.0292	1/4 chain or 16.5 international feet
Link	lk	0.201168	1/100 international chain or 66/100 international feet
Inch	in	0.0254	1/12 of an international foot

Distance Units	Abbrev.	Meters per Unit	Description
U.S. survey units			
Survey foot	ftUS	0.304800-6096	The U.S. survey foot is used in the State Plane Coordinate Systems. In the United States, fundamental survey units, such as rods, chains, statute miles, acres, sections, and townships, all depend on the U.S. survey foot. An exact conversion to meters can be accomplished by multiplying U.S. survey feet by the fraction 1200/3937.
Survey mile	miUS	1609.347-2186944	5,280 survey feet
Survey chain	chUS	20.11684-02337	66 survey feet
Survey rod	rdUS	5.029210-0584	1/4 survey chain
Survey link	lkUS	0.201168-4023	1/100 survey chain
Survey yard	ydUS	0.914401-8288	3 survey feet

Editing topology

4

In addition to simple features, ArcMap lets you edit collections of features related by a topology. In a geodatabase, a topology contains rules that define how features share space.

Topologies are useful for maintaining high-quality spatial data by ensuring that your features conform to simple rules. When you set up a geodatabase with a topology, you specify which feature classes participate in the topology and define rules that control when and how features can share geometry. For example, in a geodatabase of states and coastlines, you might have a rule that states polygons cannot overlap each other and another rule that the coastline must coincide with the boundaries of the states. These rules would help you ensure, when updating the state boundaries to match the coastline, that you don't inadvertently create places where the states overlap or where a state's coastal edge doesn't match the shape of the coastline.

ArcMap allows you to simultaneously edit multiple features from layers that share geometry. Only those features that participate in the topology will be affected by these edits. For instance, you can update lot lines that define a parcel, and update the corresponding parcel polygon feature in your geodatabase. Similarly, you could move a road centerline and, at the same time, update all of the bus routes that follow that road. In this respect, editing topologies is a bit like editing features in a geometric network. However, topologies offer many more possible ways that polygon, arc, and point features can be related than networks do. ArcMap provides some new tools for editing and managing topologies. With ArcView licensed seats of ArcMap, you can edit shared geometry by creating a map topology.

What is topology?

Topology has historically been viewed as a spatial data structure used primarily to ensure that the associated data forms a consistent and clean topological fabric. With advances in object-oriented GIS development, an alternative view of topology has evolved. The geodatabase supports an approach to modeling geography that integrates the behavior of different feature types and supports different types of key relationships. In this context, topology is a collection of rules and relationships that, coupled with a set of editing tools and techniques, enables the geodatabase to more accurately model geometric relationships found in the world.

Topology, considered from the feature behavior perspective, allows a more flexible set of geometric relationships to be modeled than the data structure perspective. It also allows topological relationships to exist between more discrete types of features within a feature dataset. In this alternative view, topology may still be employed to ensure that the data forms a clean and consistent topological fabric; but also, more broadly, it is used to ensure that the features obey the key geometric rules defined for their role in the database.

Why use topology?

Topology is used most fundamentally to ensure data quality and to allow your geodatabase to more realistically represent geographic features. A geodatabase provides a framework within which features can have behavior, such as subtypes, default values, attribute domains, validation rules, and structured relationships to tables or other features. This behavior enables you to more accurately model the world and maintain referential integrity between objects in the geodatabase. Topology may be considered an extension of this framework for behavior that allows you to control the geometric relationships between features and to maintain their geometric integrity. Unlike other

feature behavior, topology rules are managed at the level of the topology and dataset, not for individual feature classes.

How do I work with topology?

Different people work with topology in different ways, depending upon their role in an organization and its GIS design and management work flow.

Initially, creating a topology requires a geodatabase designer. A topology organizes the spatial relationships between features in a set of feature classes. The designer analyzes an organization's data modeling needs, identifies the key topological relationships required in the geodatabase, and defines the rules that will constrain different features' topological relationships.

Once the participating feature classes have been added to the topology and the rules defined, the topology is validated. Data quality managers use the topology tools to analyze, visualize, report, and, where necessary, repair the spatial integrity of the database after it is initially created as well as after editing. Topology provides these users with a set of validation rules for the topologically related features. It also provides a set of editing tools that let users find and fix integrity violations.

As the geodatabase is used and maintained, new features are added and existing features are modified. Data editors update features in the geodatabase and use the topology tools to construct and maintain relationships between features, within the constraints imposed by the database designer. Depending on the work flow of the organization, the topology may be validated after each edit session or on a schedule.

Topology basics for data editors

Topologies store three sets of parameter rules, ranks, and a cluster tolerance. When editing a geodatabase, you will not typically need to modify these parameters, but you will need to be aware of them, especially the rules.

Topologies also maintain a feature layer that stores *dirty areas*, *errors*, and *exceptions*. You use these to maintain the quality of data in your topology.

The sections that follow describe each of these parameters and concepts in more detail.

Rules

Rules define the permissible spatial relationships between features. The rules you define for a topology control the relationships of features allowed within a feature class, between features in different feature classes, or between subtypes of features.

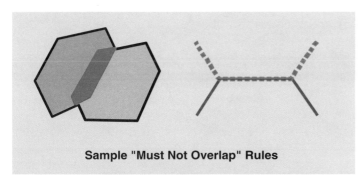

Sample "Must Not Overlap" Rules

Example of a "Must Not Overlap" rule applied to polygons and lines. The red polygon and line mark the places where the rule is violated. These are stored in the topology as error features. Such rules can apply to features within the same feature class, to pairs of feature classes, or to subtypes of features.

The initial validation of the topology checks all of the features against all of the rules. This initial check can take some time, but subsequent checks are performed only on the areas that have been edited—the dirty areas.

Cluster tolerance

The *cluster tolerance* defines how close vertices must be to each other in order to be considered coincident and limits the distance features can move during *validation*. The cluster tolerance is the minimum distance between vertices of features that are not coincident. Vertices that fall within the cluster tolerance are defined as coincident and are snapped together. The cluster tolerance is typically a small actual distance to minimize the movement of correctly placed features.

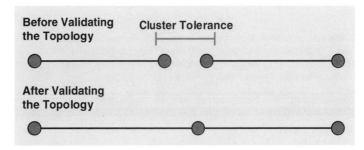

When you validate a topology, features within the cluster tolerance are snapped together.

Ranks

Ranks control which features may be moved to other features when snapping the topology together during validation. The ranks you specify for feature classes in the topology control which feature classes will be moved when snapping coincident vertices during the initial validation of the topology as well as subsequent validations.

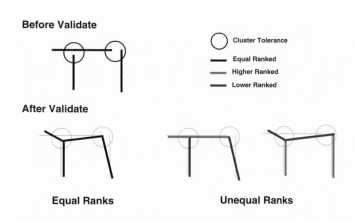

Before Validate

Cluster Tolerance

Equal Ranked
Higher Ranked
Lower Ranked

After Validate

Equal Ranks

Unequal Ranks

When you validate a topology, the ranks of the feature classes in the topology control how features are snapped together. Lower-ranking features snap to higher-ranking features. Equally ranked features snap to the geometric average of their position.

When different feature classes have different levels of intrinsic reliability, such as when one was collected by survey or differential global positioning system and another was digitized from less accurate source material or collected with uncorrected GPS, ranks can allow you to ensure that reliably placed vertices are not snapped to the location of less reliable vertices. Lower-ranked features' vertices will be snapped to the location of higher-ranked vertices, if they fall within the cluster tolerance. The location of equally ranked vertices are geometrically averaged when they fall within the cluster tolerance.

Feature layers maintained by a topology

Instead of storing topological information for all features, the topology discovers those relationships when the information is requested, such as when you are editing using the Topology Edit tool. The topology stores some feature layers that let it efficiently track the places where the topology may have been violated during editing—dirty areas—and features that were found to violate topology rules after validation—error features. Certain errors may be acceptable, in which case the error features are marked and stored as exceptions.

Dirty areas

Dirty areas are areas that have been edited, updated, or affected by the addition or deletion of features. Dirty areas allow the topology to limit the area that must be checked for topology errors during topology validation. Dirty areas track the places where topology rules may have been violated during editing. This allows selected parts, rather than the whole extent of the topology, to be validated after editing.

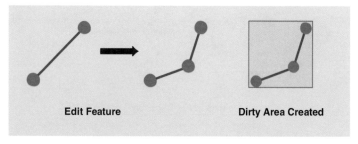

Edit Feature

Dirty Area Created

When you edit features in a topology, the topology creates a dirty area to mark the area that should be checked for violations of the topology rules.

Dirty areas are created when:

- A feature is created or deleted
- A feature's geometry is modified
- A feature's subtype is changed
- Versions are reconciled
- The topology properties are modified

Dirty areas are stored in the topology as a single feature, with each new dirty area joined with the existing dirty area, and each area that has been validated removed from the dirty area.

Errors and exceptions

Errors and exceptions are stored as features in the topology layer and allow you to render and manage the cases in which features do not obey the rules of the topology. Error features record where topological errors were discovered during validation. Certain errors may be acceptable, in which case the error features can be marked as exceptions.

ArcMap and ArcCatalog allow you to create a report of the total number of errors and exceptions for the feature classes in your topology. You can use the report of the number of error features as a measure of the data quality of a topological dataset. The error inspector in ArcMap lets you select different types of errors and zoom to individual errors. You can correct topology errors by editing the features that violate the topology's rules. After you validate the edits, the error is deleted from the topology.

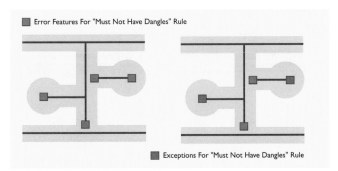

When you validate a topology, features that violate the rules are marked as error features. You can edit the features to fix the errors, or you can mark the errors as exceptions. In this example, the street line features cannot have dangles, which are endpoints that do not connect to other street features. Because cul-de-sac streets are a legitimate exception to this rule, they may be marked as exceptions in the topology. The remaining errors should be fixed by editing the street features.

Topology rules

Many topology rules can be imposed on features in a geodatabase. A well-designed geodatabase will have only those topology rules that define key spatial relationships needed by an organization.

Some topology rules govern the relationships of features within a given feature class, while others govern the relationships between features in two different feature classes. Topology rules can also be defined between subtypes of features in one or another feature class. For example, a topology rule can require street features to be connected to other street features at both ends, except in the case of streets belonging to the cul-de-sac or dead-end subtypes.

The topological rules that you may encounter and examples of them are discussed on the following pages. There are also images of sample errors generated by the particular topology rule. By default, ArcMap uses shades of coral to symbolize topology errors. When errors are selected using the Error Inspector or the Fix Topology Error tool, they are drawn with black outlines, lines, or squares.

An explanation of the *fixes* that you can use to correct errors in your topology are listed after the descriptions of the rules. Some topology rules, however, have no predefined fixes. Once you've discovered the topology errors, you can select the error on the map with the Fix Topology Error tool, or select the error from within the Error Inspector and apply one of the fixes listed in the context menu for that error type.

Polygon rules

Must Not Overlap

This rule requires that the interior of polygons in the feature class not overlap. The polygons can share edges or vertices. This rule is used when an area cannot be-

long to two or more polygons. It is useful for modeling administrative boundaries, such as ZIP Codes or voting districts, and mutually exclusive area classifications, such as land cover or landform type.

Subtract: The Subtract fix removes the overlapping portion of geometry from each feature that is causing the error and leaves a gap or void in its place. This fix can be applied to one or more selected Must Not Overlap errors.

Merge: The Merge fix adds the portion of overlap from one feature and subtracts it from the others that are violating the rule. You need to pick the feature that receives the portion of overlap using the Merge dialog box. This fix can be applied to one Must Not Overlap error only.

Create Feature: The Create Feature fix creates a new polygon feature out of the error shape and removes the portion of overlap from each of the features causing the error to create a planar representation of the feature geometry. This fix can be applied to one or more selected Must Not Overlap errors.

Must Not Have Gaps

This rule requires that there are no voids within a single polygon or between adjacent polygons. All polygons must form a continuous surface. An error will always exist on the perimeter of the surface. You can either ignore this error or mark it as an exception. Use this rule on data that must completely cover an area. For example, soil polygons cannot include gaps nor form voids—they must cover an entire area.

You can use Create Feature or mark the error on the outside boundary as an exception.

You can use Create Feature to create a new polygon in the void.

Create Feature: The Create Feature fix creates a new polygon feature in a void that is completely surrounded by polygons in error (a closed ring of line errors). This fix can be applied to one or more selected Must Not Have Gaps errors. If you select two errors and use the Create Feature fix, the result will be one polygon feature per ring. If you want one multipart feature as a result, you'll need to select each new feature and click Merge from the Editor menu.

Note that the outer boundary of your feature class is in error. Using the Create Feature fix on this specific error can create overlapping polygons. Alternatively, you can mark the outer bounds Must Not Have Gaps error as an exception.

Must Not Overlap With

This rule requires that the interior of polygons in one feature class must not overlap with the interior of polygons in another feature class. Polygons of the two feature classes can share edges or vertices or be completely disjointed. This rule is used when an area cannot belong to two separate feature classes. It is useful for combining two mutually exclusive systems of area classification, such as zoning and water-body type, where areas defined within the zoning class cannot also be defined in the water-body class and vice versa.

Subtract: The Subtract fix removes the overlapping portion of each feature that is causing the error and leaves a gap or void in its place. This fix can be applied to one or more selected Must Not Overlap With errors.

Merge: The Merge fix adds the portion of overlap to one feature and subtracts it from the others that are violating the rule. You need to pick the feature that receives the portion of overlap using the Merge dialog box. This fix can be applied to one Must Not Overlap With error only.

Must Be Covered By Feature Class Of

This rule requires that a polygon in one feature class must share all of its area with polygons in another feature class. An area in the first feature class that is not covered by polygons from the other feature class is an error. This rule is used when an area of one type, such as a state, should be completely covered by areas of another type, such as counties.

Subtract: The Subtract fix removes the overlapping portion of each feature that is causing the error so the boundary of each feature from both feature classes is the same. This fix can be applied to one or more selected Must Be Covered By Feature Class Of errors.

Create Feature: The Create Feature fix creates a new polygon feature out of the portion of overlap from the existing polygon so the boundary of each feature from both feature classes is the same. This fix can be applied to one or more selected Must Be Covered By Feature Class Of errors.

Must Cover Each Other

This rule requires that the polygons of one feature class must share all of their area with the polygons of another feature class. Polygons may share edges or vertices. Any area defined in either feature class that is not shared with the other is an error. This rule is used when two systems of classification are used for the same geographic area and any given point defined in one system must also be defined in the other. One such case occurs with nested hierarchical datasets, such as census blocks and block groups or small watersheds and large drainage basins. The rule can also be applied to nonhierarchically related polygon feature classes, such as soil type and slope class.

Subtract: The Subtract fix removes the overlapping portion of each feature that is causing the error so the boundary of each feature from both feature classes is the same. This fix can be applied to one or more selected Must Cover Each Other errors.

Create Feature: The Create Feature fix creates a new polygon feature out of the portion of overlap from the existing polygon so the boundary of each feature from both feature classes is the same. This fix can be applied to one or more selected Must Cover Each Other errors.

Must Be Covered By

This rule requires that polygons of one feature class must be contained within polygons of another feature class. Polygons may share edges or vertices. Any area defined in the contained feature class must be covered by an area in the covering feature class. This rule is used when area features of a given type must be located within features of another type. This rule is useful when modeling areas that are subsets of a larger surrounding area, such as management units within forests or blocks within block groups.

Create Feature: The Create Feature fix creates a new polygon feature out of the portion of overlap from the existing polygon so the boundary of each feature from both feature classes is the same. This fix can be applied to one or more selected Must Be Covered By errors.

Boundary Must Be Covered By

This rule requires that boundaries of polygon features must be covered by lines in another feature class. This rule is used when area features need to have line features that mark the boundaries of the areas. This is usually when the areas have one set of attributes and their boundaries have other attributes. For example, parcels might be stored in the geodatabase along with their boundaries. Each parcel might be defined by one or more line features that store information about

their length or the date surveyed, and every parcel should exactly match its boundaries.

Create Feature: The Create Feature fix creates a new line feature from the boundary segments of the polygon feature generating the error. This fix can be applied to one or more selected Boundary Must Be Covered By errors.

Area Boundary Must Be Covered By Boundary Of

This rule requires that boundaries of polygon features in one feature class be covered by boundaries of polygon features in another feature class. This is useful when polygon features in one feature class, such as subdivisions, are composed of multiple polygons in another class, such as parcels, and the shared boundaries must be aligned.

There are no topology fix commands for this rule.

Contains Point

This rule requires that a polygon in one feature class contain at least one point from another feature class. Points must be within the polygon, not on the boundary. This is useful when every polygon should have at least one associated point, such as when parcels must have an address point.

This polygon is an error because it does not contain a point.

Create Feature: The Create Feature fix creates a new point feature at the centroid of the polygon feature that is causing the error. The point feature that is created is guaranteed to be within the polygon feature. This fix can be applied to one or more selected Contains Point errors.

Line rules

Must Not Overlap

This rule requires that lines not overlap with lines in the same feature class. This rule is used where line segments should not be duplicated—for example, in a stream feature class. Lines can cross or intersect but cannot share segments.

Subtract: The Subtract fix removes the overlapping line segments from the feature causing the error. You must select the feature from which the error will be removed. If you have duplicate line features, select the line feature you want to delete from the Subtract dialog box. Note that the Subtract fix will create multipart features, so if the overlapping segments are not at the end or start of a line feature, you may want to then use the Explode command on the Advanced Editing toolbar to create single part features. This fix can be applied to one selected Must Not Overlap error only.

Must Not Intersect

This rule requires that line features from the same feature class not cross or overlap each other. Lines can share endpoints. This rule is used for contour lines that should never cross each other or in cases where the intersection of lines should only occur at endpoints, such as street segments and intersections.

Subtract: The Subtract fix—which is only available for lines with overlapping features—removes the overlapping line segments from the feature causing the error. You must select the feature from which the error will be removed. If you have duplicate line features, select the line feature you want to delete from the Subtract dialog box. Note that the Subtract fix will create multipart features, so if the overlapping segments are not at

the end or start of a line feature, you may want to then use the Explode command on the Advanced Editing toolbar to create single part features. This fix can be applied to one Must Not Intersect error only.

Split: The Split fix splits the line features that cross one another at their point of intersection, but cannot be used when the error has overlapping line segments. If two lines cross at a single point, applying the Split fix at that location will result in four features. Attributes from the original features will be maintained in the split features. This fix can be applied to one or more Must Not Intersect errors.

Must Not Have Dangles

This rule requires that a line feature must touch lines from the same feature class at both endpoints. An endpoint that is not connected to another line is called a dangle. This rule is used when line features must form closed loops, such as when they are defining the boundaries of polygon features. It may also be used in cases where lines typically connect to other lines, as with streets. In this case, exceptions can be used where the rule is occasionally violated, as with cul-de-sac or dead-end street segments.

Because the fixes use tolerance values to determine whether the fix occurs, make sure you have specified your map's distance units. Click View, Data Frame Properties, then the General tab.

Snap: The Snap fix will snap dangling line features to the nearest line feature within a given distance. If no line feature is found within the distance specified, the line will not be snapped. The Snap fix will snap to the nearest feature found within the distance. It searches for endpoints to snap to first, then vertices, and finally for edges of line features within the feature class. The Snap fix can be applied to one or more Must Not Have Dangles errors.

Extend: The Extend fix will extend the dangling end of line features if they snap to other line features within a given distance. If no feature is found within the distance specified, the feature will not extend to the distance specified. Also, if several errors were selected, the fix will simply skip the features that it cannot extend and attempt to extend the next feature in the list. The errors of features that could not be extended remain in the Error Inspector dialog box. If the distance value is 0, lines will extend until they find a feature to snap to. This fix can be applied to one or more Must Not Have Dangles errors.

Trim: The Trim fix will trim dangling line features if a point of intersection is found within a given distance. If no feature is found within the distance specified, the feature will not be trimmed, nor will it be deleted if the distance is greater than the length of the feature in error. If the distance value is 0, lines will be trimmed back until they find a point of intersection. If no intersection is located, the feature will not be trimmed and the fix will attempt to trim the next feature in error. This fix can be applied to one or more Must Not Have dangles errors.

Must Not Have Pseudonodes

This rule requires that a line connect to at least two other lines at each endpoint. Lines that connect to one other line, or to themselves, are said to have pseudonodes. This rule is used where line features must form closed loops, such as when they define the boundaries of polygons or when line features logically must connect to two other line features at each end, as with segments in a stream network, with exceptions being marked for the originating ends of first-order streams.

Merge To Largest: The Merge To Largest fix will merge the geometry of the shorter line into the geometry of the longest line. The attributes of the longest line feature will be retained. This fix can be applied to one or more Must Not Have Pseudonodes errors.

Merge: The Merge fix adds the geometry of one line feature into the other line feature causing the error. You must pick the line feature to merge into. This fix can be applied to one selected Must Not Have Pseudonodes error.

Must Not Intersect Or Touch Interior

This rule requires that a line in one feature class must only touch other lines of the same feature class at endpoints. Any line segment in which features overlap, or any intersection not at an endpoint, is an error. This rule is useful where lines must only be connected at endpoints, such as in the case of lot lines, which must split (only connect to the endpoints of) back lot lines and which cannot overlap each other.

Subtract: The Subtract fix—which is only available for lines with overlapping features—removes the overlapping line segments from the feature causing the error. You must select the feature from which the error will be removed. If you have duplicate line features, choose the line feature you want to delete from the Subtract dialog box. The Subtract fix creates multipart features, so if the overlapping segments are not at the end or start of a line feature, you may next want to use the Explode command on the Advanced Editing toolbar to create single part features. This fix can be applied to one selected Must Not Intersect or Touch Interior error only.

Split: The Split fix splits the line features that cross one another at their point of intersection, but cannot be used when the error has overlapping line segments. If two lines cross at a single point, applying the Split fix at that location will result in four features. Attributes from the original features will be maintained in the split features. This fix can be applied to one or more Must Not Intersect or Touch Interior errors.

Must Not Overlap With

This rule requires that a line from one feature class not overlap with line features in another feature class. This rule is used when line features cannot share the same space—for example, roads must not overlap with railroads or depression subtypes of contour lines cannot overlap with other contour lines.

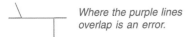

Where the purple lines overlap is an error.

Subtract: The Subtract fix removes the overlapping line segments from the feature causing the error. You must select the feature from which the error will be removed. If you have duplicate line features, choose the line feature you want to delete from the Subtract dialog box. The Subtract fix creates multipart features, so if the overlapping segments are not at the end or start of a line feature, you may next want to use the Explode command on the Advanced Editing toolbar to create single part features. This fix can be applied to one selected Must Not Overlap With error only.

Must Be Covered By Feature Class Of

This rule requires that lines from one feature class must be covered by the lines in another feature class. This is useful for modeling logically different but spatially coincident lines, such as routes and streets. A bus route feature class must not depart from the streets defined in the street feature class.

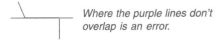

Where the purple lines don't overlap is an error.

There are no fixes for this rule.

Must Be Covered By Boundary Of

This rule requires that lines be covered by the boundaries of area features. This is useful for modeling lines, such as lot lines, that must coincide with the edge of polygon features, such as lots.

Subtract: The Subtract fix removes line segments that are not coincident with the boundary of polygon features. If the line feature does not share any segments in common with the boundary of a polygon feature, the feature will be deleted. This fix can be applied to one or more Must Be Covered By Boundary Of errors.

Endpoint Must Be Covered By

This rule requires that the endpoints of line features must be covered by point features in another feature class. This is useful for modeling cases where a fitting must connect two pipes or a street intersection must be found at the junction of two streets.

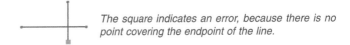

The square indicates an error, because there is no point covering the endpoint of the line.

Create Feature: The Create Feature fix adds a new point feature at the endpoint of the line feature that is in error. The Create Feature fix can be applied to one or more Endpoint Must Be Covered By errors.

Must Not Self Overlap

This rule requires that line features not overlap themselves. They can cross or touch themselves, but must not have coincident segments. This rule is useful for features such as streets, where segments might touch, in a loop, but where the same street should not follow the same course twice.

This individual line feature overlaps itself, with the error indicated by the coral line.

Simplify: The Simplify fix removes self overlapping line segments from the feature in error. Applying the Simplify fix can result in multipart features, which you can detect using the Must Be Single Part rule. The Simplify fix can be applied to one or more Must Not Self Overlap errors.

Must Not Self Intersect

This rule requires that line features not cross or overlap themselves. This rule is useful for lines, such as contour lines, that cannot cross themselves.

Simplify: The Simplify fix removes self overlapping line segments from the feature in error. Note that applying the Simplify fix can result in multipart features. You can detect multipart features using the Must Be Single Part rule. This fix can be applied to one or more Must Not Self Intersect errors.

Must Be Single Part

This rule requires that lines must have only one part. This rule is useful where line features, such as highways, may not have multiple parts.

Multipart lines are created from a single sketch.

Explode: The Explode fix creates single part line features from each part of the multipart line feature that is in error. This fix can be applied to one or more Must Be Single Part errors.

Point rules

Must Be Covered By Boundary Of

This rule requires that points fall on the boundaries of area features. This is useful when the point features help support the boundary system, such as boundary markers, which must be found on the edges of certain areas.

The square is an error because it is a point that is not on the boundary of the polygon.

There are no fixes for this rule.

Must Be Properly Inside Polygons

This rule requires that points fall within area features. This is useful when the point features are related to polygons, such as wells and well pads or address points and parcels.

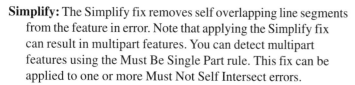
The squares are errors where there are points that are not inside the polygon.

Delete: The Delete fix removes point features that are not properly within polygon features. Note that you can use the Edit tool and move the point inside of the polygon feature if you do not wish to delete it. This fix can be applied to one or more Must Be Properly Inside errors.

Must Be Covered By Endpoint Of

This rule requires that points in one feature class must be covered by the endpoints of lines in another feature class. This rule is similar to the line rule Endpoint Must Be Covered By, except that where the rule is violated, the point feature—rather than the line—is marked as an error. Boundary corner markers might be constrained to be covered by the endpoints of boundary lines.

The square indicates an error where the point is not on an endpoint of a line.

Delete: The Delete fix removes point features that are not coincident with the endpoints of line features. Note that you can snap the point to the line by setting edge snapping to the line layer, then moving the point with the Edit tool. This fix can be applied to one or more Must Be Covered By Endpoint Of errors.

Must Be Covered By Line

This rule requires that points in one feature class must be covered by lines in another feature class. It does not constrain the covering portion of the line to be an endpoint. This rule is useful for points that fall along a set of lines, such as highway signs along highways.

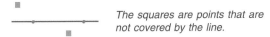

The squares are points that are not covered by the line.

There are no fixes for this rule.

Topology errors and exceptions

Topology rules may represent an ideal situation, but geodatabases are flexible enough to handle exceptions to the rules found in real-world data. Violations of topology rules are initially stored as errors in the topology, but where appropriate, you can mark them as exceptions. Exceptions are thereafter ignored, though you can return them to error status if you decide that they are actually errors and that the features should be modified to comply with the topology rules.

Exceptions are a normal part of the data creation and update process. An assessor's geodatabase might have a topology rule requiring that building features not cross parcel lines as a quality control for the building digitizing effort. This rule might be true for 90 percent of the features in the city, but it could be violated by some high-density housing and commercial buildings.

If you create a condominium building feature that crosses parcel boundaries, it will be discovered as an error when you validate your edits, but you can mark it as a legitimate exception to the rule. Similarly, a street database for a city might have a rule that centerlines must connect at both ends to other centerlines. This rule would normally ensure that street segments are correctly snapped to other street segments when they are edited. However, at the boundaries of the city you might not have street data. Here, the external ends of streets might not snap to other centerlines. These cases could be marked as exceptions, and you would still be able to use the rule to find cases where streets were incorrectly digitized or edited.

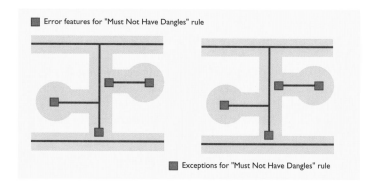

■ Error features for "Must Not Have Dangles" rule

■ Exceptions for "Must Not Have Dangles" rule

Topology errors can be fixed quickly using the Fix Topology Error tool. This tool allows you to select a topology error and choose from a number of fixes that have been predefined for that error type. You can also use the tool to get more information about the rule that has been violated or mark the error as an exception.

■ Exceptions, building footprints must be covered by parcels.

■ Error features, building footprints must be covered by parcels.

Geometric elements of a topology

When you create a topology, you specify the feature classes that participate in the topology. These feature classes may contain point, line, or polygon features. In the topology, the geometric relationships are between the parts of the features rather than the features themselves. Polygons in a topology have edges that define the boundary of the polygons, nodes where edges intersect, and vertices, which define the shape of the edges.

Polygon features share edges and nodes, in red. Vertices define the shape of the edges, in green.

Similarly, line features are made up of an edge, at least two nodes that define the endpoints of the edge, and vertices that define the shape of the edge. Point features behave as nodes when they are coincident with other features in a topology.

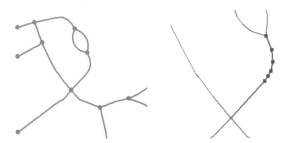

Line features share edges and nodes, in red. Vertices define the shape of the edges, in green.

When features in the topology have parts that intersect or overlap, the edges and nodes that define these parts are shared.

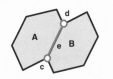

Polygons A and B have shared nodes c and d and shared edge e.

Lines A and B have endpoint nodes c, d, and e.
Lines A and B share node e.

You can use the Topology Edit tool to move nodes and whole edges that are shared between features or to move the vertices that define the shape of shared edges.

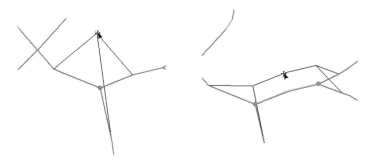

Moving a node stretches the connected edges so they stay connected. Moving an edge with its endpoint nodes also stretches the edges attached to the nodes.

When you move nodes or vertices, you can choose whether you want the segment between the vertex and the closest vertex to be stretched or whether you want the whole edge to be proportionately stretched.

You can choose whether to stretch the feature geometry proportionally when moving a vertex, or whether to just stretch the segments between the vertex and the next vertices.

You can also temporarily add new topology nodes to split edges. This simply splits the edge for the topology; it does not break the feature into two features. This can be useful when you want to move one part of an edge without affecting other parts of the edge or when you want to create a new node to snap to.

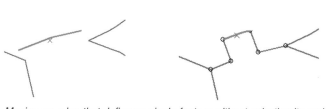

Moving an edge that defines a single feature without selecting its nodes moves the whole edge without maintaining connections to the nodes. Moving a split edge that is a part of a single feature does maintain connectivity within the feature.

You can find out which features share a given topology element and control whether or not the geometry should be considered shared with the Show Shared Features tool.

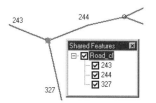

If two or more features share an edge or node, you can use the Show Shared Features tool to turn off geometry sharing for one or more of the features. Changes that you make to that topology edge or node with the Topology Edit tool will only affect the features for which the geometry is still shared.

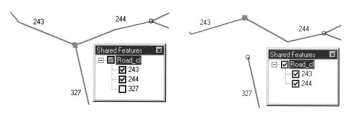

Uncheck a feature with the Shared Features tool in order to make a shared topology element independent of that feature.

Editing features in a topology

Editing features that participate in a topology is similar to editing simple features—in fact, you can use the same sketch tools to create new features that participate in a topology that you would use for features that do not. When you want to modify a feature that shares edges or nodes with other features in the topology, you can use the Topology Edit tool.

When editing topological features, you often have a choice of several ways of doing something. For example, suppose you manage a forest and there are two polygon feature classes, Forest and Stand, in your forest dataset.

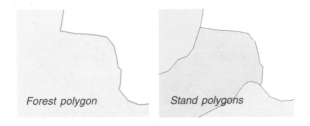

The Forest and Stand polygons are related by three topology rules: Stand must not overlap, Forest must cover Stand, and Stand must cover Forest. These rules prevent Stand polygons from overlapping, since no area can be in two stands at once. They also prevent stands from extending outside the official boundary of the whole forest and the forest boundary from covering an area not in a stand.

Suppose you are editing the Stand feature class and need to change the boundary between two of the stands. You could start editing; use the Topology Edit tool to select the shared edge;

double-click the edge to edit its vertices; then add, remove, and move vertices along that edge to shape it to fit the new boundary.

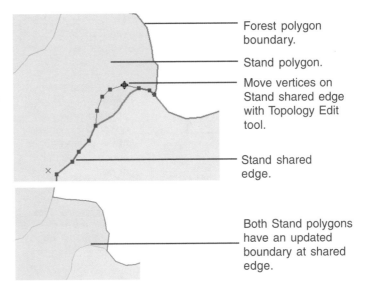

Forest polygon boundary.

Stand polygon.

Move vertices on Stand shared edge with Topology Edit tool.

Stand shared edge.

Both Stand polygons have an updated boundary at shared edge.

Use the Topology Edit tool to edit an edge shared by two polygons from the same feature class.

You could also use the Topology Edit tool to modify edges shared by the Stand and Forest polygons. For example, suppose the actual boundary of the forest has been determined to be 150 meters east and 20 meters north of the corner where two stand features meet at the edge of the forest. You could use the Topology Edit tool to select the topology node at this intersection of features and move it to the correct location.

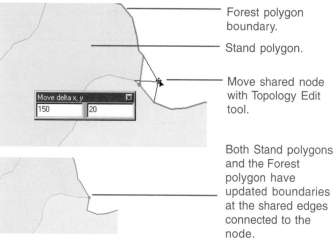

Forest polygon boundary.

Stand polygon.

Move shared node with Topology Edit tool.

Both Stand polygons and the Forest polygon have updated boundaries at the shared edges connected to the node.

Use the Topology Edit tool to edit a topology node shared by two polygons from the same feature class and a third polygon from another feature class. You can move the node freehand, move it relative to its current position, or move it to an absolute location. When the node moves, the edges connected to it in both the Forest and Stand polygon feature classes are stretched to stay connected to it.

You can also use the regular editing tools to edit individual features that participate in a topology. When you edit topologically related features using the nontopological editing tools, you are only modifying one feature at a time. If this feature shares geometry with other features, the shared geometry is not updated. If the edits create a violation of the topology rules, you can use the Error Inspector to find the error and the Fix Topology Error tool to fix the error. There are several predefined ways that you can fix a given type of topology error. The Fix Topology Error tool allows you to right-click an error and choose which fix to use for the error.

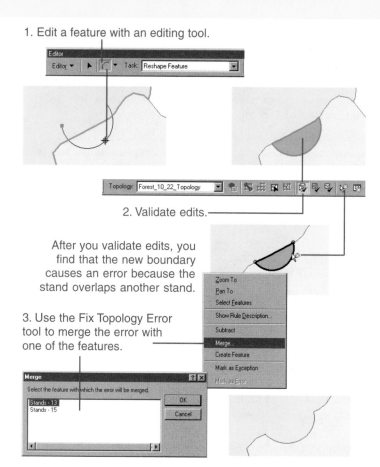

1. Edit a feature with an editing tool.

2. Validate edits.

After you validate edits, you find that the new boundary causes an error because the stand overlaps another stand.

3. Use the Fix Topology Error tool to merge the error with one of the features.

You can also edit features with the nontopological Edit tool. If the features participate in a topology rule, you can validate the topology to identify errors that your edits may have caused. If the edit created an error, you can use the Fix Topology Error tool to fix it using one of the predefined topology error fixes. The shared geometry is updated by the fix. You can also apply edits to shared edges using an edit sketch with the Modify Edge and Reshape Edge topology edit tasks.

The Modify Edge and Reshape Edge topology edit tasks allow you to update a selected shared edge using an edit sketch.

1. Reshape an edge using the Reshape Edge editing task and the editing tools.

2. Finish the sketch. All features that share the edge are updated.

You can use the editor tools and the Reshape Edge and Modify Edge edit tasks to simultaneously edit several features that share an edge.

Correcting topology errors

There are a couple of ways to correct topology errors once you've discovered them. You can select the error on the map with the Fix Topology Error tool, or select the error from within the Error Inspector and apply one of the fixes listed in the context menu for that error type.

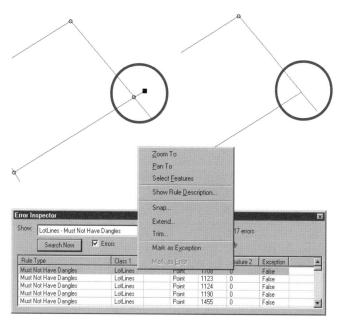

Different error types have different predefined fixes available for them. For example, a dangling line can be snapped, trimmed, or extended to another line. Errors caused by overlapping polygons can be merged into one of the polygons, subtracted from both, or turned into a separate new polygon feature. Errors caused by violations of the "must be covered by" rules can be fixed by creating a new feature or deleting a feature.

Making new features with topology tools

There are several ways that you can use topology tools to make new features from existing ones. In ArcCatalog you can create a whole new polygon feature class from an input set of line features. In ArcMap you can construct new polygon features from the intersection of selected existing line and polygon features or create new line features by splitting selected line features where they cross each other.

Creating polygons from lines in ArcCatalog

In ArcCatalog, the Polygon Feature Class From Lines tool takes one or more existing line or polygon feature classes in a feature dataset and creates new polygon features from the closed shapes that are defined by the intersection of all of the lines or polygon edges.

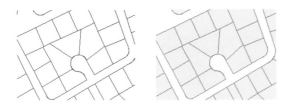

You have the option to use a point feature class to supply attributes for the new polygons. If a point falls within one of the new polygons, the polygon is assigned the point's attributes.

Creating features in ArcMap

In ArcMap, the Construct Features tool takes selected features from one or more feature classes and creates new features in the target feature class.

The tool uses the input geometries of the selected features to construct polygons or lines following polygon boundaries, depending upon the geometry of the target feature class.

Construct Features tool

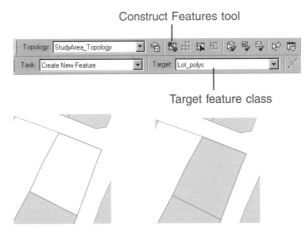

Target feature class

Selected lines can be turned into a polygon in the target feature class.

You can use this tool to build parcel polygons from selected lot line features or lake shorelines from selected lake polygon features.

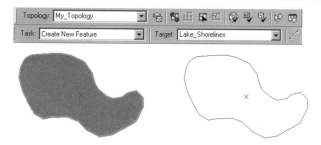

Selected polygon features can be turned into line features in the target feature class.

You can also use the *Planarize* Lines tool to create separate line features from selected touching or crossing line features. This can be useful when you have nontopological line work that has been spaghetti digitized or imported from a CAD drawing.

Planarize Lines tool

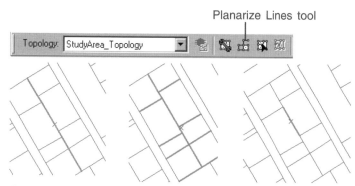

Selected line features can be split into separate features where they touch or cross other selected line features.

Adding the Topology toolbar

The Topology toolbar contains tools that you can use to create a map topology as well as tools that you can use to work with map and geodatabase topologies.

The topology tools operate within an edit session, so you will need to start editing before any of the topology tools are available.

1. Click Editor, point to More Editing Tools, and click Topology.

   The Topology toolbar appears.

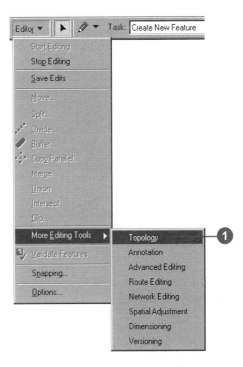

Map topology concepts

A *map topology* is a simple topology that you can impose on simple features on a map during an edit session. A map topology allows you to simultaneously edit simple features that overlap or touch each other using the tools on the topology toolbar. The features can be in one or more feature classes and may have different geometries. Line features and the outlines of polygon features become topological edges when you create a map topology. Point features, the endpoints of lines, and the places where edges intersect become nodes.

There are two steps to creating a map topology. First, you specify which feature classes on the map will participate in the topology, then you specify a cluster tolerance. The cluster tolerance is a distance within which features will be coincident.

After you create a map topology, you can use the Topology Edit tool to edit the edges and nodes shared by the features. Editing an edge or node shared by two or more different features results in each feature being modified. This lets you move a border to update two forest polygons or move a corner vertex and update several parcel polygons and a few lot boundaries at the same time.

A map topology can be applied to simple features in a shapefile or to simple feature classes in a geodatabase. The feature classes that participate in the map topology must be in the same folder or geodatabase. A map topology cannot be applied to feature classes that participate in a geometric network.

Although they cannot edit geodatabase topologies, ArcView seats of ArcMap can be used to edit a map topology.

A map topology creates topological relationships between the parts of features that are coincident. You can choose the distance, or cluster tolerance, that defines how close together edges and vertices must be in order to be considered coincident. You can also specify the feature classes that you want to participate in the map topology.

You do not specify any topology rules for a map topology. All edges or vertices of features in the map topology that fall within the cluster tolerance are considered to be topologically shared. You edit shared edges and vertices in a map topology in the same way, and with the same tools, as you would edit a geodatabase topology. Since there are no topology rules, there is no need to validate a map topology, and there is no creation of error features.

At the geometry level, topologies are about simple relationships, such as coincidence, covering, and crossing, between the geometric primitives that make up features. While all simple feature class geometries—point, line, polygon—may participate in topologies, internally, the types of geometry that are acted on when editing a topology are:

- *Edges*—line segments that define lines or polygons.
- *Nodes*—points at the end of an edge.
- *Pseudonodes*—a node connecting only two edges or a logical split defined in the topology cache while editing. Pseudonodes of the latter sort become a vertex after editing.

When you create a map topology, the cluster tolerance that you specify is used to determine which parts of the features are coincident and which edges and nodes in the topology are shared. The cluster tolerance is typically a small actual ground distance. Setting large cluster tolerances can result in features being collapsed or distorted when vertices within a given feature snap together.

Creating a map topology

Once the data that you want to create a map topology for is on the map and you've started an edit session, you can create a map topology.

1. On the Editor toolbar, click Editor and click Start Editing.

2. Click the source folder or geodatabase that contains the data that you want to edit.

3. Click OK.

4. On the Topology toolbar, click the Map topology button. ▶

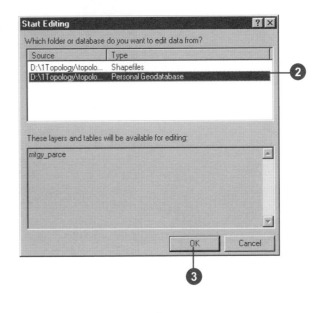

5. Check the feature classes that will participate in the map topology.

   Annotation, dimension, and relationship classes, as well as feature classes in a geometric network or geodatabase topology, cannot be added to a map topology.

6. Optionally, set a cluster tolerance for the map topology.

   The default cluster tolerance is the minimum possible cluster tolerance. Increasing the cluster tolerance may cause more features to be snapped together and considered coincident, but this may reduce the spatial accuracy of your data.

7. Click OK.

8. Click the Topology Edit tool and click the features you want to edit using the map topology.

   The map topology is created for the features that are visible in the current display extent.

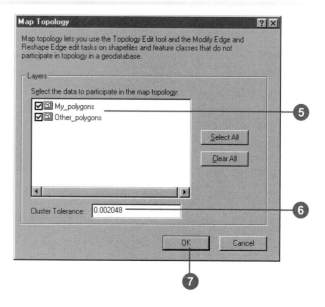

Editing shared geometry

The Topology Edit tool allows you to select and modify edges and nodes that may be shared by more than one feature. It also allows you to select and move the individual vertices that define the shape of edges. When you move vertices, edges, or nodes with the Topology Edit tool, all of the features that share the node or edge are updated. ▶

Tip
Adding to a topology selection
Pressing the Shift key while selecting a node or edge adds that node or edge to the currently selected topology elements.

Tip
Selecting only nodes
You can select nodes by holding the N key while clicking the node or while dragging a box around the node with the Topology Edit tool.

Tip
Selecting only edges
You can select edges by holding the E key while clicking the edge or while dragging a box around the edge with the Topology Edit tool.

Selecting a node

1. Click the Topology Edit tool on the Topology toolbar.

2. Click the node that you want to select.

   You can ensure that edges are not selected by holding the N key while selecting the node. Another easy way to select a node is to drag a rectangle around it while holding the N key.

Selecting an edge

1. Click the Topology Edit tool on the Topology toolbar.

2. Click the edge that you want to select.

   You can ensure that nodes are not selected by holding the E key while selecting the node.

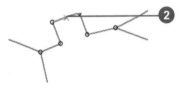

Moving a vertex on a shared edge

1. Click the Topology Edit tool on the Topology toolbar.

2. Double-click the edge that you want to move the vertices of.

3. Click and drag the vertex that you want to move.

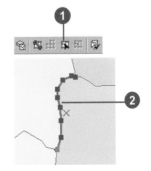
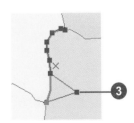

When you move a node in a topology, all of the edges that connect to it are stretched to stay connected to the node. When you move an edge, edge segments stretch to maintain the connection of shared endpoint nodes to their previous location. Sometimes you may want to move a node and a connected edge without stretching the other connected edge. Moving a shared endpoint node of an edge requires you to temporarily split the topological relationship between the node and the other shared edges, then reestablish it. This is known as a split-move of the node. You'll need to snap the node to an edge or to another topology node.

Moving a node

1. Click the Topology Edit tool on the Topology toolbar.

2. Click the node that you want to move.

   You can ensure that edges are not selected by holding the N key while selecting the node. Another easy way to select a node is to drag a rectangle around it while holding the N key.

3. Click and drag the node that you want to move.

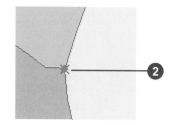

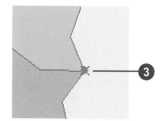

Moving an edge

1. Click the Topology Edit tool on the Topology toolbar.

2. Click the edge that you want to move.

3. Click and drag the edge to a new location. Edge segments stretch to connect the edge's endpoint nodes to their previous positions, where they are shared.

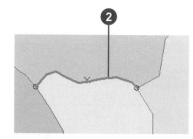

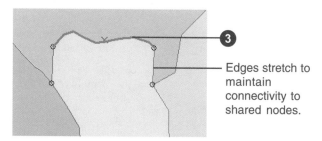

Edges stretch to maintain connectivity to shared nodes.

146

Moving a topology element by a given X and Y distance

1. Click the Topology Edit tool on the Topology toolbar.

2. Click the node or edge that you want to move.

3. Right-click and click Move.

4. Type an X and a Y distance to move the topology element relative to its current location and press Enter.

   If you are moving an edge or more than one topology element, the Move command moves the selection anchor to the specified location and moves the topology element to maintain its position relative to the selection anchor.

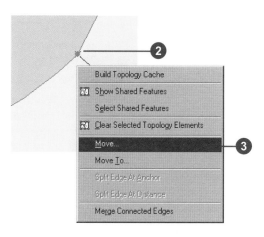

Build Topology Cache
Show Shared Features
Select Shared Features
Clear Selected Topology Elements
Move...
Move To...
Split Edge At Anchor
Split Edge At Distance
Merge Connected Edges

Move delta x, y
-183 m   171 m

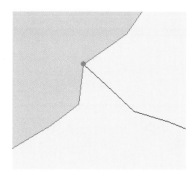

Moving a topology element to a given location

1. Click the Topology Edit tool on the Topology toolbar.

2. Click the node or edge that you want to move.

3. Right-click and click Move To.

4. Type the absolute X and Y coordinate to which you want to move the topology element and press Enter.

   If you are moving an edge or more than one topology element, the Move To command moves the selection anchor to the specified location and moves the topology element to maintain its position relative to the selection anchor.

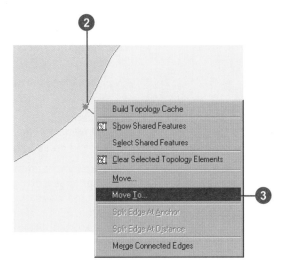

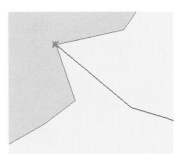

Splitting an edge with the selection anchor

1. Click the Topology Edit tool on the Topology toolbar.

2. Click the edge that you want to split.

3. Hold the Ctrl key and click and drag the selection anchor to the place where you want to split the edge.

4. Right-click and click Split Edge At Anchor.

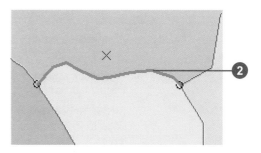

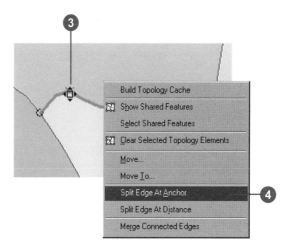

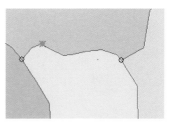

Splitting an edge at a distance from an endpoint

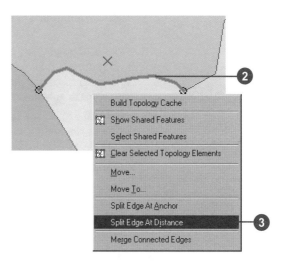

1. Click the Topology Edit tool on the Topology toolbar.

2. Click the edge that you want to split.

3. Right-click and click Split Edge At Distance.

   Arrows appear along the edge to indicate the edge direction. The edge can be split at a distance or a percentage of its length, measured from the start point or the endpoint of the edge. ▶

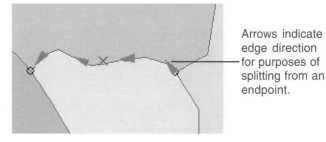

Arrows indicate edge direction for purposes of splitting from an endpoint.

4. Optionally, click the button to specify a percentage of the edge length.

5. Type a distance or a percentage if you chose to make the split at a percentage of the edge length.

6. Optionally, click the button to indicate that you want the distance to be measured from the endpoint of the edge.

7. Click OK.

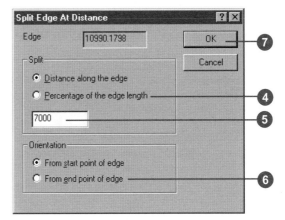

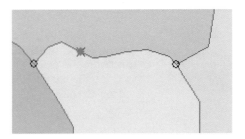

Moving a shared endpoint node of an edge

1. Set the snapping environment to snap to Topology nodes. See Chapter 3, 'Creating new features'.

   You can also set snapping to edges of the feature to which you want to move the endpoint node.

2. Click the Topology Edit tool on the Topology toolbar.

3. Click the edge to which you want to move the endpoint node.

4. Hold the Ctrl key and click and drag the selection anchor to the place where you want to snap the edge's endpoint node.

   Holding the Ctrl key allows you to move the selection anchor.

5. Right-click and click Split Edge At Anchor.

   Splitting the edge creates a new node to which you can snap the endpoint node of the edge. ►

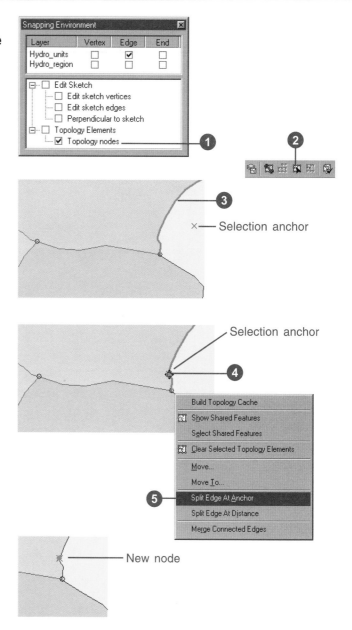

6. Click the edge that you want to move the end of.

7. Hold the N key and drag a rectangle around the endpoint node you want to move.

   The N key limits the Topology Edit tool selection to nodes.

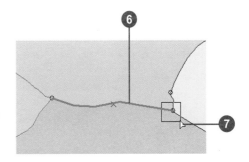

8. Hold the S key and click and drag the node that you want to move to the node you created.

   Holding the S key changes the pointer to the Split-Move tool pointer.

   The endpoint node of the edge is moved to the new location, and the topology is maintained. If you do not snap the node to the new node or edge, the split-move will be cancelled.

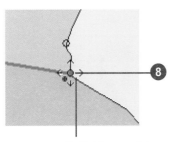

Split-Move pointer

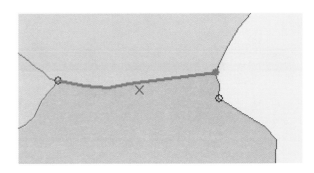

Rebuilding the topology cache

When you select a topology element using the Topology Edit tool, ArcMap creates a *topology cache*. The topology cache stores the topological relationships between edges and nodes of the features that fall within the current display extent. If you are editing with the map zoomed in to a small area and you go back to a previous extent, some of the features in the new extent may not be in the topology cache. You can rebuild the topology cache to include these features. You can also rebuild the topology cache to remove temporary topology nodes that you created for snapping and editing.

1. Click the Topology Edit tool on the Topology toolbar.

2. Right-click the map and click Build Topology Cache.

   The topological relationships between edges and nodes are rediscovered for all of the features in the current display extent.

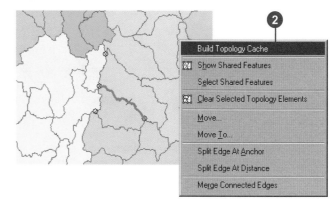

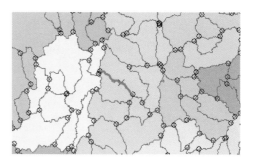

Clearing selected topology elements

When you are editing topological edges and nodes, you may sometimes want to deselect some elements. You can deselect a given element by holding the Shift key and clicking it, or deselect all selected edges and nodes by clearing all selected topology elements.

You can also click the map with the Topology Edit tool away from edges and nodes to clear the selection.

Deselecting a single topology element

1. Click the Topology Edit tool on the Topology toolbar.

2. Hold the Shift key and click a selected edge or node to deselect it.

   The topology element is deselected.

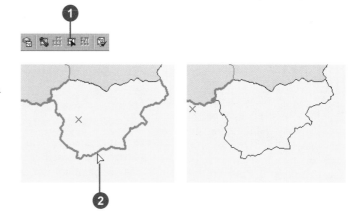

Deselecting all topology elements

1. Click the Topology Edit tool on the Topology toolbar.

2. Right-click and click Clear Selected Topology Elements.

   All of the topology elements are deselected.

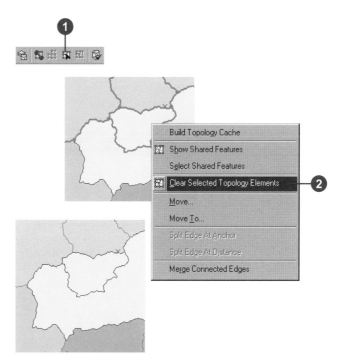

Finding out which features share topology elements

Topology elements may be shared by multiple features. It can be useful to know which features share a given node or edge. You can find out which features share a given topology element by selecting them, then using the Show Shared Features command.

You can also control whether or not the shared features will be affected by edits that you make to a given edge or node. By default, all features that share a topology element are updated when you edit that element with the Topology Edit tool. However, when you turn off a feature in the Shared Features dialog box, the feature will not be modified if you edit the topology element.

Showing shared features

1. Click the Topology Edit tool on the Topology toolbar.

2. Click an edge or node to select it.

3. Right-click and click Show Shared Features.

    You can also click the Show Shared Features button on the Topology toolbar.

4. Click the plus sign to show all of the features in a given feature class that are shared. A given topology element may be shared by features in multiple feature classes, so more than one feature class may be listed.

5. Click a feature in the list to make it flash on the map.

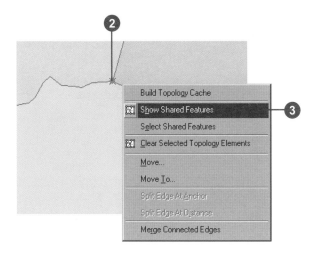

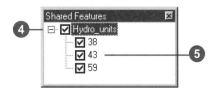

Temporarily turning off topology element sharing for a feature

1. Click the Topology Edit tool on the Topology toolbar.

2. Click an edge or node to select it.

3. Right-click and click Show Shared Features.

   You can also click the Show Shared Features button on the Topology toolbar.

4. Click the plus sign to show all of the features in a given feature class that are shared. A given topology element may be shared by features in multiple feature classes, so more than one feature class may be listed.

5. Uncheck a feature in the list to turn off topology element sharing. Edits that you make with the Topology Edit tool to the topology element will not update this feature.

   The unshared status of the feature is temporary. It only lasts while the topology element is selected.

6. Click the Close button to close the Shared Features dialog box.

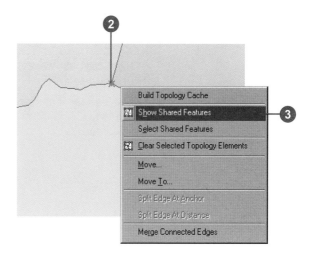

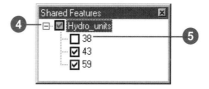

Selecting features that share a topology element

1. Click the Topology Edit tool on the Topology toolbar.

2. Click an edge or node to select it.

3. Right-click and click Select Shared Features.

   The features that share the topology element are selected.

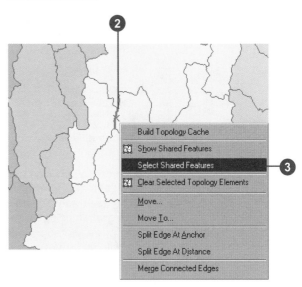

	Build Topology Cache
	Show Shared Features
	Select Shared Features
	Clear Selected Topology Elements
	Move...
	Move To...
	Split Edge At Anchor
	Split Edge At Distance
	Merge Connected Edges

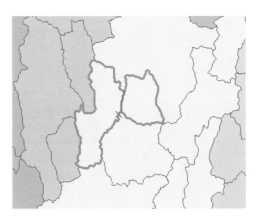

Merging connected edges within a feature

1. Click the Topology Edit tool on the Topology toolbar.

2. Click an edge of a feature that has been topologically split by adding nodes.

3. Right-click and click Merge Connected Edges.

   The selected edge is merged with the adjacent edge, and the topology node is removed.

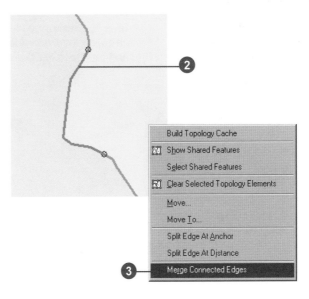

	Build Topology Cache
▨	Show Shared Features
	Select Shared Features
▨	Clear Selected Topology Elements
	Move...
	Move To...
	Split Edge At Anchor
	Split Edge At Distance
	Merge Connected Edges

Using the edit sketch to make topology edits

In addition to editing topology elements with the Topology Edit tool, you can also modify and reshape a selected topology edge using an edit sketch.

The Modify Edge topology edit task takes the selected edge and makes an edit sketch from it. You can then use the standard editing tools to insert, delete, or move the vertices that make up the edge.

With the Reshape Edge topology edit task, you can use the basic editing tools to create a new line to replace an existing edge line.

Modifying an edge

1. Click the Topology Edit tool on the Topology toolbar.

2. Click an edge to select it.

3. Click the Task dropdown arrow on the Editor toolbar and click Modify Edge. ▶

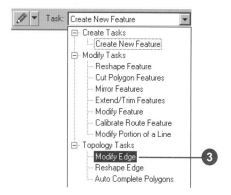

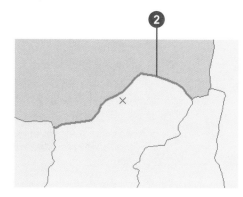

4. Optionally, right-click a segment of the edge that has no vertices and click Insert Vertex.

A new vertex is inserted into the edge and into all features that share it.

5. Optionally, right-click a vertex and click Delete Vertex.

The vertex is removed from the edge and from all features that share it.

6. Optionally, click a vertex and drag it to a new location. ▶

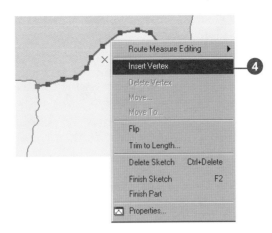

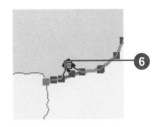

7. Optionally, right-click a vertex, then click Move.

8. Type an X and a Y distance and press Enter to move the vertex relative to its current position.

9. Optionally, right-click a vertex and click Move To.

10. Type the new coordinates for the vertex and press Enter. ▶

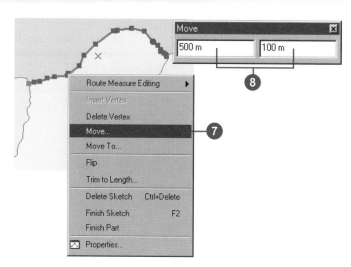

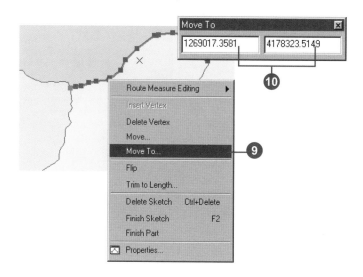

11. Right-click anywhere on the
    map and click Finish Sketch.

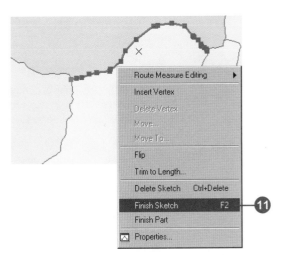

Reshaping an edge

1. Click the Topology Edit tool.

2. Click an edge to select it.

3. Click the Task dropdown arrow on the Editor toolbar and click Reshape Edge. ▶

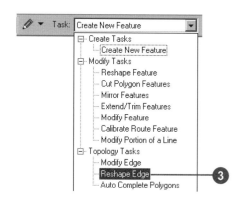

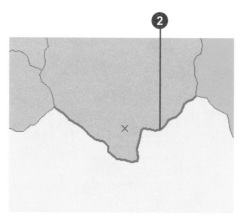

4. Click the Sketch Tool on the Editor toolbar.

5. Start an edit sketch.

   You can either snap the edit sketch to the selected edge or cross the edge to indicate where to start reshaping the edge.

6. Use the Sketch tools to digitize a new shape for part of the selected edge.

   Once you've started the edit sketch, you can use any of the tools on the Sketch Tool Palette to create your edit sketch.

   You can either snap the edit sketch to the selected edge or cross the edge to indicate where to stop reshaping the edge.

7. Right-click anywhere on the map and click Finish Sketch.

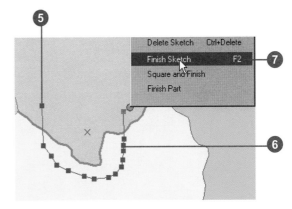

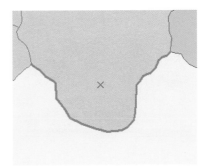

Stretching features when editing topology elements

Just as you can stretch a single feature geometry proportionately when moving a vertex, you can also stretch the geometry of features that share a topology element when moving a node or vertex on a topology edge.

1. Click Editor and click Options.

2. Click the General tab.

3. Check Stretch geometry proportionately when moving a vertex.

4. Click OK. ▶

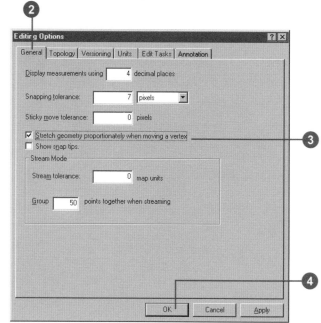

5. Click the Topology Edit tool on the Topology toolbar.

6. Click a topology node or double-click a topology edge and click a vertex.

7. Click and drag the node or vertex to a new location.

The features that share the node or vertex stretch proportionately.

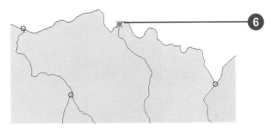

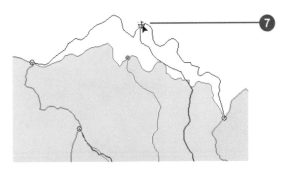

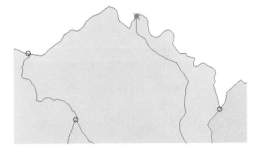

Snapping to topology nodes

When you are editing topology elements, it can be useful to snap to topology nodes. You can turn on snapping to topology nodes on the Snapping Environment dialog box.

1. Click Editor and click Snapping.

2. Check Topology nodes.

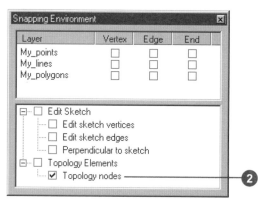

Changing the symbology for selected error features

You can change the way selected error features are drawn on the map. Error features are drawn with point, line, and area symbols of a given color by default. When you select errors, for example, when you are using the Fix Topology Error tool, the selected errors change color so you can more easily identify the errors that you are fixing. You can change the symbology of selected topology errors to make them stand out better against a given map background.

1. Click Editor and click Options.

2. Click the Topology tab.

3. Click the Active Errors Symbology buttons to change the way error features look when they are selected.

4. Pick a new symbol for the selected error feature and click OK.

5. Click OK to close the Editing Options dialog box.

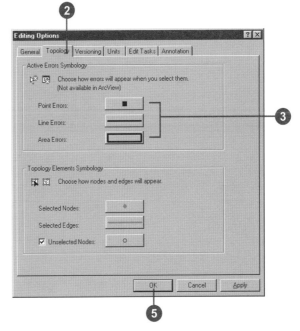

Changing the symbology for topology elements

You can change the way topology elements are drawn on the map. Topology nodes and edges are drawn with point and line symbols of a given color by default, and unselected topology nodes are not drawn by default. You can change the symbol for selected topology nodes and edges and for unselected nodes. Turning on the symbol for unselected nodes can make it easier to identify nodes to snap to when you are editing topology elements.

1. Click Editor and click Options.

2. Click the Topology tab.

3. Click the Topology Elements Symbology buttons to change the way topology elements look on the map.

4. Pick a new symbol for the topology element and click OK.

5. Optionally, check Unselected Nodes to show the nodes in the topology cache that have not been selected.

6. Click OK.

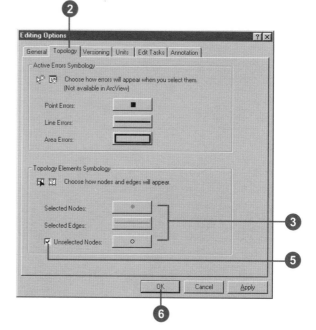

Changing the symbology for topology layers

You can change the way error features, exceptions, and dirty areas are drawn on the map. Point, line, and polygon errors are drawn with symbols of a single color by default. Exceptions and dirty areas are not drawn by default. Changing the symbology of error features and exceptions that relate to different topology rules can make it easier to understand what the problems are with your data. Drawing dirty areas can make it easier to see the areas that have been affected by edits and that have yet to be validated.

See Also

For more information on symbolizing data, see Using ArcMap.

Changing topology error and exception symbology

1. Right-click the Topology layer in the ArcMap table of contents and click Properties.

2. Click the Symbology tab.

3. Check the error types that you want to see on the map.

4. Click the error type for which you want to change the symbol.

5. Optionally, click the button to draw all of the errors of this type with a single symbol.

6. Choose a new symbol for this type of error feature and click OK.

7. Optionally, click the button to draw the errors of this type with unique symbols.

8. Double-click the error symbol for the rule that you want to draw with a new symbol.

9. Choose a new symbol for this type of error feature and click OK.

10. Click OK to close the Layer Properties dialog box.

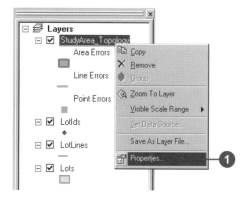

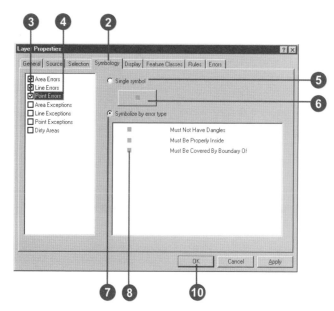

Showing dirty areas and changing their symbology

1. Right-click the Topology layer in the ArcMap table of contents and click Properties.

2. Click the Symbology tab.

3. Check Dirty Areas to draw dirty areas in the Topology layer.

4. Click Dirty Areas to set the symbology for dirty areas.

5. Click the button to change the dirty area symbol.

6. Pick a new symbol for dirty areas and click OK.

7. Click OK to close the Layer Properties dialog box.

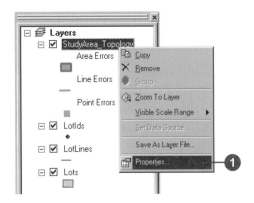

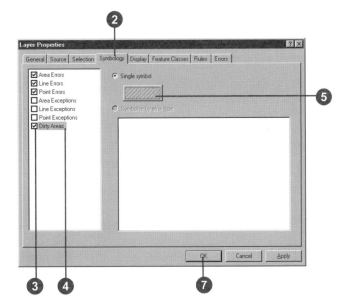

Validating edits to a topology

Once you've made edits to a feature that participates in a topology, the next step is to validate the topology. Validating the topology checks the features to identify any violations of the rules that have been defined for the topology.

You can validate the whole topology, validate the visible extent of your map, or drag a box around the area to validate.

Validating the whole topology

1. Click the Validate Entire Topology button on the Topology toolbar.

   Validating the entire extent may take a while for complex or large datasets or where there are many topology rules.

   You will be prompted to specify whether or not you wish to validate the whole topology.

2. Click Yes.

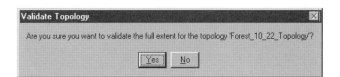

Validating topology in the visible extent of the map

1. Click the Validate Topology in Current Extent button on the Topology toolbar.

   The visible extent is validated. Areas that are not currently visible on the map are not validated.

Validating topology in a selected area

1. Click the Validate Topology in Specified Area button on the Topology toolbar.

2. Drag a box around the area you want to validate.

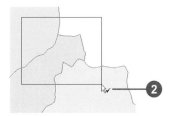

ArcInfo and ArcEditor

Summarizing topology errors

Once you've made edits to a feature that participates in a topology and validated your edits, you may see one or more topology errors. You can manage topology errors with the Error Inspector.

The Error Inspector lets you view topology errors in a table that tells you the rule violated, the feature class or classes involved in the error, the geometry of the error, the feature ID of the features involved in the error, and whether or not the error has been marked as an exception. You can sort the errors by any of the fields in the table, so you can work with all of the errors of a given type. You can also limit the errors shown in the table to errors of a given type, errors that occur in the currently visible map extent, or errors that have been marked as exceptions.

In addition to letting you view and sort errors, the Error Inspector lets you select errors, pan or zoom to selected errors, and apply topology fixes of various types to errors.

Opening the Error Inspector

1. Click the Error Inspector button on the Topology toolbar.

   The Error Inspector can be docked to the ArcMap window or it can float free as a separate window.

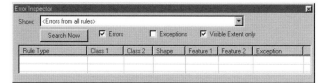

Finding all topology errors

1. On the Error Inspector, check Errors.

2. Click the Show dropdown arrow and click Errors from all rules.

3. Click Search Now.

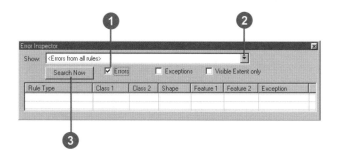

Finding only the errors in the visible extent

1. On the Error Inspector, check Visible Extent only.

2. Click Search Now.

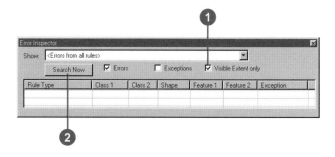

174

EDITING IN ARCMAP

Finding errors for a particular topology rule

1. On the Error Inspector, click the Show dropdown arrow and click the rule that you want to search for violations of.

2. Click Search Now.

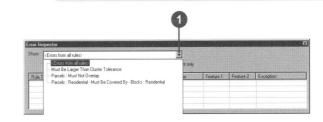

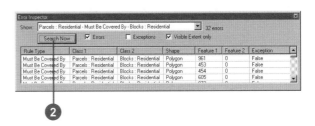

Finding exceptions

1. On the Error Inspector, check Exceptions.

   Exceptions are errors that have been marked as acceptable exceptions to the topology rule.

2. Uncheck Errors.

3. Click Search Now.

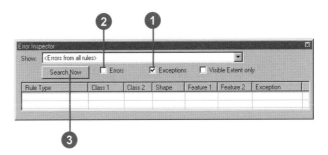

ArcInfo and ArcEditor

Correcting errors

You can apply a variety of predefined topology fixes to the errors you find. The sort of fix that will be appropriate for a given error depends on the error type and the geometry of the features involved. You can choose from different fixes or mark the error as an exception.

The topology fixes are available from the Fix Topology Error tool and by right-clicking a selected error in the Error Inspector. Depending on the type of error and the features involved, you can select, delete, merge, extend, trim, subtract, or create features.

You can also pan and zoom to a selected error, show a description of the error, and mark an error as an exception.

Merging an error area into a polygon

1. Click the Fix Topology Error button on the Topology toolbar.

2. Click the error feature that you want to merge into one of the overlapping polygons.

3. Right-click and click Merge.

4. Click the feature that you want to merge the error feature into.

5. Click OK.

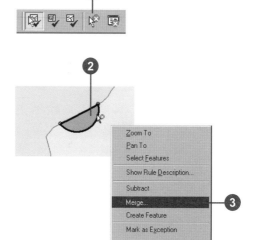

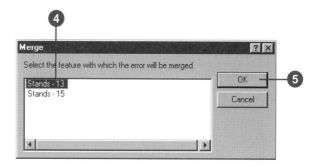

Merging an error area into a polygon from the Error Inspector

1. On the Error Inspector, click the error that you want to fix.

2. Right-click the error and click Merge.

3. Click the feature that you want to merge the error feature into.

4. Click OK.

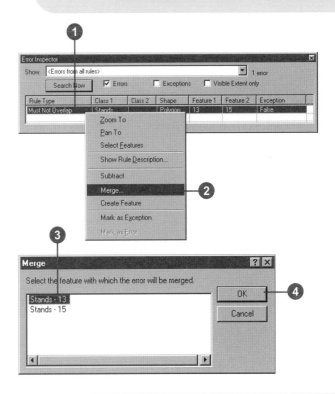

Finding the features that are affected by an error

1. On the Error Inspector, click the error.

2. Click the Feature 1 field in the error to see the first feature that is affected by it.

3. Click the Feature 2 field to see the second feature that is affected by it.

   The features flash on the map.

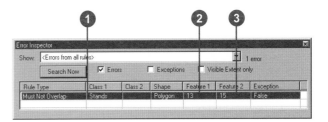

Marking an error as an exception

1. On the Error Inspector, click the error that you want to mark as an exception.

2. Right-click the error and click Mark as Exception.

   The error is marked as an exception. It is no longer symbolized as an error in the Topology layer on the map.

   You can use the Error Inspector to find exceptions as well as errors.

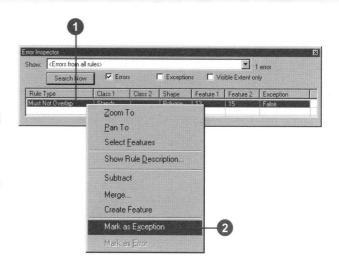

Getting a description of the rule that is violated for an error

1. On the Error Inspector, click the error that you want a description of.

2. Right-click the error and click Show Rule Description.

   A dialog box appears with a description of the error and some pictures of geometries that would and would not result in this error.

   The errors are marked in red.

3. Optionally, uncheck Show Errors to compare the feature geometries without the errors.

4. Click OK.

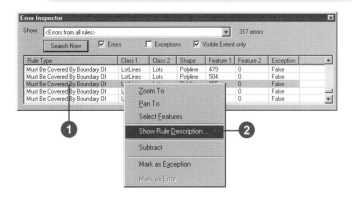

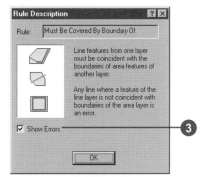

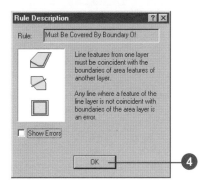

ArcInfo and ArcEditor

Creating new polygons from lines

Sometimes you need to create polygon features from line feature data. For example, you might have digitized the boundaries of a set of features into a line feature class, or you may have only been able to obtain line features from a data provider. Perhaps you have a detailed coastline feature class that you would like to use to update some existing, less detailed data. In ArcCatalog the Polygon Feature Class From Lines tool lets you create new polygon features from line and polygon features in one or more feature classes. You have the option of specifying a point feature class that will supply attributes for the new polygon features.

Creating a polygon feature class from lines

1. In ArcCatalog, navigate to the dataset in which you want to create a polygon feature class from an existing line feature class.

2. Right-click the dataset, point to New, and click Polygon Feature Class From Lines.

3. Type a name for the new polygon feature class.

4. Optionally, type a cluster tolerance.

   The default cluster tolerance is the minimum possible cluster tolerance.

5. Check the line feature classes that you want to be considered in creating the polygons.

6. Optionally, choose a point feature class in the dataset to provide attributes for the polygons.

7. Click OK.

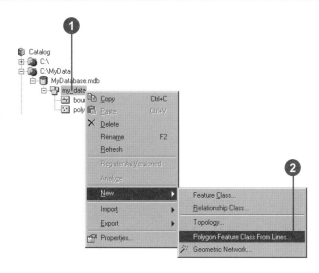

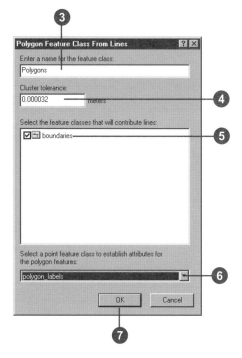

180

Creating new features from the geometry of existing features

Sometimes you need to create new features from the geometry of existing features. For example, you might need to create a new parcel feature from some parcel boundary lines or some parcel boundary lines from parcel features. In ArcMap you can select features and use their geometry to create new polygons or lines in the Editor Target Feature Class. You can create new features from existing features' geometry using the Construct Features tool.

You can create multiple line features by splitting longer features at the places where they intersect using the Planarize Lines tool.

Constructing polygons from the geometry of other features

1. In ArcMap, click the Select Features tool.

2. Select the features whose geometry you want to use to construct new polygon features.

3. On the Editor toolbar, click the Task dropdown arrow and click Create New Feature.

4. On the Editor toolbar, click the Target dropdown arrow and click the polygon feature class that you want to create a new feature in.

5. On the Topology toolbar, click the Construct Features button.

6. Optionally, type a cluster tolerance.

7. Optionally, check the box to Consider existing features of the target layer in the current extent.

   This will use the boundaries of existing polygons as input geometry and will split such features where selected lines or polygons cross them.

8. Click OK.

   The new features are created in the target feature class.

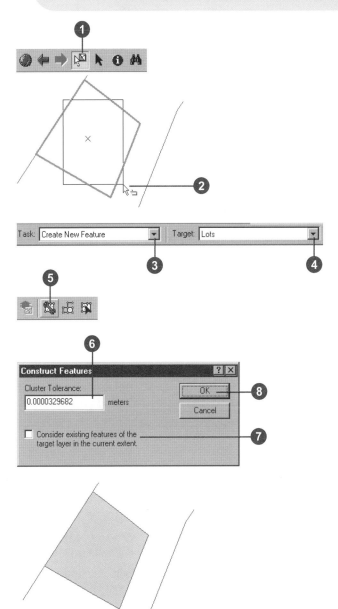

Constructing lines from the geometry of other features

1. In ArcMap, click the Select Features tool.

2. Select the features whose geometry you want to use to construct new line features.

3. On the Editor toolbar, click the Task dropdown arrow and click Create New Feature.

4. On the Editor toolbar, click the Target dropdown arrow and click the line feature class that you want to create a new feature in.

5. On the Topology toolbar, click the Construct Features button.

6. Optionally, type a cluster tolerance.

7. Optionally, check the box to Consider existing features of the target layer in the current extent.

   This will use existing lines as input geometry and will split such features where selected lines or polygons cross them.

8. Click OK.

   The new features are created in the target feature class.

   Two lines are created where polygons share boundaries.

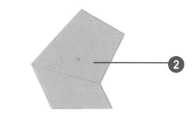

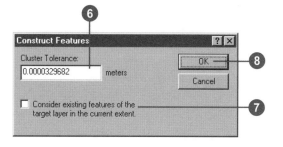

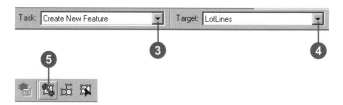

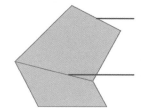

New line feature follows selected polygon feature boundary.

Where polygons share boundaries, two lines are created—one for each polygon. You can remove duplicate lines using the Planarize Lines tool.

Tip

Removing overlapping line segments with Planarize

If you use the Planarize Lines tool on lines constructed from polygons that share boundaries, overlapping line segments are removed.

Using Planarize to split lines at intersections

1. In ArcMap, click the Select Features tool.

2. Select the line features that you want to split at intersections.

3. Click the Planarize Lines button.

4. Optionally, type a cluster tolerance.

5. Click OK.

   Planarize also removes overlapping line segments—such as those created by constructing lines from polygons that have shared boundaries.

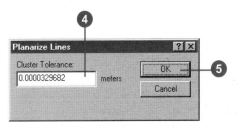

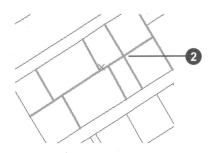

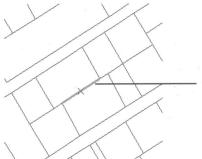

The lines are split into new features where they intersect.

Using a digitizer

5

Digitizing is the process of converting features on a paper map into digital format. To digitize a map, you use a digitizing tablet connected to your computer to trace over the features that interest you. The x,y coordinates of these features are automatically recorded and stored as spatial data.

Digitizing with a digitizing tablet offers another way, besides digitizing freehand, to create and edit spatial data. You can convert features from almost any paper map into digital features. You can use a *digitizer* in conjunction with the tools in ArcMap to create new features or edit existing features on a digital map.

You may want to digitize features into a new layer and add the layer to an existing map document, or you may want to create a completely new set of layers for an area for which no digital data is available. You can also use a digitizer to update an existing layer on your digital map.

Chapter 3, 'Creating new features', introduced you to the Sketch tool and other useful editing tools in ArcMap and discussed how these are used to digitize features freehand. This chapter will teach you the fundamentals of editing features in ArcMap using a digitizer. You may want to read Chapter 3, 'Creating new features', first to get an understanding of editing before reading this chapter.

Setting up your digitizing tablet and preparing your paper map

Before you can start digitizing, you must set up your digitizing tablet and prepare your paper map. This can be done after you have installed the digitizer driver software.

Installing the driver software and configuring puck buttons

To use a digitizing tablet with ArcMap, it must have WinTab™-compliant digitizer driver software. To find out if a WinTab-compliant driver is available for your digitizer, see the documentation that came with the tablet or contact the manufacturer. If you need to know if ArcMap supports your digitizing tablet, consult the ESRI Web site at *www.esri.com* for the most recent information.

If you installed ArcMap before installing your digitizer, the Digitizer tab may not appear in the Editing Options dialog box. To add the tab, you must register the digitizer.dll file. To do this, start the DOS Command Prompt, which is usually accessed by clicking Start and pointing to Programs. In the Command Prompt, type "cd" and a space, followed by the path to the directory where you installed ArcGIS. For example, to register digitizer.dll when ArcGIS is installed in the default directory, type "cd C:\Program Files\ArcGIS\Bin" and press the Enter key. Then type "regsvr32 digitizer.dll" and press Enter. If the registration was successful, the Editing Options dialog box will have the Digitizer tab when you restart ArcMap.

After installing the driver software, use the WinTab manager setup program to configure the buttons on your digitizer *puck*. You may have to turn on your digitizer and reboot your machine before you can use the setup program. One puck button should be configured to perform a left mouse click to digitize point features and vertices; another button should be configured to perform a left double-click to finish digitizing line or polygon features. You may also want to configure a button to perform a right-click so you can access context menus.

With any development programming language, you can configure additional buttons to run specific ArcMap commands—such as the Zoom In or Sketch tools—normally accessed through toolbar buttons and menus. *Exploring ArcObjects* contains sample Visual Basic® for Applications (VBA) code that you can use to run a variety of ArcMap commands from the digitizer puck.

Preparing the map

After you have set up your digitizing tablet and configured the puck buttons, you can prepare your paper map for digitizing. Your map ideally should be reliable, up-to-date, flat, and not torn or folded. Paper expands or shrinks according to the weather. To minimize distortion in digitizing, experienced digitizers often copy paper maps to a more stable material such as Mylar®.

If you know what coordinate system (projection) your paper map is in, you should set the same projection for the layer you're digitizing into. If you are digitizing features into an existing feature layer, you must ensure that your paper map and digital layer share the same coordinate system. For more information on specifying a coordinate system in ArcMap, see *Using ArcMap*.

Establishing control points on your paper map

Before you can begin digitizing from your paper map, you must first establish *control points* that you will later use to register the map to the geographic space in ArcMap. If your map has a grid or a set of known ground points, you can use these as your control points. If not, you should choose between four and 10 distinctive locations such as road intersections and mark them on your map with a pencil. Give each location a unique number and write down its actual ground coordinates.

Once you've identified at least four well-placed control points, you can place your map on the tablet and attach it with special residue-free putty, masking tape, or drafting tape—drafting tape looks like masking tape but leaves less residue when it's removed. You don't have to align the map precisely on your tablet; ArcMap corrects any alignment problems when you register the map and displays such adjustments in the error report.

The error report includes two different error calculations: a point-by-point error and a root mean square (RMS) error. The point-by-point error represents the distance deviation between the transformation of each input control point and the corresponding point in map coordinates. The RMS error is an average of those deviations. ArcMap reports the point-by-point error in current map units. The RMS error is reported in both current map units and digitizer units (generally inches). If the RMS error is too high, you can reregister the appropriate control points. To maintain highly accurate data, the RMS error should be kept under 0.004 digitizer inches. For less accurate data, the value can be as high as 0.008 digitizer inches.

Registering your paper map

Before you can start digitizing, you must register your paper map into real-world coordinates. This allows you to digitize features directly in geographic space.

Registering your map involves recording the ground coordinates for the control points you identified while preparing your map. These are recorded using the Digitizer tab of the Editing Options dialog box. You must first use the digitizer puck to digitize the control points on the paper map; with the puck over each control point on the map, press the button you configured to perform a left mouse click. You must then type the actual ground coordinates for each control point.

When registering your map, you have the option of saving the ground coordinates you entered for later use—for example, if you want to reregister your map or register ▶

See Also

For information on configuring puck buttons and establishing control points, see 'Setting up your digitizing tablet and preparing your paper map' in this chapter.

Registering your map for the first time

1. After adding a layer to your map, click Editor and click Start Editing.

2. Click Editor and click Options.

3. Click the Digitizer tab.

4. With the digitizer puck, digitize the control points you established earlier on your paper map.

   A record appears in the X Digitizer and Y Digitizer columns for each control point you digitized.

5. Type the actual ground coordinates for each control point in the X Map and Y Map fields.

   An error in map units is displayed at each control point. An RMS error is displayed in map units and in digitizer inches.

6. Click OK to register the map and close the Editing Options dialog box.

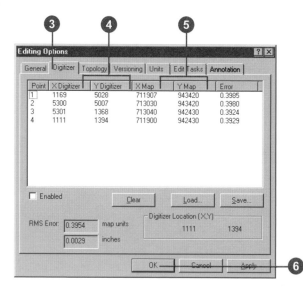

another map that uses the same control points. These ground coordinates are stored in tic text files.

After you've entered the ground coordinates, ArcMap displays an error at each control point as well as an RMS error. If the RMS error is too high—greater than 0.004 digitizer inches for highly accurate data or greater than 0.008 digitizer inches for less accurate data—you can register the appropriate control points again. For more information on errors, see 'Setting up your digitizing tablet and preparing your paper map' in this chapter.

Tip

Missing Digitizer tab

If you installed ArcMap before installing your digitizer, the Digitizer tab may not appear in the Editing Options dialog box. To add the tab, you must register the digitizer.dll file. See 'Setting up your digitizer and preparing your paper map' in this chapter for more information.

Saving new ground coordinates

1. Follow steps 1 through 5 for 'Registering your map for the first time' in this chapter.

2. Click Save.

3. Navigate to the directory in which you want to save the coordinates and type a filename.

4. Click Save.

5. Click OK.

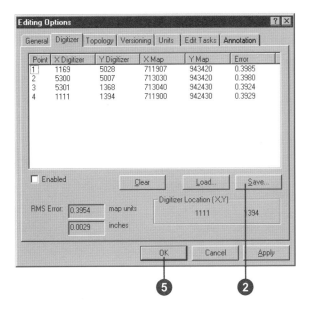

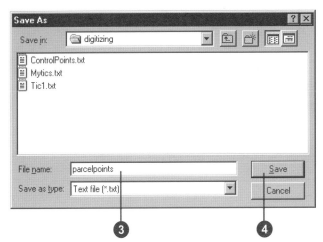

Registering your map using existing tic files or saved coordinates

1. After adding a layer to your map, click Editor and click Start Editing.

2. Click Editor and click Options.

3. Click the Digitizer tab.

4. Click Load.

5. Navigate to the file you want to use.

6. Click Open. ▶

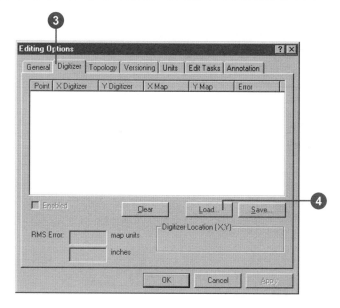

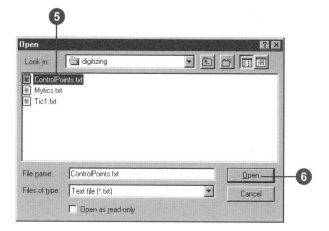

The ground coordinates appear under the X Map and Y Map fields.

7. Click the first record and digitize the first control point with the digitizer puck.

8. Digitize each of the other control points.

The digitized coordinates appear in the X Digitizer and Y Digitizer columns. An error is displayed for each control point, and an RMS error is displayed in map units and in digitizer inches.

9. Click OK to register the map.

The ground coordinates are displayed.

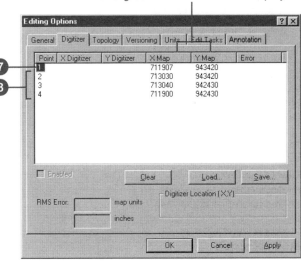

The digitized coordinates are displayed.

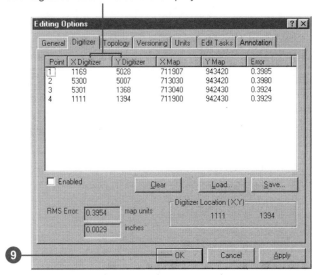

Creating features using a digitizer

It's easy to digitize features in ArcMap. You can digitize features into a new map layer or edit an existing layer.

Digitizing modes

Digitizing tablets generally operate in two modes: digitizing (absolute) mode and mouse (relative) mode.

In *digitizing mode*, the location of the tablet is mapped to a specific location on the screen. In other words, moving the digitizer puck on the tablet surface causes the screen pointer to move to precisely the same position. When you are in digitizing mode, you can only digitize features; you can't choose buttons, menu commands, or tools from the ArcMap user interface because the screen pointer is locked to the drawing area.

In *mouse mode*, the digitizer puck behaves just like a mouse; there is no correlation between the position of the screen pointer and the surface of the digitizing tablet, but you can choose interface elements with the pointer.

ArcMap lets you switch between digitizing and mouse modes using the Editing Options dialog box. This means you can use the digitizer puck both to digitize features and access user interface choices (as a substitute to the mouse) as you digitize.

Whether your digitizer is in mouse mode or digitizing mode, you can still use your mouse at any time to choose interface elements.

Two ways to digitize features on a paper map

You can digitize features on a paper map in two ways: using point mode digitizing or stream mode digitizing (streaming). You can toggle between point and stream mode by pressing the F8 key or by right-clicking with the Sketch tool active and clicking Streaming from the menu.

Digitizing by point

When you start a digitizing session, the default is point mode. With *point mode digitizing*, you convert a feature on a paper map by digitizing a series of precise points, or vertices. ArcMap then connects the vertices to create a digital feature. You would use point mode when precise digitizing is required—for example, when digitizing a perfectly straight line.

Digitizing using stream mode

Stream mode digitizing (streaming) provides a quick and easy way to capture features on a paper map when you don't require as much precision—for example, to digitize rivers, streams, and contour lines. With stream mode, you create the first vertex of the feature and trace over the rest of the feature with the digitizer puck. When you're finished tracing, you use the puck to complete the feature.

As you stream, ArcMap automatically adds vertices at an interval you specify; this interval, expressed in current map units, is called the *stream tolerance*. You can change the stream tolerance at any time, even while you're in the process of digitizing a feature.

You can also digitize using stream mode when you create features freehand with the sketch construction tools. You can digitize in stream mode with the Sketch tool, for example, in the same way you do from a paper map. The only difference is that you use the mouse pointer to digitize freehand.

Adding topology to digitized features

Digitizing creates lines or points that have no topological relationships. ArcMap provides tools to improve such spaghetti digitized data, for example, by splitting lines at intersections or creating polygons from lines. To learn more about topology, see Chapter 4, 'Editing topology'.

Digitizing features in point mode

Point mode digitizing works the same way with a digitizer as freehand digitizing with the Sketch tool; the only difference is that with the digitizer you're converting a feature from a paper map using a digitizer puck instead of a mouse.

Point mode digitizing involves converting point, line, and polygon features from a paper map by digitizing a series of precise points, or vertices. You digitize each vertex by pressing the puck button you configured to perform a left mouse click. To finish the feature, press the puck button you configured to perform a left double-click. ArcMap connects the vertices to create a digital feature.

Before you begin digitizing, you must set the digitizer to work in digitizing mode rather than in mouse mode; this constrains the screen pointer to the digitizing area. When the puck ▶

See Also

For information on configuring puck buttons and establishing control points, see 'Setting up your digitizing tablet and preparing your paper map' in this chapter.

1. Click Editor and click Options.

2. Click the Digitizer tab.

3. Check Enabled to use the puck in digitizing mode.

4. Click OK. ▶

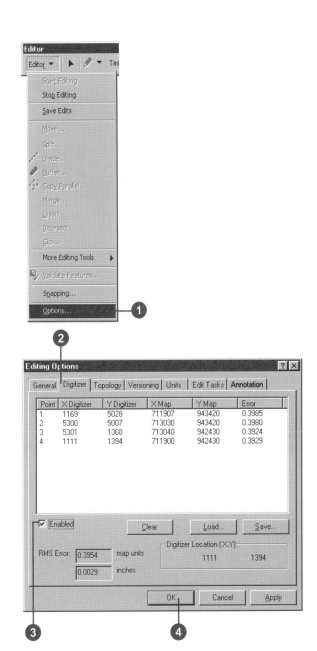

is in digitizing mode, you must use your mouse to choose items in the ArcMap interface—unless you have used VBA or another development programming language to configure additional puck buttons to run specific ArcMap commands.

Tip

Snapping

To help you digitize features in a precise location on an existing layer, you can use the snapping environment. For information on snapping, see Chapter 3, 'Creating new features'.

Tip

Deleting vertices

Click the Undo button on the ArcMap Standard toolbar to delete a vertex as you digitize.

See Also

For information on creating features by digitizing freehand with the sketch creation tools, see Chapter 3, 'Creating new features'.

See Also

For information on configuring puck buttons with programming code, see 'Setting up your digitizing tablet and preparing your paper map' in this chapter.

5. Click the tool palette dropdown arrow and click the Sketch tool.

6. With the digitizer puck, digitize the first vertex of the feature.

7. Trace the puck over the feature on the paper map, creating as many vertices as you need.

8. Finish the feature by pressing the appropriate puck button.

   The feature is created.

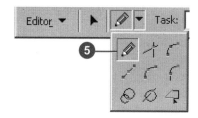

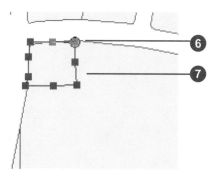

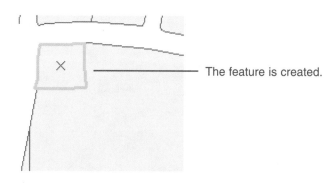

The feature is created.

Digitizing features in stream mode

When you digitize line or polygon features from a paper map in stream mode (streaming), you create the first vertex of the feature by pressing the digitizer puck button you configured to perform a left mouse click. You then trace over the rest of the feature with the digitizer puck. When you're finished tracing, press the puck button you configured to perform a left double-click to complete the feature.

Before starting to digitize in stream mode, you must set the stream tolerance—the interval at which ArcMap adds vertices along the feature you're digitizing. Because the default stream tolerance is 0, you must enter a tolerance value before you start digitizing, or the vertices will join together or overlap each other. You can change the stream tolerance any time in the digitizing process.

You must also specify the number of streaming vertices you want to group together. The number you set tells ArcMap how many vertices to delete when you click the ▶

Setting the stream tolerance

1. Click Editor and click Start Editing.
2. Click Editor and click Options.
3. Click the General tab.
4. Type the stream tolerance— in map units—in the Stream tolerance text box.
5. Click OK.

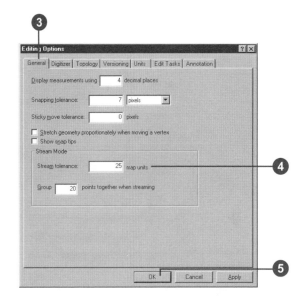

Setting the number of vertices to be grouped

1. Click Editor and click Options.
2. Click the General tab.
3. Type the number of vertices you want to group together.
4. Click OK.

   Now when you click the Undo button while digitizing in stream mode, the number of vertices you specified are deleted.

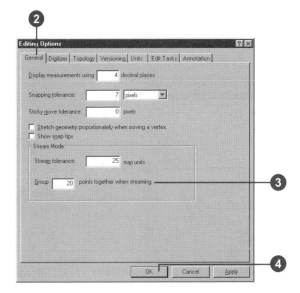

Undo button. For example, if you set this number to 20 and click the Undo button while you're digitizing a feature, ArcMap deletes the last 20 digitized vertices from your feature.

To begin digitizing in stream mode, you must choose Streaming from the sketch context menu. You can switch back to point mode at any time by pressing F8; press F8 again to switch to stream mode again.

Before streaming, remember to set the digitizer to work in digitizing mode rather than in mouse mode; this constrains the screen pointer to the digitizing area.

Tip

Snapping

To help you digitize features in a precise location on an existing layer, you can use the snapping environment. For information on snapping, see Chapter 3, 'Creating new features'.

Digitizing a feature in stream mode

1. Click Editor and click Options.

2. Click the General tab.

3. Type the stream tolerance— in map units—in the Stream Tolerance text box.

4. Type the number of vertices you want to group together.

5. Click the Digitizer tab.

6. Check Enabled to use the puck in digitizing mode.

7. Click OK.

8. Click the tool palette dropdown arrow and click the Sketch tool. ▶

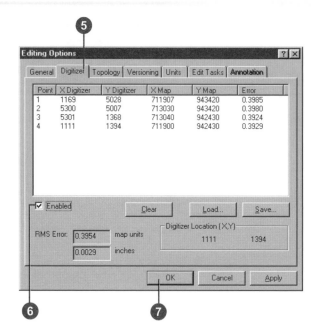

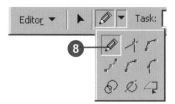

Choosing interface elements while streaming

When you're in the process of digitizing a feature in stream mode and want to interact with the ArcMap interface using your mouse—for example, to change the stream tolerance or undo an action—you must first switch back to point mode by pressing F8. After you have finished interacting with the interface, you can resume streaming by pressing F8 again.

Tip

Configuring a puck button for streaming

Instead of choosing Streaming from the context menu, you can configure one of your puck buttons using any development programming language, such as C++ or VBA, to activate stream mode digitizing. To learn more about configuring your puck buttons and customization in general, see Exploring ArcObjects.

9. With the mouse pointer, right-click anywhere on the map and click Streaming.

10. With the digitizer puck, digitize the first vertex of the line or polygon feature.

11. Trace the puck over the feature on the paper map.

    ArcMap creates vertices at the stream tolerance you specified.

12. Finish the feature by pressing the appropriate puck button.

    The feature is created.

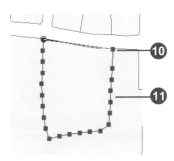

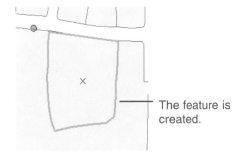

The feature is created.

Creating features from other features

6

In spatial data editing, many new features can be created using the shapes of other features. ArcMap has many tools you can use to create new features based on features already in your database.

For example, you can construct a line that is a parallel copy of an existing line to create a centerline on a street. You can create a buffer around a point, line, or polygon feature to show a specific area, such as a floodplain around a river. You can create a new feature by combining or intersecting existing features; you can also create a mirror image of a feature or set of features.

In this chapter, you'll learn how easy it is to perform these tasks using various tools in ArcMap.

Copying a line at a specific interval

The Copy Parallel command copies a line parallel to an existing feature at a distance you specify. If you give a distance that is positive, the line is copied to the right side of the original feature. A negative distance value copies the line to the left.

You might use the Copy Parallel command to create a street centerline or to create a gas line that runs parallel to a road.

1. Click the Edit tool.

2. Click the line you want to copy.

3. Click the Target layer dropdown arrow and click the layer to which you want the new line to belong. ▶

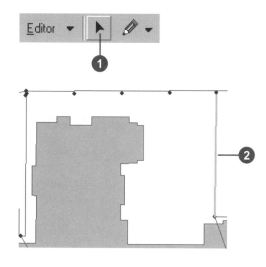

4. Click Editor and click Copy Parallel.

5. Specify the copy parameters including the distance—in map units—from the original feature where you want to copy the line, the corner style, and the behavior of intersecting loops.

6. Click OK or press Enter.

A parallel copy of the line is created at the specified distance.

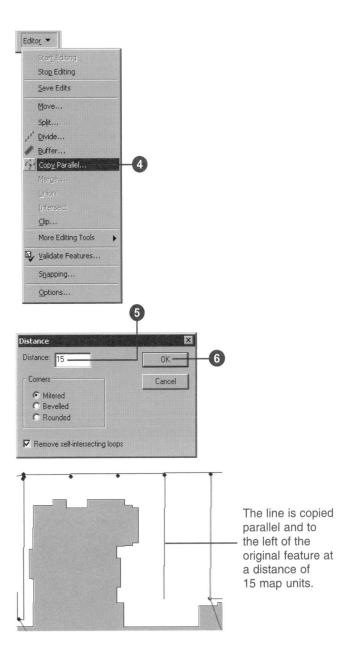

The line is copied parallel and to the left of the original feature at a distance of 15 map units.

Creating a buffer around a feature

You can create a buffer around a feature using the Buffer command. For instance, you might use Buffer to show the area around a well that's contaminated or to represent a floodplain around a river.

You can buffer more than one feature at a time, but a separate buffer will be created around each feature.

1. Click the Edit tool.

2. Click the feature or features around which you want to create a buffer.

3. Click the Target layer dropdown arrow and click the layer with the type of features you want the buffer to be. (This can only be a line or polygon layer.) ►

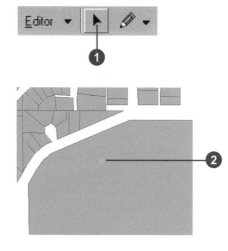

4. Click Editor and click Buffer.

5. Type the distance—in map units—from the feature around which you want to create the buffer and press Enter.

A buffer is created at the specified distance.

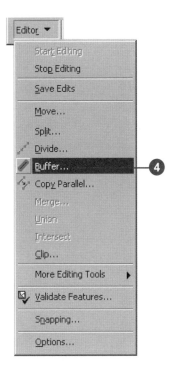

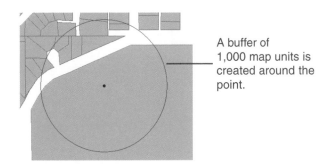

A buffer of 1,000 map units is created around the point.

Creating a mirror image of a feature

The Mirror task creates a mirror image of selected features on the other side of a straight line you create. You might use the Mirror task to create houses in a housing development where houses are mirror images of the ones on the opposite side of the street.

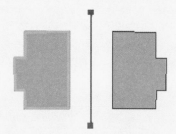

Also, as shown in the example, the Mirror task provides an easy way to add gas services to parcels that mirror the services on the other side of the street.

Tip

Other ways to construct a line

You can also use the Distance–Distance and Intersection tools to create the endpoints of the line. For more information, see Chapter 3, 'Creating new features'.

1. Click the Edit tool.
2. Click the feature or features that you want to mirror.
3. Click the Task dropdown arrow and click Mirror Features.
4. Click the tool palette dropdown arrow and click the Sketch tool.
5. Construct a line by clicking once on the start point and once on the endpoint. ▶

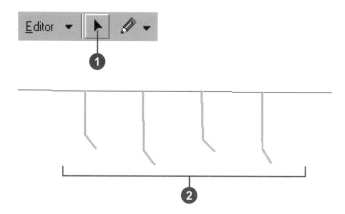

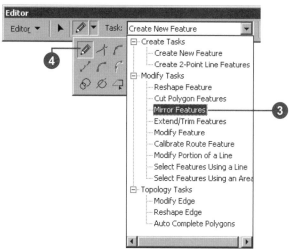

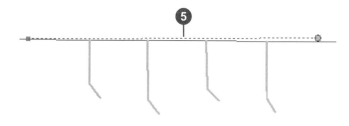

After you digitize the end-point, a mirror image of the feature or features is created.

New features

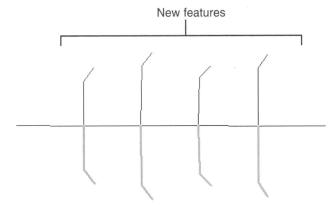

Merging features from the same layer into one feature

The Merge command combines features from the same layer into one feature. The features must be part of a line or polygon layer. You could use the Merge command to combine two parcels into one.

You might also want to merge nonadjacent features to create a multipart feature. For example, you could merge the individual islands that make up Hawaii to create a multipart polygon feature.

When you merge features in a geodatabase, the original features are removed and the new feature's attributes are copied from the feature that was selected first. If you merge shapefile features, the attributes of the feature with the lowest ID number (the oldest feature) are used.

1. Click the Edit tool.
2. Click the features that you want to merge.

    The features must be from the same layer, either a line or polygon layer.

3. Click the Target layer dropdown arrow and click the layer to which you want the new feature to belong. ▶

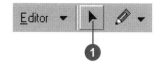

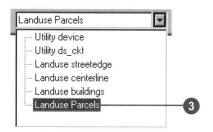

4. Click Editor and click Merge.

5. Click the feature that you want to merge the other feature or features into.

   The selected features are merged into one.

6. Click OK.

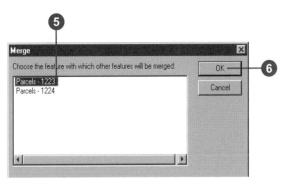

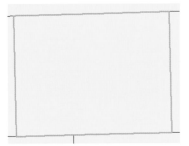

Parcels are merged into one.

Combining features from different layers into one feature

The Union command lets you combine features from different layers into one feature while maintaining the original features and attributes. You might use this command to create a sales territory from several ZIP Codes.

You can also create a multipart feature using the Union command by combining nonadjacent features from different layers. For example, suppose you want to create a sedimentary rock polygon in a new rock classification layer given selected clay and quartz polygons in an existing rock composite layer. You would use the Union command to combine the clay and quartz features to create a new, multipart sedimentary rock feature in the rock classification layer.

When you use the Union command, the features you combine must be from layers of the same type—line or polygon. The new feature is created in the current layer with no attribute values.

1. Click the Edit tool.

2. Click the features that you want to combine into one.

   The features may be from different layers, although they must be the same layer type—line or polygon.

3. Click the Target layer dropdown arrow and click the layer to which you want the new feature to belong. ▶

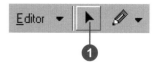

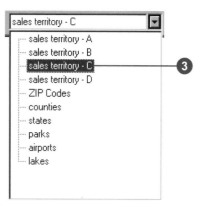

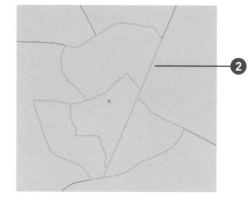

4. Click Editor and click Union.

The selected features are combined into one.

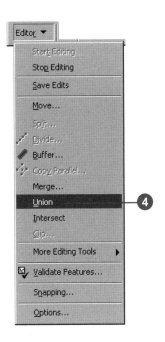

ZIP Codes are combined into one sales territory.

Creating a feature from features with common areas

The Intersect command creates a new feature from the area where features overlap. For instance, you might create a new sales territory out of overlapping trade areas.

You can find the intersection between features of different layers, but the layers must be of the same type—line or polygon. The original features are maintained, and the new feature is created in the current layer with no attribute values. You must enter attribute values for the new feature yourself.

1. Click the Edit tool.

2. Click the features from whose intersection you want to create a new feature.

   The features may be from different layers, although they must be of the same layer type—line or polygon.

3. Click the Target layer dropdown arrow and click the layer to which you want the new feature to belong.

   The layer must be of the same type as the selected features—line or polygon. ▶

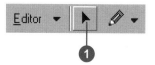

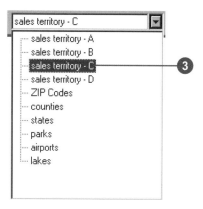

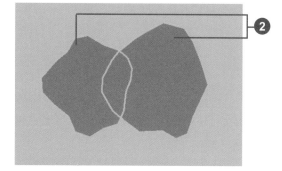

4. Click Editor and click Intersect.

A new feature is created from the areas in common between all selected features.

④

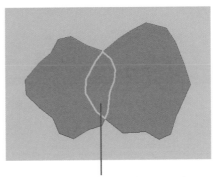

A single sales territory is created from the areas in common between two other sales territories.

Editing existing features

7

This chapter shows you how to modify features that already exist in your database. Suppose you need to change the shape of a parcel to accommodate a newly added cul-de-sac—you can use the Reshape Feature task to modify the parcel to the proper shape. Suppose the street you've digitized doesn't intersect with the correct cross street—you can use the Extend task to extend the line to the correct location. If you need to divide a parcel, you can use the Cut Polygon Feature task to cut the feature into two.

These are just a few examples of how easy it is to modify features while editing in ArcMap. The editing tools, commands, and tasks provide a variety of ways to make changes to existing features.

Many of the functions described in this chapter will react differently with data involved in a topology. If your project involves working with topological data, you should also read Chapter 4, 'Editing topology', to further understand the tools and functions related to topological rules and relationships.

Splitting a line or polygon

Using the editing tools, you can easily split line and polygon features.

To manually split one line into two, use the Split tool. The line is split at the location where you clicked with the mouse. The attributes of the original line are copied to each of the new lines. In the example shown, the Split tool is used to divide a street centerline into two features in anticipation of a new centerline being added between the parcels.

You can also split a line into two using the Split command on the Editor menu. Use the Split command when you know the distance at which you want to split the line, measured from either the first or last vertex. You can also use this command when you want to split a line at a certain percentage of the ▶

▶

Tip

Using snapping to split a line

If you want to use the Split tool to split a line at a specific vertex, use the snapping environment to snap the pointer precisely to the vertex. For more information on snapping, see Chapter 3, 'Creating new features'.

Splitting a line manually

1. Click the Edit tool.
2. Click the line you want to split.
3. Click the Split tool.
4. Click the spot on the line where you want it to split.

   The line is split into two features.

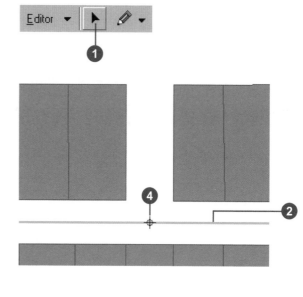

214

original length. You might use the Split command to split a power line at a known distance along the line when you want to add an electrical pole that requires its own service.

The Split dialog box displays the length of the original feature in current map units to help you split it accurately. When you split the line using the Split command, the attributes of the original line are copied to each of the new lines.

To split one polygon into two, use the Cut Polygon Features task. The polygon is split according to a line sketch you create. The attributes of the original feature are copied to each of the new features.

Splitting a line at a specified distance or percentage

1. Click the Edit tool.

2. Click the line you want to split.

3. Click Editor and click Split. ▶

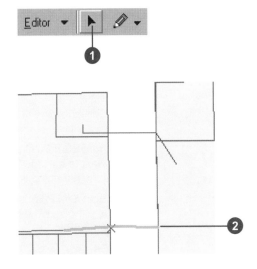

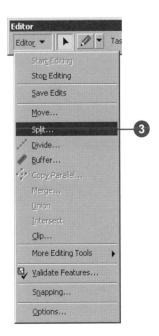

Controlling how attributes are handled

If you're working with geodatabase features, you can set up split policies that control the behavior of an object's attributes when it is split. For more information on split policies, see Building a Geodatabase.

4. Click the first Split option to split the feature at a certain distance.

   Click the second Split option to split the feature at a certain percentage of the whole.

5. Type a distance or percentage, as desired.

6. Click From Start Point of Line if you want to split the feature starting from the first vertex.

   Click From End Point of Line if you want to split the feature starting from the last vertex.

7. Click OK.

   The line is split into two features according to the parameters you specified.

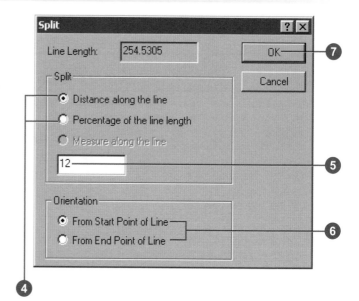

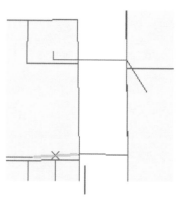

The line is split into two according to the distance and orientation you specified.

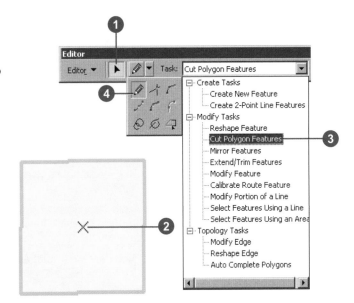

Tip

Cutting a polygon shape out of a polygon

You can use the Cut Polygon Features task to create a sketch that acts like a cookie cutter, splitting the polygon in two. Simply create a line sketch that closes in on itself by double-clicking precisely on the first vertex of the sketch to finish it.

Tip

Other ways to construct a sketch

You can also use the Distance–Distance tool, the Arc tool, or the Intersection tool to create a sketch. For more information, see Chapter 3, 'Creating new features'.

Tip

Using snapping while cutting polygons

Make sure your sketch cuts completely through the selected polygon. Turning on edge snapping often helps ensure that the cut operation is completed.

Splitting a polygon

1. Click the Edit tool.

2. Click the polygon you want to split.

3. Click the Task dropdown arrow and click Cut Polygon Features.

4. Click the tool palette dropdown arrow and click the Sketch tool.

5. Construct a line or polygon sketch that cuts the original polygon as desired.

6. Right-click anywhere on the map and click Finish Sketch.

   The polygon is split into two features.

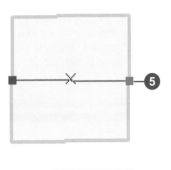

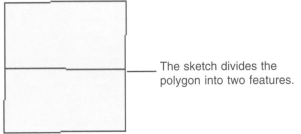

The sketch divides the polygon into two features.

Trimming a line

The Trim to Length command on the Sketch context menu reduces the length of a line, trimming a distance you specify from the last vertex.

The Trim task in the Current Task dropdown list also trims lines, but instead of trimming them a given distance, the Trim task uses a sketch you draw. ▶

Tip

Shortcut for modifying features

Instead of using the Modify Feature task to change a feature to its sketch, you can click the Edit tool and double-click the feature you want to modify.

Tip

Trimming from the first vertex of a line

You can trim a line from the first vertex instead of the last. See 'Flipping a line' in this chapter.

Tip

Shortcuts for finishing a sketch

When you're finished modifying a sketch, you can press F2 to finish it. Simply selecting another feature with the Edit tool will also finish the sketch.

Trimming a specific length from the last point

1. Click the Task dropdown arrow and click Modify Feature.

2. Click the Edit tool.

3. Click the line that you want to trim.

   The line appears as a sketch with vertices.

4. Right-click over any part of the line and click Trim to Length.

5. Type the length to trim the line to and press Enter.

   If you type a positive value it trims the line to the specified length. If you type a negative value it removes that much from the length of the line, starting from the last vertex.

   The line is trimmed.

6. When finished modifying the line, right-click over any part of the sketch and click Finish Sketch.

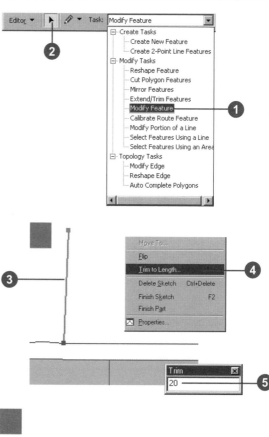

The original line is trimmed to 20 map units. You can also type the length in other units by specifying a distance unit abbreviation—km, m, ft, and so on—with the value you enter.

This is useful if you don't know the exact distance you want to trim but have a physical boundary where the features should end or begin.

Suppose your database has some roads that should end at the coastline, but overshoot it instead. Using the Trim task, you can draw a line sketch on top of the coastline and the lines will be trimmed where you have drawn the sketch.

Portions of the lines that are on the right side of the sketch are trimmed. The right side of the sketch is based on the direction in which the sketch was drawn. Imagine riding a bicycle along the sketch in the direction in which the vertices were added. ▶

Tip

Other ways to construct a sketch

You can also use the Distance–Distance tool, the Arc tool, the Trace tool, or the Intersection tool to create a sketch. For more information, see Chapter 3, 'Creating new features'.

Tip

Shortcuts for finishing a sketch

You can double-click on the last vertex of a sketch to finish it. You can also press F2.

Trimming based on a line you draw

1. Click the Task dropdown arrow and click Extend/Trim Features.

2. Click the Edit tool.

3. Click the line or lines you want to trim.

4. Click the tool palette dropdown arrow and click the Sketch tool.

5. Construct a line that trims the selected line or lines as desired. The direction of the sketch line determines the part of the features to be removed. The portion of the selected features to the right of the sketch is trimmed.

6. Right-click anywhere on the map and click Finish Sketch. ▶

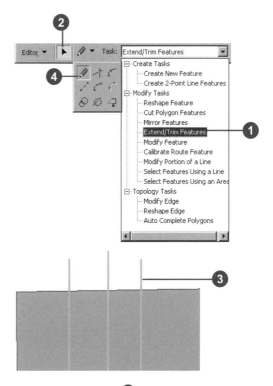

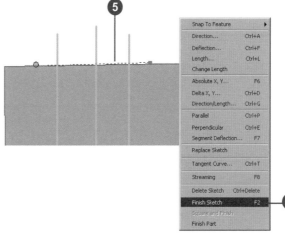

If you looked to your right, you would be looking at the right side of the sketch.

The lines are trimmed on the right side of the line you constructed.

The lines are trimmed where the sketch was drawn.

Extending a line

The Extend task is the opposite of the Trim task, extending selected lines to a line you construct. Consider the roads and coastline example shown in the Trim task. If your database has some roads that should end at the coastline, but instead stop short, you could use the Extend task. By drawing a sketch on top of the coastline, you can extend the roads to the sketch you drew.

Tip

Other ways to construct a sketch

You can also use the Distance–Distance tool, the Arc tool, the Trace tool, or the Intersection tool to create a sketch. For more information, see Chapter 3, 'Creating new features'.

1. Click the Task dropdown arrow and click Extend/Trim Features.

2. Click the Edit tool.

3. Click the line or lines you want to extend.

4. Click the tool palette dropdown arrow and click the Sketch tool.

5. Construct a line to which you want to extend the selected line or lines.

6. Right-click anywhere on the map and click Finish Sketch. ▶

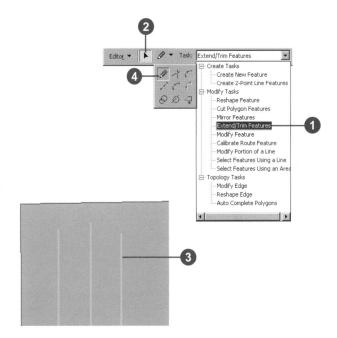

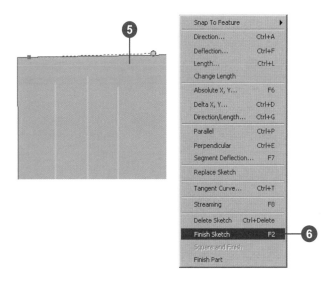

Tip

Other methods of extending or trimming a line

Beyond the basic Extend/Trim Features task, lines can be extended using the advanced editor Trim and Extend tools as well as specific topology correction methods when working with topologies. These additional functions are only available with ArcEditor and ArcInfo software packages.

The lines are extended to the line you constructed.

The lines are extended to where the sketch was drawn.

Flipping a line

When you modify a line by trimming or extending it, the line is automatically trimmed or extended from its last vertex.

However, if you prefer to trim or extend a line from the first vertex instead of the last, you can use the Flip command. The Flip command reverses the direction of a line so that the last vertex of the sketch becomes the first.

Tip

Working with topologies

For line feature classes or shapefiles that are part of a topology, the line direction is involved with the topological rules, and the flip function will not be permitted. For more information on working with topologies, see Chapter 4, 'Editing topology'.

1. Click the Task dropdown arrow and click Modify Feature.

2. Click the Edit tool.

3. Click the line whose direction you want to change.

4. Right-click over any part of the sketch and click Flip.

   The sketch becomes inverted. The first vertex becomes the last, marked in red.

5. When finished modifying the line, right-click over any part of the sketch and click Finish Sketch.

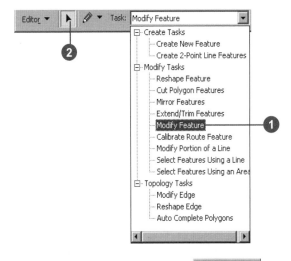

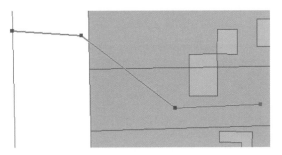

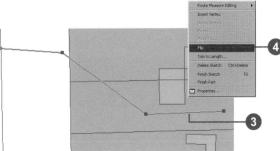

The first and last vertices of the line are reversed.

Placing points along a line

The Divide command creates points at a given interval along a line. For instance, you could use Divide to place utility poles along a primary line.

You can create a specific number of points that are evenly spaced, or you can create points at a distance interval you choose.

1. Click the Edit tool.

2. Click the line you want to divide.

3. Click the Target layer dropdown arrow and click the point layer containing the type of points you want to place along the line.

4. Click Editor and click Divide. ▶

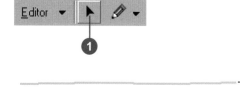

5. Click the first option and type a number to place a specific number of points evenly along the line.

   Or click the second option and type a number to place the points at a specific interval in map units.

   If the data has M values, you can click the third option and type a number to place the points at a specific interval of measure units.

6. Click OK.

   The line is divided by points placed along the line as specified.

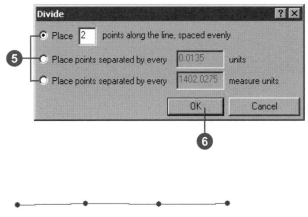

The line is divided by points.

Reshaping a line or polygon

The Reshape Feature task lets you reshape a line or polygon by constructing a sketch over the feature. The feature takes the shape of the sketch from the first place the sketch intersects the feature to the last.

When you reshape a polygon, if both endpoints of the sketch are within the polygon, the shape is added to the feature. ▶

Tip

Other ways to construct a sketch

You can also use the Distance–Distance tool, the Arc tool, the Trace tool, or the Intersection tool to create a sketch. For more information, see Chapter 3, 'Creating new features'.

1. Click the Task dropdown arrow and click Reshape Feature.

2. Click the Edit tool.

3. Click the feature you want to reshape.

4. Click the tool palette dropdown arrow and click the Sketch tool.

5. Create a line according to the way you want the feature reshaped.

6. Right-click anywhere on the map and click Finish Sketch. ▶

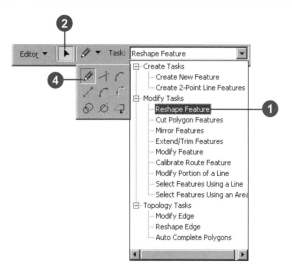

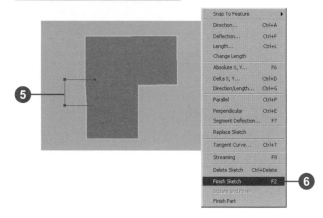

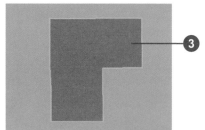

If the endpoints are outside the polygon, the feature is cut away.

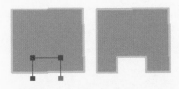

When you reshape a line, both endpoints of the sketch must be on the same side of the line. The line takes the shape of the sketch you draw.

The feature is reshaped.

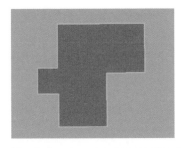

The feature is reshaped according to the sketch you constructed.

Adding and deleting sketch vertices

You can easily add vertices to or delete vertices from a sketch using the Insert Vertex and Delete Vertex commands on the Sketch context menu. By adding or deleting vertices, you can reshape a feature when you obtain new or better geographic data.

Suppose you have an existing layer with curb lines and receive an aerial photo that shows that the lines in the layer are incorrectly shaped. Using the ►

Using the ►

Tip

Adding vertices from the last vertex

You can add vertices to a feature beginning from the last vertex of the sketch. Click the Edit tool and double-click the feature to see its sketch. Then, click the Sketch tool to begin digitizing vertices.

Adding a vertex to a sketch

1. Click the Task dropdown arrow and click Modify Feature.

2. Click the Edit tool and click the line or polygon to which you want to add a vertex.

3. Move the pointer to where you want the vertex inserted and right-click.

4. Click Insert Vertex.

   A vertex is added to the sketch.

5. When finished modifying the line, right-click over any part of the sketch and click Finish Sketch.

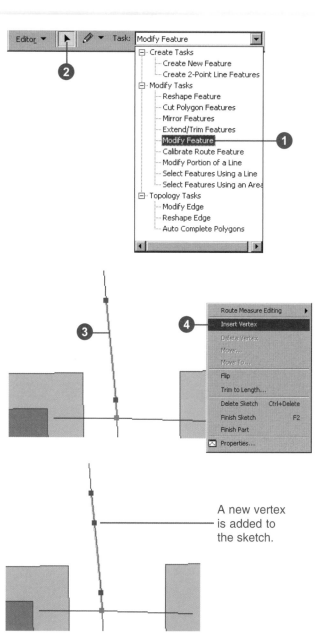

A new vertex is added to the sketch.

aerial photo as a backdrop, you can add vertices to the curb lines as needed, then reshape the feature to match the photo by moving the vertices to new locations. You can also reshape the curb line features by deleting existing vertices from their sketches.

See Also

To learn how to move a vertex, see 'Moving a vertex in a sketch' in this chapter.

Deleting a vertex from a sketch

1. Click the Task dropdown arrow and click Modify Feature.

2. Click the Edit tool.

3. Click the line or polygon from which you want to delete a vertex.

4. Position the pointer over the vertex you want to delete.

   The pointer will change appearance to have four small arrows surrounding a circle.

5. Right-click and click Delete Vertex.

   The vertex is deleted from the sketch.

6. Right-click over any part of the sketch and click Finish Sketch.

   The feature is reshaped.

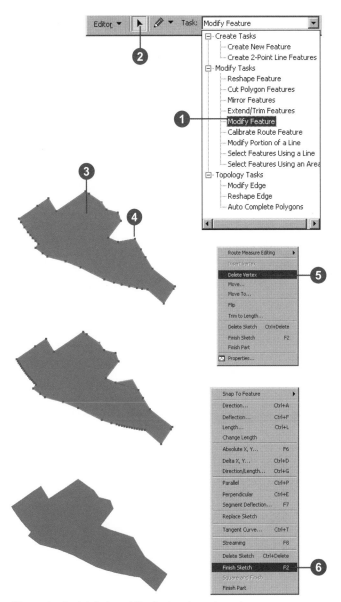

The vertex is deleted, and the feature is reshaped.

Moving a vertex in a sketch

Moving a vertex in a sketch offers another way to modify or reshape a feature.

ArcMap lets you move a vertex in several ways: by dragging it, by specifying new x,y coordinates, or by moving it relative to its current location.

You might choose to drag a vertex to a new location when you want to reshape a feature according to additional data you receive. For instance, you can drag a vertex to reshape a road feature in an existing layer in order to match it to the feature in a more accurate aerial photo. ►

Dragging a vertex

1. Click the Task dropdown arrow and click Modify Feature.

2. Click the Edit tool and click the line or polygon whose vertex you want to move.

3. Position the pointer over the vertex you want to move.

   The pointer will change appearance to have four small arrows surrounding a circle.

4. Click and drag the vertex to the desired location.

5. Right-click over any part of the sketch and click Finish Sketch.

   The feature is reshaped.

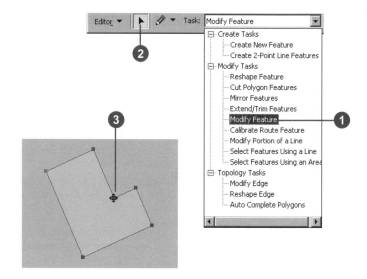

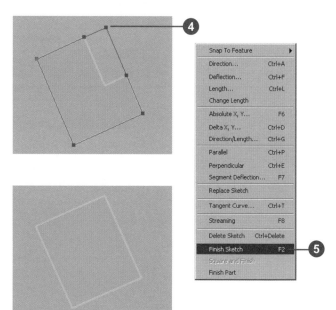

The vertex is moved, and the feature is reshaped.

You might move a vertex by specifying new x,y locations when you obtain additional data that provides the exact coordinate location at which the vertex should be. For example, suppose a parcel is resurveyed and a new GPS point is obtained for the parcel corner. You can move the corner of the parcel to match the location found by the GPS by specifying the equivalent location in x,y coordinates.

Tip

Maintaining a feature's shape when moving a vertex

You can also move a vertex without changing the shape of the feature. For more information, see 'Stretching a feature's geometry proportionately' in this chapter.

Moving a vertex by specifying x,y coordinates

1. Click the Current Task dropdown arrow and click Modify Feature.

2. Click the Edit tool and click the line or polygon whose vertex you want to move.

3. Position the pointer over the vertex you want to move until the pointer changes.

4. Right-click and click Move To.

5. Type the x,y coordinates where you want to move the vertex.

   The vertex is moved. ▶

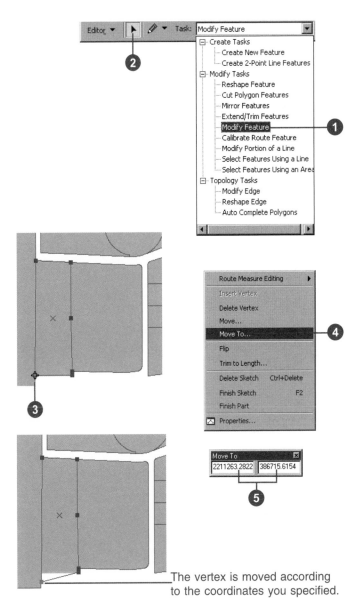

The vertex is moved according to the coordinates you specified.

Undoing a vertex move

If you move a vertex and don't want it to stay in the new location, click the Undo button on the ArcMap Standard toolbar. The vertex returns to its last position. Click the Redo button if you want to move the vertex back to the new location.

6. Right-click over any part of the sketch and click Finish Sketch.

The feature is reshaped.

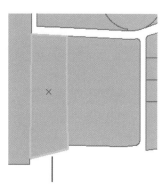

The feature is reshaped.

The sketch context menu also provides a way to move a vertex relative to its current location. Suppose an electrical pole must be moved 15 feet east and 5 feet north of its current location due to a road widening. Before moving the pole, you must reshape its electrical line so that the pole can connect to the line in the new location; you can do this by moving the vertex of the electrical line on which the pole sits using relative (delta) x,y coordinates.

The original location of the vertex as the origin (0,0) is used, and the vertex is moved to the new location using the map unit coordinates you specify—(15,5) in this example. After the vertex is moved and the electrical line is reshaped, you can snap the pole feature to the vertex in its new location.

Moving a vertex relative to its current location

1. Click the Task dropdown arrow and click Modify Feature.

2. Click the Edit tool and click the line or polygon whose vertex you want to move.

3. Position the pointer over the vertex you want to move until the pointer changes.

4. Right-click and click Move.

5. Type the delta x,y coordinates where you want to move the vertex. ▶

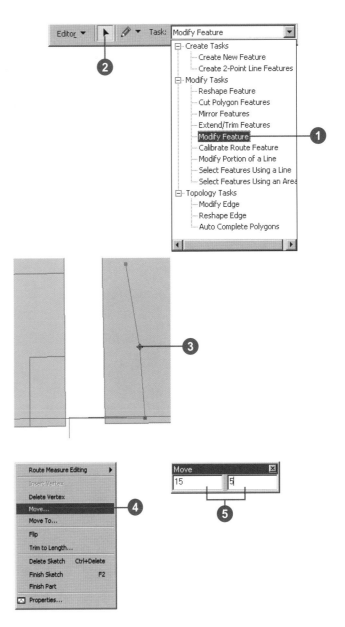

The vertex is moved.

6. Right-click over any part of the sketch and click Finish Sketch.

The feature is reshaped.

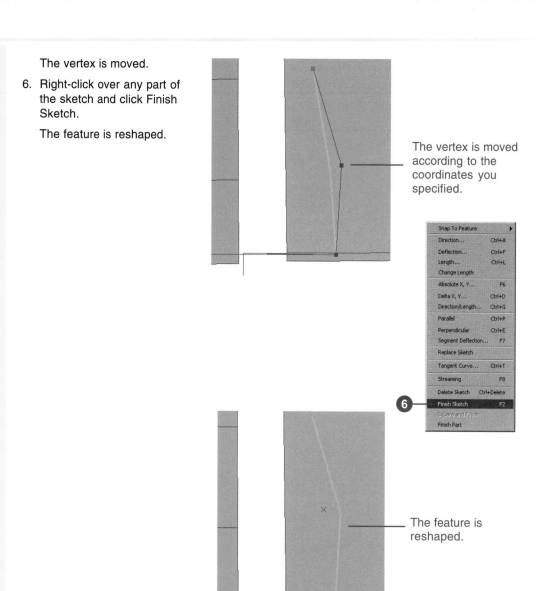

The vertex is moved according to the coordinates you specified.

The feature is reshaped.

Changing the properties of a sketch

When creating a new feature or modifying an existing one, you can easily change the properties of the sketch shape using the Sketch Properties dialog box.

Using the Sketch Properties dialog box, you can remove parts from a multipart feature, insert and delete vertices, and alter the m- and z-values of vertices.

Suppose you are editing a layer that contains river features whose shapes contain too many vertices. You could use the Sketch Properties dialog box to select unwanted vertices and delete them.

Tip

How do I know which vertices I have selected?

As you select vertices in the dialog box, they change color on the map.

Deleting multiple vertices from a feature

1. Click the Edit tool and select the feature whose shape you want to modify.

2. Click the Task dropdown arrow and click Modify Feature to place the shape of the feature in the edit sketch.

3. Right-click the sketch and click Properties.

4. Select the vertices that you want to remove by holding down the Shift key and clicking vertices from the table. Use the Shift or Ctrl key to select more than one vertex.

5. Press the Delete key or right-click the selected vertices and click Delete.

   The selected vertices are deleted from the sketch.

6. Click Finish Sketch.

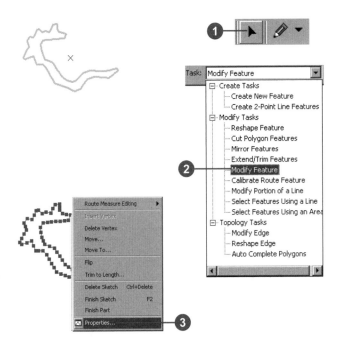

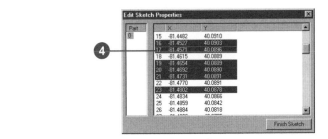

Tip

Modifying the x,y coordinates

If you don't want the added point to be exactly at the midpoint between two vertices, click the x or y column and type a new coordinate for the point.

Tip

Insert vertices after a selected vertex

You can insert vertices either before or after the vertex that you right-click.

Inserting a vertex at the midpoint of a segment

1. Right-click over a segment of the edit sketch and click Properties.

2. Select the vertex before which you wish to insert a new vertex.

3. Right-click the selected vertex and click Insert Before.

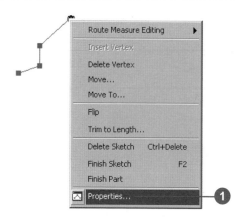

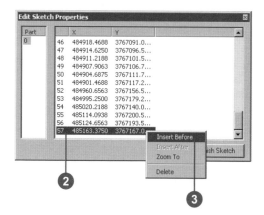

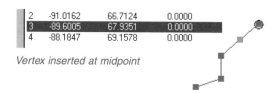

Vertex inserted at midpoint

Tip

How do I know which parts I have selected?

When you select a part from the Sketch Properties dialog box, the segments for that part will appear thicker.

Removing a part from a multipart feature

1. Click the Edit tool and select the feature you want to remove a part from.

2. Click the Task dropdown arrow and click Modify Feature to place the multipart shape in the edit sketch.

3. Right-click the sketch and click Properties.

4. Right-click the part that you want to remove and press the Delete key or right-click and click Delete.

5. Click Finish Sketch.

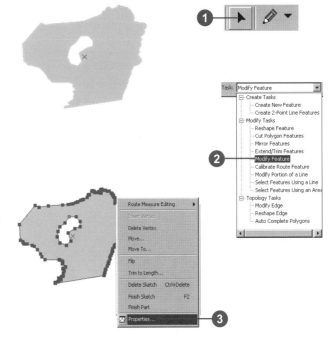

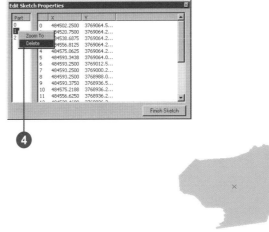

Editing z- and m-values of a feature

1. Click the Edit tool and select the feature whose z- or m-values you wish to edit.

2. Click the Task dropdown arrow and click Modify Feature.

3. Right-click the sketch and click Properties.

4. Select the vertex you wish to modify.

5. Click the z or m field in the table and type a new value.

6. Click Finish Sketch.

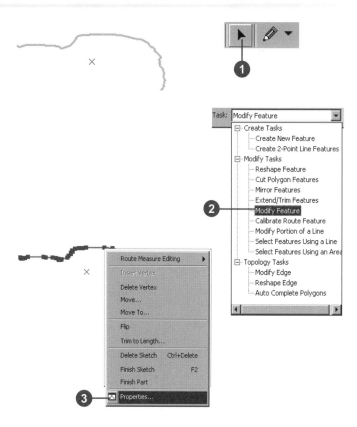

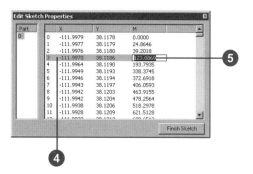

Scaling features

You can scale a feature—make the entire feature larger or smaller—using the Scale tool. The feature is scaled based on the location of the selection anchor—the small x located in the center of selected features.

You might use the Scale tool when working with data from a new source in which the scale is slightly different—for example, subdivision parcels from a surveyor. You can use the Scale tool to scale parcels so they fit together properly.

To use the Scale tool, you must first add it to a toolbar from the Commands tab of the Customize dialog box. The Scale tool is available from the Editor category. For more information on adding a tool to a toolbar, see *Exploring ArcObjects* or *Using ArcMap*.

Tip

Moving the selection anchor

To move the selection anchor of a feature you want to scale, hold the scaling pointer over the anchor until the icon changes. Then, click and drag the anchor to a new location.

1. Click the Edit tool.
2. Click the feature you want to scale.
3. Click the Scale tool.
4. Move the selection anchor if necessary.
5. Click and drag the pointer over the feature to scale it as desired. ▶

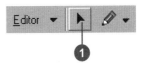

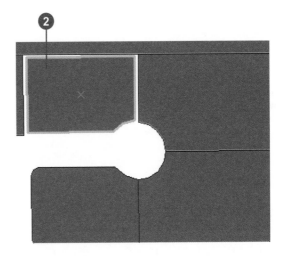

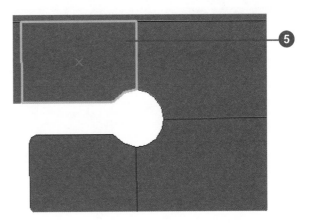

Tip

Scaling more than one feature

You can scale more than one feature at the same time. Simply select all the desired features and move the selection anchor to the desired location before using the Scale tool.

Tip

Undoing scaling

To return a feature to its original size after scaling it, click the Undo button on the ArcMap Standard toolbar.

Tip

Scale factor

You can scale features using a scale factor instead of dragging the mouse. Press the F key to set the scale factor.

Tip

Scaling with snapping

Press the S key to add an auxiliary selection anchor to the feature that you are scaling. The auxiliary selection anchor can be dragged anywhere on the feature and will snap to the features specified in the current snapping environment.

6. Release the mouse button when you're finished scaling the feature.

   The feature is scaled.

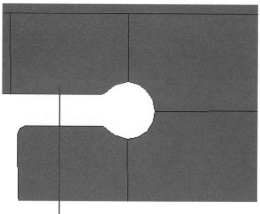

The feature is scaled.

Clipping features

You can easily clip features that touch or are within a buffered distance of selected features.

Suppose that you want to model the effect of a proposed road-widening project on the lots of a subdivision block. You can do this using the Clip command. Select the road centerline where the proposed widening is to occur, then click Clip from the Editor menu. Type the length measurement of the widening and click the option to Discard the area that intersects to clip the subdivision lots.

When using the Discard the area that intersects option, the Clip command will buffer the selected road feature and clip all portions of editable features that are within the buffered region. Using the Preserve the area that intersects option, all features that touch the buffered feature will be deleted.

1. Select the feature you want to use to clip features.

2. Click Editor and click Clip.

3. Type a buffer value. You can leave the value as 0 if you are using a polygon feature to clip with.

4. Click the type of clip operation you wish to use.

5. Click OK to clip the feature.

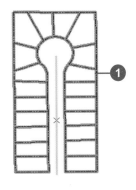

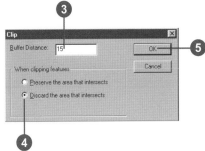

Stretching geometry proportionately

Sometimes you want to stretch a feature without changing its geometry (shape). Suppose you want to change the position of a feature in relation to other features by moving a vertex. For example, perhaps the data you have for an electric transmission system is not as accurate as you would like. However, you have other layers containing accurate surveyed points that coincide with some of the transmission towers, power generating plants, and substations. By moving the vertices of the transmission lines, you can adjust the positions of the lines to the known surveyed positions of the features in the more accurate layer. You can change the positions of these vertices without changing the general shape of the transmission lines by stretching the features proportionately.

When you stretch a feature proportionately, the proportions of the feature's segments are maintained, thereby maintaining the general shape of the feature. This is different from moving a vertex to reshape a feature.

The graphics below show the difference between moving a vertex to reshape a feature and moving a vertex while maintaining the shape of the feature. The three graphics on the top show how a feature is modified when its upper-right vertex is moved with proportionate stretching turned on. The three graphics on the bottom show how the same feature is reshaped when its upper-right vertex is moved with proportionate stretching turned off.

Proportionate stretching on

Proportionate stretching off

 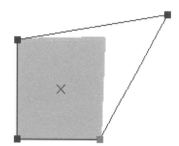 

Stretching a feature's geometry proportionately

Within the Editing Options menu, you can choose to stretch the geometry of features proportionately when moving vertices. When you drag a vertex to a new location with this option turned on, the proportions of the feature's segments are maintained, thereby maintaining the general shape of the feature.

You might want to stretch features proportionately when merging data from different data sources—for example, utility lines from one source and subdivision parcels from another.

Suppose the data for the subdivision parcels is accurate, but the data for the utility lines is not as accurate. While the shapes of the utility lines are generally correct, you want to change the position of one line relative to the parcels by moving a vertex. By stretching the utility line feature proportionately, you can make it fit accurately with the parcels without losing the general shape of the line. ▶

1. Click the Task dropdown arrow and click Modify Feature.

2. Click the Edit tool and click the feature you want to stretch.

3. Click Editor and click Options.

4. Click the General tab.

5. Check the check box to stretch the feature proportionately.

   Uncheck the check box if you want to reshape the feature without maintaining proportionate geometry.

6. Click OK. ▶

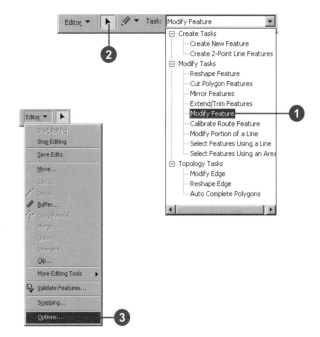

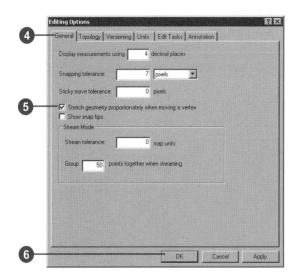

You can turn on proportionate stretching by checking a box on the General tab of the Editing Options dialog box. Uncheck the box if you simply want to reshape a feature without maintaining proportionate geometry.

See Also

To see how stretching a feature proportionately looks in comparison to stretching a feature to reshape it, see 'Stretching geometry proportionately' in this chapter.

7. Position the pointer over the vertex you want to move until the pointer changes.

8. Drag the vertex to the desired location.

9. Right-click over any part of the sketch and click Finish Sketch.

   The feature is stretched proportionately.

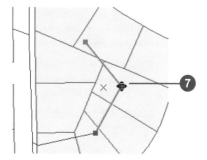

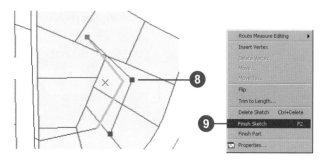

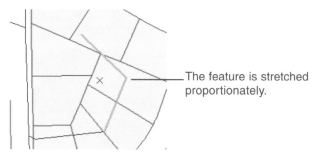

The feature is stretched proportionately.

Spatial adjustment

8

The *Spatial Adjustment* toolbar lets you transform, rubber sheet, and edgematch features in your map. It works within ArcMap Editor to provide a highly productive adjustment environment. Spatial adjustment supports a variety of adjustment methods and will adjust all editable data sources.

Spatial adjustment commands and tools are located on an additional editing toolbar called the Spatial Adjustment toolbar. These tools and commands allow you to define a spatial adjustment. Since spatial adjustment operates within an Edit session, you can leverage existing editing functionality, such as snapping, to enhance your adjustments.

Along with the ability to spatially adjust your data, the Spatial Adjustment toolbar also provides a way for you to transfer the attributes from one feature to another. This tool is called the Attribute Transfer tool and relies on matching common fields between two layers. Together, the adjustment and attribute transfer functions available in the Spatial Adjustment tool allow you to improve the quality of your data.

About spatial adjustments

The following section briefly describes the spatial adjustment methods and related concepts.

Transformations

Transformations convert data from one coordinate system to another. They are often used to convert data from digitizer or scanner units to real-world coordinates. Transformations can also be used to shift your data within a coordinate system, such as converting feet to meters.

The transformation functions are based on comparing the coordinates of source and destination points, also called control points, in special graphical elements called displacement links. You may create these links interactively, pointing at known source and destination locations, or by loading a link text file or control points file.

By default, ArcMap supports three types of transformations: affine, similarity, and projective.

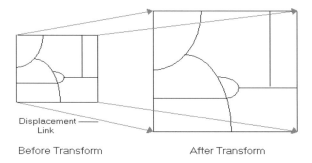

Displacement Link

Before Transform   After Transform

An affine transformation can differentially scale, skew, rotate, and translate the data. The graphic below illustrates the four possible changes:

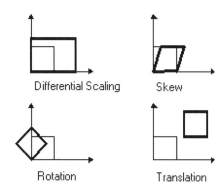

Differential Scaling   Skew

Rotation   Translation

The affine transformation function is:

$$x' = Ax + By + C$$
$$y' = Dx + Ey + F$$

where x and y are coordinates of the input layer and x' and y' are the transformed coordinates. A, B, C, D, E, and F are determined by comparing the location of source and destination control points. They scale, skew, rotate, and translate the layer coordinates.

The affine transformation requires a minimum of three displacement links.

The similarity transformation scales, rotates, and translates the data. It will not independently scale the axes, nor will it introduce any skew. It maintains the aspect ratio of the features transformed.

The similarity transform function is:

$$x' = Ax + By + C \quad y' = -Bx + Ay + F$$

where:

$A = s \cdot \cos t$
$B = s \cdot \sin t$
$C =$ translation in x direction
$F =$ translation in y direction

and:

$s =$ scale change (same in x and y directions)
$t =$ rotation angle, measured counterclockwise from the x-axis

A similarity transformation requires a minimum of two displacement links.

The projective transformation is based on a more complex formula that requires a minimum of four displacement links:

$$x' = (Ax + By + C) / (Gx + Hy + 1)$$
$$y' = (Dx + Ey + F) / (Gx + Hy + 1)$$

This method is used to transform data captured directly from aerial photography. For more information, please refer to one of the photogrammetric texts listed in 'References' at the end of this section.

Understanding residual and root mean square

The transformation parameters are a best fit between the source and destination control points. If you use the transformation parameters to transform the actual source control points, the transformed output locations won't match the true output control point locations. This is known as the residual error; it is a measure of the fit between the true locations and the transformed locations of the output control points. This error is generated for each displacement link.

An RMS error is calculated for each transformation performed. It indicates how good the derived transformation is. The following example illustrates the relative location of four destination control points and the transformed source control points:

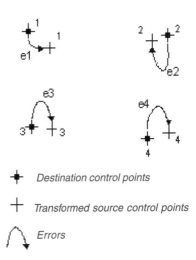

+ Destination control points

+ Transformed source control points

⌒ Errors

The RMS error measures the errors between the destination control points and the transformed locations of the source control points.

$$\text{RMS error} = \sqrt{\frac{e_1^2 + e_2^2 + e_3^2 + \cdots + e_n^2}{n}}$$

The transformation is derived using least squares, so more links can be given than are necessary.

Rubber sheeting

Geometric distortions commonly occur in source maps. They may be introduced by imperfect registration in map compilation, lack of geodetic control in source data, or a variety of other causes. *Rubber sheeting* corrects flaws through the geometric adjustment of coordinates.

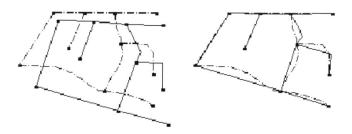

The source layer—drawn with solid lines—is adjusted to the more accurate target layer.

During rubber sheeting, the surface is literally stretched, moving features using a piecewise transformation that preserves straight lines. Similar to transformations, displacement links are used in rubber sheeting to determine where features are moved.

Conflation applications use rubber sheeting to align layers in preparation for transferring attributes.

Edgematching

The *edgematching* process aligns features along the edge of one layer to features of an adjoining layer. The layer with the least-accurate features is adjusted, and the other adjoining layer is used as the control.

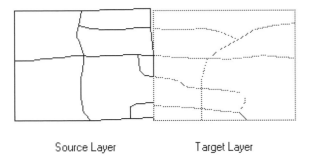

Source Layer   Target Layer

Attribute transfer

Attribute transfer is typically used to copy attributes from a less accurate layer to a more accurate one. For example, it can be used to transfer the names of hydrological features from a previously digitized and highly generalized 1:500,000-scale map to a more detailed 1:24,000-scale map.

In ArcMap, you can specify what attributes to transfer between layers, then interactively choose the source and target features.

References

Maling, D.H. *Coordinate Systems and Map Projections*. George Philip, 1973.

Maling, D.H. "Coordinate systems and map projections for GIS." *Geographical Information Systems: Principles and Applications*, Maguire, D.J., M.F. Goodchild, and D.W. Rhind (eds.) vol. 1, pp. 135–146. Longman Group UK Ltd., 1991.

Moffitt, F.H., and E.M. Mikhail. *Photogrammetry*. Third edition. Harper & Row, Inc., 1980.

Pettofrezzo, A.J. *Matrices and Transformations*. Dover Publications, Inc., 1966.

Slama, C.C., C. Theurer, and S.W. Henriksen (eds.). *Manual of Photogrammetry*. Fourth edition. Chapter XIV, pp. 729–731. ASPRS, 1980.

The Spatial Adjustment toolbar

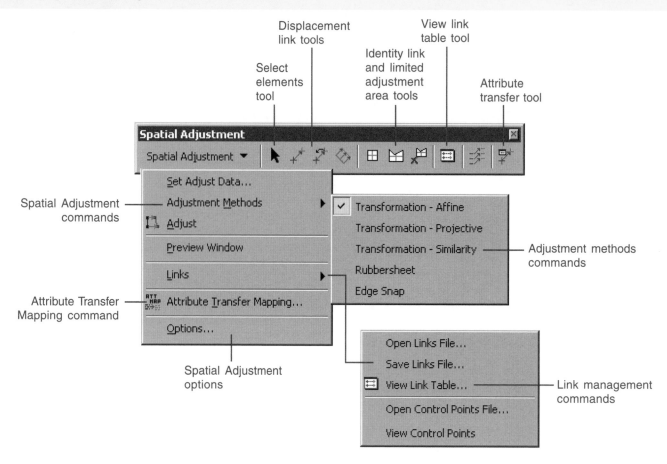

Select elements tool

Displacement link tools

Identity link and limited adjustment area tools

View link table tool

Attribute transfer tool

Spatial Adjustment commands

Attribute Transfer Mapping command

Spatial Adjustment options

Adjustment methods commands

Link management commands

An overview of the spatial adjustment process

The following is a general overview of how to use ArcMap, the Editor toolbar, and the Spatial Adjustment toolbar to adjust your data. Each of the following steps is outlined in detail in this chapter or other chapters in this book.

1. Start ArcMap.

2. Create a new map or open an existing one.

Open button

New Map File button

3. Add the data you want to edit to your map.

Add Data button

If there are no existing layers for the feature classes you want to edit, you can create them using ArcCatalog. For more information on creating a feature layer, see *Using ArcCatalog*.

4. Add the Editor toolbar to ArcMap.

Editor Toolbar button

5. Add the Spatial Adjustment toolbar to ArcMap.

6. Choose Start Editing from the Editor menu.

7. Click Spatial Adjustment, point to Adjustment Methods, and click one of the Transformation methods to choose a spatial adjustment method.

8. Click the displacement link tools to create displacement links.

Displacement
link tools

9. Perform the adjustment.

10. Choose Stop Editing from the Editor menu and click Yes when prompted to save your edits.

There is no need to save the map—all edits made to the database will automatically be reflected the next time you open the map.

Adding the Spatial Adjustment toolbar

Before adjusting geographic feature data within ArcMap, you must first add the Spatial Adjustment toolbar.

Tip

Adding the Spatial Adjustment toolbar using the Customize dialog box

Click the Tools menu and click Customize. In the Customize dialog box, click the Toolbars tab and check Spatial Adjustment.

1. Start ArcMap.

2. Click the View menu, point to Toolbars, and click Spatial Adjustment to display the Spatial Adjustment toolbar.

3. Click the toolbar's title bar and drag it to the top of the ArcMap application window.

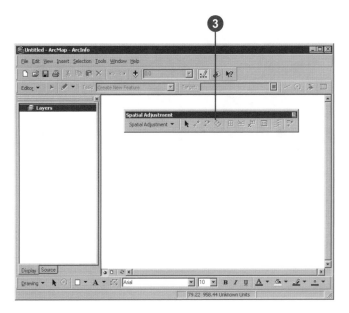

Choosing the input data for adjustment

The first step in the spatial adjustment process is to choose the input data for the adjustment. You have the option to adjust selected features or all the features in the layer. These settings are available in the Choose Input For Adjustment dialog box.

Tip

All selection methods are supported

The Spatial Adjustment tool will honor selections performed interactively or by an attribute query.

1. Click the Spatial Adjustment menu and click Set Adjust Data.

   The Choose Input For Adjustment dialog box appears.

2. Choose whether to adjust selected features in a layer or all features in a layer.

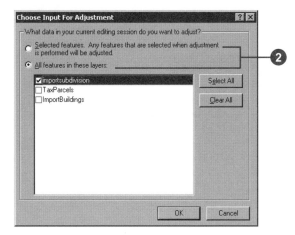

Choosing a transformation method

The Spatial Adjustment tool supports three types of transformation methods: affine, projective, and similarity. Choose a transformation method from the Adjustment Methods submenu.

See Also

For more information on the spatial adjustment methods, see the introductory material with this chapter.

1. Click the Spatial Adjustment menu, point to Adjustment Methods, and click a Transformation method.

Choosing a rubber sheet method

The Spatial Adjustment tool supports two types of rubber sheet methods: Natural Neighbor and Linear. Choose Rubbersheet from the Adjustment Methods submenu. Once you have chosen Rubbersheet, you may specify a rubber sheet method in the Adjustment Properties dialog box. The Natural Neighbor method is the default.

1. Click the Spatial Adjustment menu, point to Adjustment Methods, and click Rubbersheet.

2. Click the Spatial Adjustment menu and click Options.

   The Adjustment Properties dialog box appears.

3. Click the Adjustment method dropdown arrow and choose Rubbersheet.

4. Click the Adjustment method Options button.

   The Rubbersheet properties dialog box will appear.

5. Click the Natural Neighbor or Linear method and click OK.

6. Click OK to close the Adjustment Properties dialog box.

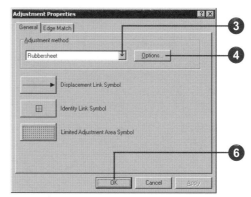

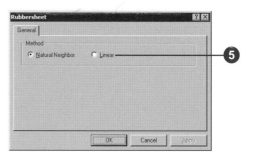

Choosing an edge snap method

The Spatial Adjustment tool supports two types of Edge Snap methods: Smooth and Line. Choose Edge Snap from the Adjustment methods submenu. Once you have chosen Edge Snap, you may specify an edge snap method in the Adjustment Properties dialog box.

When using the Smooth edge snap method, vertices at the link source point are moved to the destination point. The remaining vertices are also moved to give an overall smoothing effect.

When using the Line edge snap method, only the vertices at the link source point are moved to the destination point. The remaining vertices on the feature remain unchanged.

The Smooth method is the default.

1. Click the Spatial Adjustment menu, point to Adjustment Methods, and click Edge Snap.

2. Click the Spatial Adjustment menu and click Options.

   The Adjustment Properties dialog box appears.

3. Click the Adjustment method dropdown arrow and click Edge Snap.

4. Click the Adjustment method Options button.

   The Edge Snap dialog box will appear.

5. Click the Smooth or Line method.

6. Check the box if you want to adjust to the midpoint of the links, then click OK.

7. Click OK to close the Adjustment Properties dialog box.

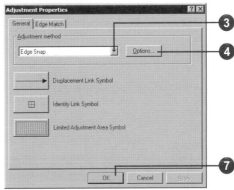

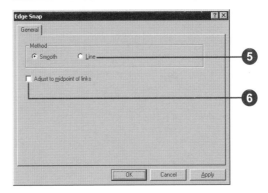

Setting the edge snap properties

The Edge Snap adjustment method requires more property settings than other methods. These property settings are located in the Edge Match tab of the Adjustment Properties dialog box.

Choose the source and target layers. The source layer's features will be edgematched to the target layer's features. If you choose to adjust to the midpoints of the links, features from both layers will be adjusted.

You have the option to specify one link per destination point and to prevent duplicate links. These settings can help you avoid creating unnecessary links. The Spatial Adjustment tool supports the ability to use attributes to enhance the edgematching process. Based on the Attribute Transfer Mapping dialog box, you have the option to match fields between the source and target layers and use common attributes to define the edgematch. This function can help ensure the accuracy of the edgematch.

1. Click the Spatial Adjustment menu and click Options.

   The Adjustment Properties dialog box appears.

2. Click the Edge Match tab.

3. Click the Source Layer dropdown arrow and choose a source layer.

4. Click the Target Layer dropdown arrow and choose a target layer.

5. Check Use Attributes if you want to use attributes to enhance the edgematch.

6. If you only want one link for each destination point, check the appropriate box.

7. If you want to prevent duplicate links, check the appropriate box.

8. Click the Attributes button if you chose to use attributes.

   The Edgematch Attributes dialog box appears.

9. Match the source and target layer fields.

10. Click Add.

11. Click OK when finished matching fields.

12. Click OK to close the Adjustment Properties dialog box.

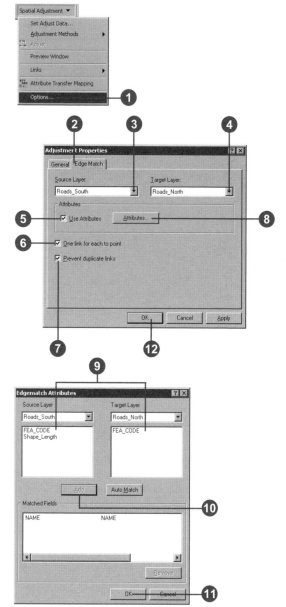

Creating displacement links

Before you adjust your data, you must create *displacement links* to define the source and destination coordinates for the adjustment. Links are represented as arrows with the arrowhead pointing toward the destination location. Links can be created manually or loaded by means of a link file.

Displacement links are represented as graphic elements in the map. You can change the symbol, size, and color of displacement links.

Tip

Use snapping to ensure accurate link placement

Use the Snapping Environment tool to set the snapping agents and features. Snapping will ensure that links are created at the vertices, edges, or endpoints of features.

1. Click the New Displacement link tool on the Spatial Adjustment toolbar.

2. Position the cursor over the source location and click once to start adding a link.

3. Position the cursor over the destination location and click once to finish adding the link.

   A displacement link now connects the source location to the destination location.

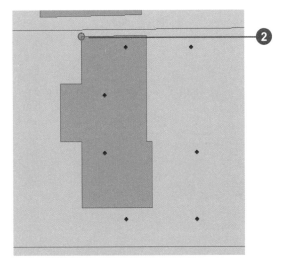

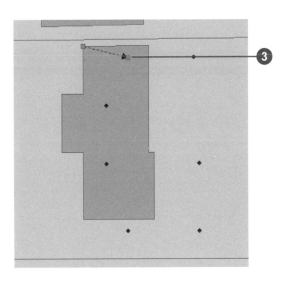

Creating multiple displacement links

You can create multiple displacement links using the Multi Displacement Links tool. The Multi Displacement Links tool is useful for areas that require many links, such as curve features. This tool can also help you save time by allowing you to create many links at once.

Tip

Snap to edges when using the Multi Displacement Links tool

It is best to snap to the edges of features when creating multiple links.

1. Click the Multi Displacement Links tool on the Spatial Adjustment toolbar.

2. Position the cursor over the source feature and click once.

3. Position the cursor over the target feature and click once.

   The No. of links dialog box will appear. This dialog box allows you to specify how many links to create. ▶

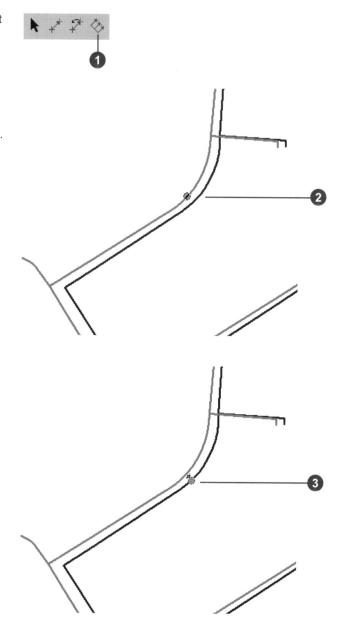

4. Enter the number of links you want and press Enter. The default is 10.

   Based on the value you entered, the multiple links are created and now connect the source feature to the target feature.

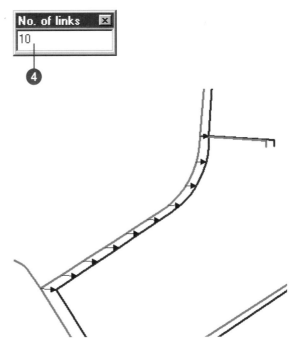

Creating identity links

Identity links can be used to hold features in place at specified locations. Identity links can serve as anchors because they prevent the movement of features during an adjustment.

Identity links are only available when using the Rubbersheet adjustment method. Like displacement links, identity links are represented as graphic elements in the map.

1. Click the New Identity Link tool on the Spatial Adjustment toolbar.

2. Position the cursor over the source location and click once.

   Add identity links to locations to prevent the movement of features during an adjustment.

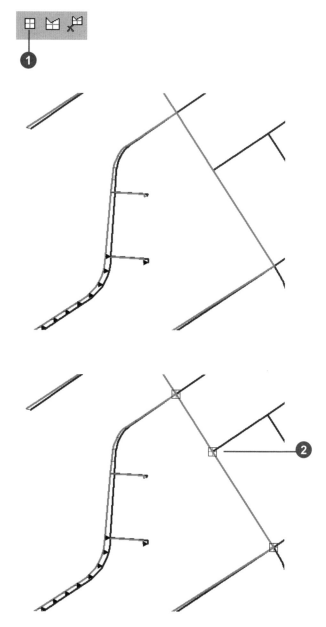

Using the Limited Adjustment Area tools

You can limit the scope of an adjustment area by using the Limited Adjustment Area tool. This tool is only available for the Rubbersheet adjustment method.

This tool allows you to draw a polygon shape around the features you wish to adjust. Any features that are outside this polygon area will not be affected by the adjustment, regardless of whether or not they are selected. The Limited Adjustment Area tool provides similar feature anchoring as identity links. However, in cases where you must add many identity links, using the Limited Adjustment Area tool may help you save time.

Creating a limited adjustment area

1. Click the New Limited Adjustment Area tool on the Spatial Adjustment toolbar.

2. Using the cursor on the map, draw a polygon around the area you wish to rubber sheet. Double-click to complete the polygon.

   Features outside of this polygon will not be affected during the adjustment.

3. Click the Clear Limited Adjustment Area tool on the Spatial Adjustment toolbar to remove the limited adjustment area polygon.

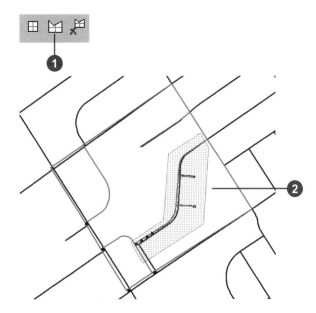

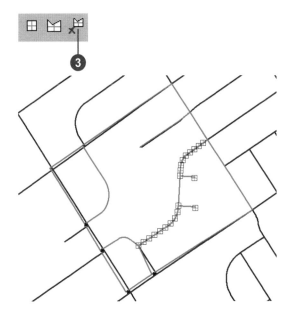

Using the Edge Match tool

The Edge Match tool allows you to create multiple displacement links that connect the edges of two adjacent layers. Once you have set the appropriate snapping agents and tolerance, use the tool to drag a box around the features you wish to edgematch. This will create links between the closest source and target features by default.

You can also use additional properties to enhance the link creation process, such as restricting one link per destination point and preventing duplicate links.

These properties, combined with the proper snapping settings, can help ensure an accurate edgematch.

Tip

Use attributes to refine the edgematch

The Use Attributes option located in the Edge Match properties dialog box can assist in the creation of links by ensuring they connect to features that share common attribute values.

1. Click the Edge Match tool on the Spatial Adjustment toolbar.

2. Drag a box around the features you want to edgematch.

   Links will now connect the edges of the source layer to the edges of the target layer.

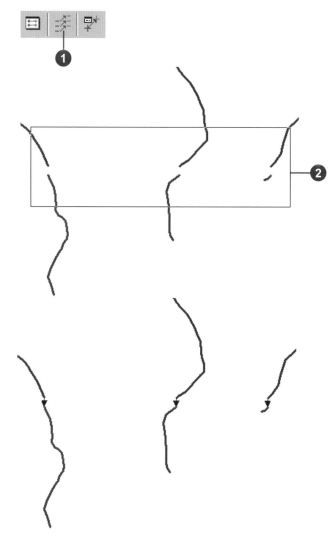

Modifying the link and limited adjustment area symbols

You can customize the symbology of the displacement links, identity links, and limited adjustment area. These settings are in the Adjustment Properties dialog box. When you click the Displacement Link Symbol, Identity Link Symbol, or Limited Adjustment Area Symbol buttons, the Symbol Selector dialog box appears. Use this window to choose a new style, size, and color for the links and limited adjustment area. The Symbol Selector will present options to modify the symbols based on the graphical element's geometry type.

1. Click the Spatial Adjustment menu and click Options.

   The Adjustment Properties dialog box appears.

2. Click the Displacement Link Symbol, Identity Link Symbol, or Limited Adjustment Area Symbol button.

   The Symbol Selector dialog box appears.

3. Choose a different symbol, change the symbol size, specify a new symbol color, or any combination of these, then click OK.

4. Click OK to close the Adjustment Properties dialog box.

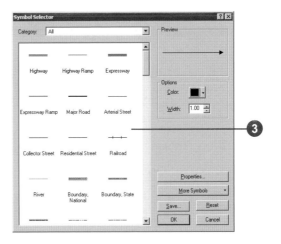

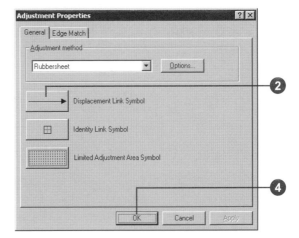

Selecting links

Displacement and identity links are selected with the Select Elements tool located on the Spatial Adjustment toolbar.

Links must be selected prior to modifying or deleting a link.

Tip

Use the Select Elements tool on the ArcMap Standard toolbar

You can also select links by using the Select Elements tool.

Selecting a link

1. Click the Select Elements tool on the Spatial Adjustment toolbar.

2. Position the cursor over the link you want to select and click once.

   Selection grips will appear at the endpoints of the link.

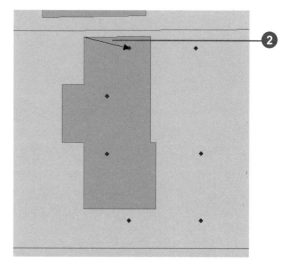

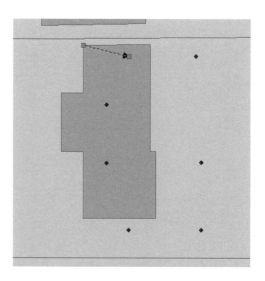

Tip

Use the Shift key to select more than one link at a time

You can select multiple links by holding down the Shift key while clicking links with the Select Elements tool.

Tip

Use the Select All Elements command

You can select all the links in the map by using the Select All Elements command. Click the Edit menu and click Select All Elements.

Selecting multiple links

1. Click the Select Elements tool on the Spatial Adjustment toolbar.

2. Drag a box around the links you want to select.

   Selection grips will appear at the endpoints of the links.

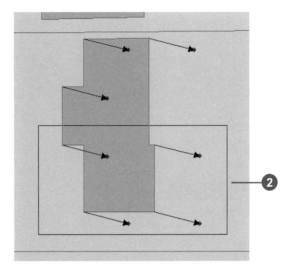

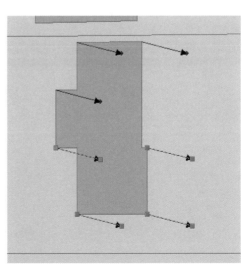

Modifying displacement links

Displacement links can be modified by using the Modify Link tool. They must be selected prior to modifying them. Links can be modified both inside or outside an edit session. You can modify links at their source or destination location or move the entire link to a new location.

Tip

Use the Select Elements tool to modify identity links
You can modify identity links with the Select Elements tool. Simply click an identity link and drag it to a new location.

1. Click the Select Elements tool on the Spatial Adjustment toolbar.

2. Position the cursor over the link you want to modify and click once.

   Selection grips will appear at the endpoints of the link. ▶

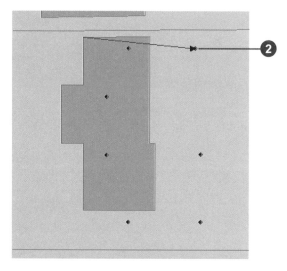

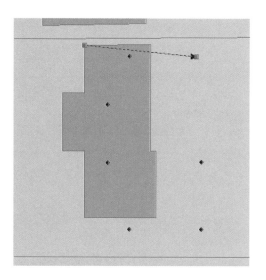

3. Click the Modify link tool on the Spatial Adjustment toolbar.

4. Position the cursor over the source or destination point of the link.

   The link cursor changes to an arrow cursor.

5. Move the endpoint of the link to the desired location.

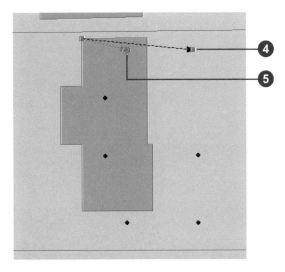

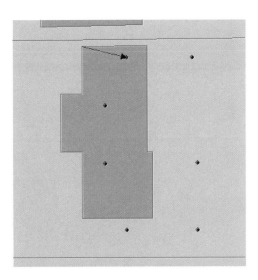

Deleting displacement links

Displacement links can be deleted by using the Delete command or pressing the Delete key. Links must first be selected in order to delete them. Links can be deleted both inside or outside an edit session.

Tip

Use the Delete command to remove links

Click the Edit menu and click Delete to remove links.

Tip

Delete links with the Link Table

You can also delete links with the Link Table. Right-click a link record to open the context menu and click Delete link(s) to open the link table; see 'Viewing the Link Table' later in this chapter.

Deleting a link

1. Click the Select Elements tool on the Spatial Adjustment toolbar.

2. Position the cursor over the link you want to delete and click once.

   Selection grips will appear at the endpoints of the link.

3. Press the Delete key.

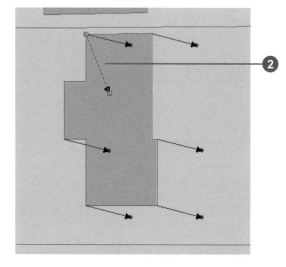

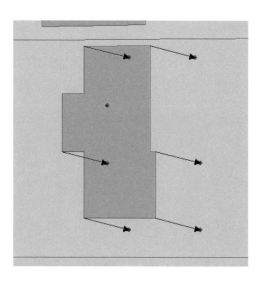

Deleting multiple links

1. Click the Select Elements tool on the Spatial Adjustment toolbar.

2. Drag a box around the links you want to delete.

   You can also select multiple links by holding down the Shift key while selecting links.

3. Press the Delete key.

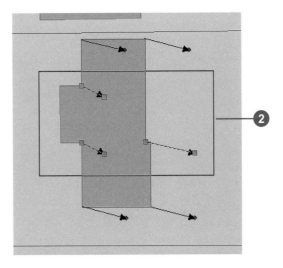

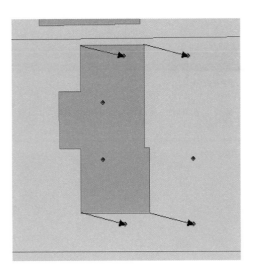

Viewing the Link Table

The Link Table displays displacement links in a tabular format. This table displays the source and destination coordinates of the links, the link IDs, and the residual error of the adjustment. Residual errors will only be displayed for Transformation adjustments.

You can select links by clicking a row in the table. Coordinate values can be edited for the selected links. You can select multiple links by holding down Shift while selecting rows. When a link is selected, right-click to open the Link Table context menu. This menu supports commands to flash links, pan and zoom to links, and delete links.

Tip

Open the Link Table from the toolbar

You can also open the Link Table by clicking the View Link Table button (shown below), located on the Spatial Adjustment toolbar.

1. Click the Spatial Adjustment menu, point to Links, and click View Link Table.

   The Link Table dialog box appears.

2. Click a row in the link table to highlight a link.

3. With a link record highlighted, you can edit the coordinates of the link or delete the link by clicking Delete Link.

4. Right-click the highlighted link to access the Link Table context menu. You can pan to the link, zoom to the link, select the link, and delete the link with the commands offered in this menu.

5. When finished working with the Link Table, click Close to close the window.

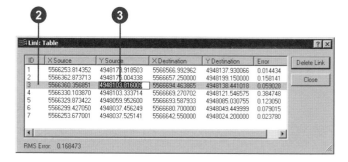

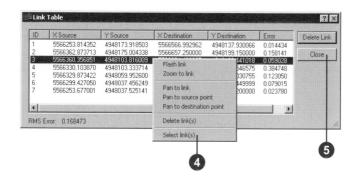

Opening a link file

Link files are text files that contain source and destination coordinates that define an adjustment. The Spatial Adjustment tool supports tab-delimited link files that contain either four or five columns. A four-column link file consists of two pairs of source and destination coordinate values. A five-column link file consists of an ID column—string or numeric—that precedes two pairs of source and destination coordinate values.

When you open a link file, the Spatial Adjustment tool automatically creates displacement links in the map based on the source and destination coordinate values in the file. Link files can help you save time by automating the link creation process.

1. Click the Spatial Adjustment menu, point to Links, and click Open Links File.

   The Open dialog box appears.

2. Click the Look in dropdown arrow and navigate to the folder where the link file resides.

3. Double-click the link file to load it.

   Displacement links will be automatically created in the map.

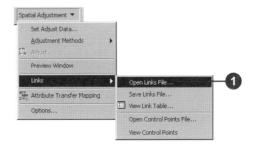

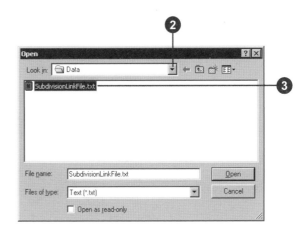

Saving a link file

You can create a link file from the existing displacement links in the map using the Save Links File command. This command opens a Save dialog box and allows you to navigate to the folder of your choice and name the new link file. You also have the option to save link IDs. The link file is saved as a tab-delimited text file.

1. Click the Spatial Adjustment menu, point to Links, and click Save Links File.

   The Save Links dialog box appears.

2. Click the Save in dropdown arrow and navigate to the folder where you want to save the link file.

3. Enter a name for the link file.

4. Click Save.

5. Choose whether or not to save link IDs.

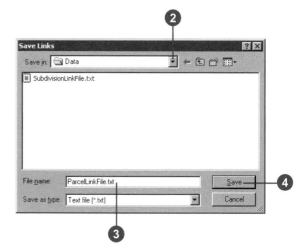

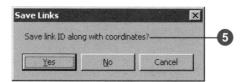

Opening a Control Point file

Control Point files are text files that contain destination coordinates that define part of an adjustment. The Spatial Adjustment tool supports tab-delimited Control Point files that contain either two or three columns. A two-column Control Points file consists of a pair of destination coordinate values. A three-column Control Points file consists of an ID column—string or numeric—that precedes a pair of destination coordinate values. Control points may represent known locations of features from GPS or ground survey and are displayed in the Control Points Window.

1. Click the Spatial Adjustment menu, point to Links, and click Open Control Points File.

   The Open dialog box appears.

2. Click the Look in dropdown arrow and navigate to the folder where the control point file resides.

3. Double-click the control point file to load it.

   The Control Points Window appears.

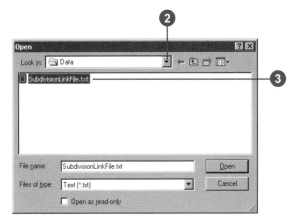

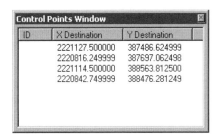

Creating displacement links from control points

Opening a control point file does not automatically create displacement links as in the case of link files. You must manually create the links from the control points. This requires that you open the Control Points Window with the View Control Points command, then double-click each row to create a destination link in the map. Once the link is created at the destination location, you must then finish adding the link to the source location. This will connect the source feature to the target feature. Repeat this process until all the control point rows are removed from the Control Points Window.

1. Click the Spatial Adjustment menu, point to Links, and click View Control Points.

   The Control Points Window appears.

2. Double-click a row in the Control Points Window.

   This will create a link that is snapped to a destination location. ▶

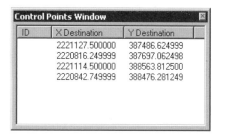

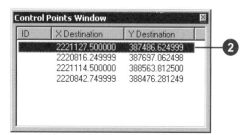

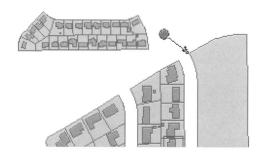

3. Snap the link to a source location.

   The row is now removed from the Control Points Window.

4. Repeat steps 2 and 3 until all the rows in the Control Points Window are removed and converted into displacement links.

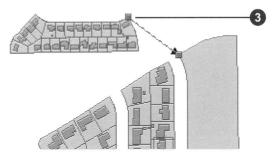

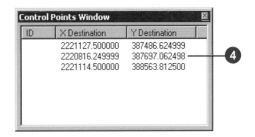

Previewing the adjustment

You can preview an adjustment using the Adjustment Preview Window. This window allows you to view the results of an adjustment prior to performing the adjustment in the map. You can use standard ArcMap Zoom and Pan commands in this window to closely examine how the adjustment will affect your features. This allows you an opportunity to go back in the map and make modifications before you adjust your data. Additionally, the Adjustment Preview Window supports its own display commands from a context menu, such as zooming to the data frame's extent, and tracking the data frame's extent.

The Adjustment Preview Window can help you save time and unnecessary edits by giving you a glimpse of how the adjustment will turn out.

1. Click the Spatial Adjustment menu and click Preview Window.

   The Adjustment Preview Window appears.

2. Examine the adjustment more closely by using the Zoom and Pan commands on the standard map display toolbar.

3. You can access additional commands by right-clicking inside the Adjustment Preview Window to open the context menu.

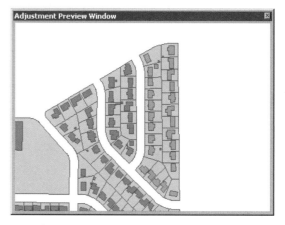

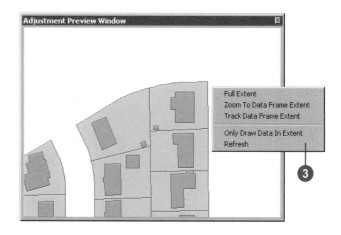

Performing the adjustment

Once you have chosen which data to adjust, selected an adjustment method, set the adjustment properties, and created links and limited adjustment areas, you can adjust the data. Clicking the Adjust command will execute the spatial adjustment.

Tip

Use the Undo command to undo an adjustment

All adjustments can be undone by clicking the Undo button:

1. Click the Spatial Adjustment menu and click Adjust.

   The data is now adjusted.

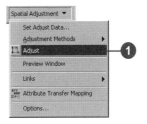

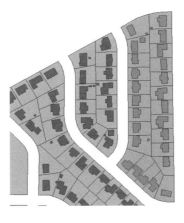

Attribute Transfer Mapping

The Attribute Transfer Mapping functions support the interactive transfer of attributes between features. The Attribute Transfer Mapping dialog box allows you to set the source and target layers and specify which fields to use as criteria for the attribute transfer. Once you have identified the common fields in the source and target layers, they are matched. These matched fields define which attributes are transferred when using the Attribute Transfer tool. You also have the option to transfer the geometry of the feature by checking the Transfer Geometry check box.

Tip

Using the Auto Match command to match multiple fields at once

You can use the Auto Match command to match multiple fields at once based on common field names.

1. Click the Spatial Adjustment menu and click Attribute Transfer Mapping.

   The Attribute Transfer Mapping dialog box appears.

2. Click the Source Layer dropdown arrow and choose a layer.

3. Click the Target Layer dropdown arrow and choose a layer.

4. Click a field in the Source Layer's field list box. ▶

5. Click a corresponding field in the Target Layer's field list box.

Both fields will be highlighted.

6. Click Add.

Repeat the process for all other fields that are to be used as criteria for the attribute transfer.

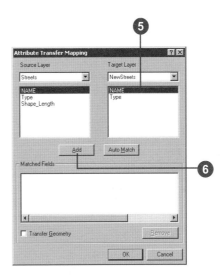

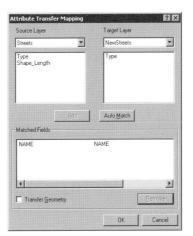

Using the Attribute Transfer tool

The Attribute Transfer tool allows you to transfer the attributes of a feature to another feature. This transfer is performed by matching the fields that are specified in the Attribute Transfer Mapping dialog box.

Use the Attribute Transfer tool to select a source feature followed by a target feature. When the transfer is complete, verify the target feature's attributes using the Identify tool.

Tip

Transfer attributes to multiple features

You can transfer attributes to multiple features by holding down the Shift key while selecting the target features.

See Also

For information on using the Attribute Transfer Mapping dialog box, see 'Attribute Transfer Mapping' in this chapter.

1. Click the Attribute Transfer tool on the Spatial Adjustment toolbar.

2. Position the cursor over the source feature and click once.

   This is the feature that contains the desired attribute data.

3. Position the cursor over the target feature and click once to transfer the attribute data of the source feature.

   The target feature is now updated with the source feature's attribute data.

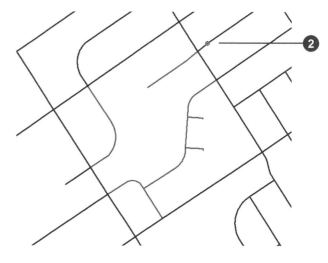

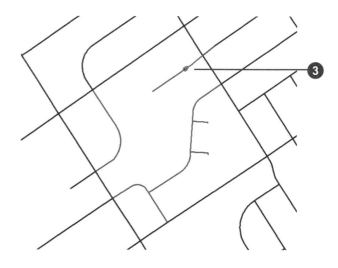

Editing attributes

9

Creating and editing features in a GIS usually entails creating or editing some attributes of the features, in addition to creating their shape.

ArcMap makes it easy to view and update the attributes of features in your database. You can edit feature attributes in two ways: using the Attributes dialog box or using a feature layer's attribute table. This chapter focuses on editing attributes using the Attributes dialog box. With the Attributes dialog box, you can view the attributes of selected features on your map; add, delete, or modify an attribute for a single feature or multiple features at the same time; and copy and paste individual attributes or all the attributes of a feature.

You can perform similar functions using a feature layer's attribute table. However, with tables you can also do computations—such as adding and sorting records—with attribute values. To learn how to edit attributes in an attribute table—including performing computations with attribute values—see *Using ArcMap*.

In the next chapter you will learn how to take advantage of the tight integration of ArcMap with geodatabases to make editing attributes quicker and more accurate.

Viewing attributes

The Attributes dialog box lets you view the attributes of features you've selected in your map. The left side of the dialog box lists the features you've selected. Features are listed by their primary display field and grouped by layer name. The number of features selected is displayed at the bottom of the dialog box.

The right side of the Attributes dialog box is called the property inspector. The property inspector contains two columns: the attribute properties of the layer you're viewing, such as Type or Owner, and the values of those attribute properties.

Tip

Finding the feature on the map

You can find a selected feature on the map by either highlighting or zooming to it. To highlight the feature, click the primary field and the feature will flash on the map. Right-click the field and click Zoom To in the context menu to get a close-up view of the feature. Click the Back button on the Tools toolbar to return to the previous map extent.

1. Click the Edit tool.

2. Select the features whose attributes you want to view.

3. Click the Attributes button.

4. Click the layer name that contains the features whose attributes you want to view.

   The layer's attribute properties appear on the right side of the dialog box. ▶

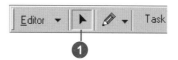

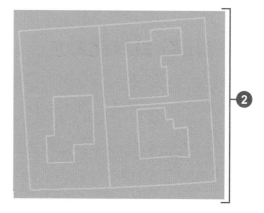

The layer's attribute properties appear.

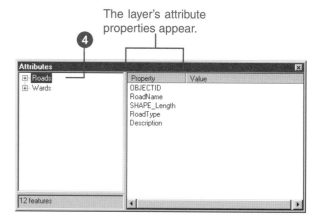

5. Double-click a layer name to see the primary display fields, representing the selected features in the layer.

   Double-click again to hide the primary display fields.

6. Click a primary display field to see the corresponding feature's attribute values.

   The corresponding feature flashes on the map.

7. Click the Close button to close the dialog box.

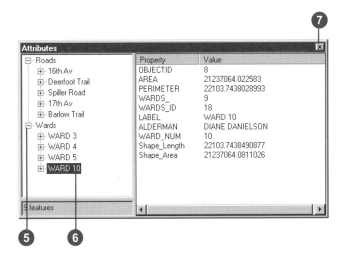

Adding and modifying attributes

The easiest way to make changes to the attributes of a selected feature is by using the Attributes dialog box.

You can add or modify attributes of selected features as needed. For example, you might want to update the attribute values—such as its name and maintenance information—for a park feature you created.

To add or modify an attribute value for a single feature, click the primary display field for the feature on the left side of the dialog box and make your changes in the Value column on the right. ▶

Tip

Saving your edits
Click the Editor menu and click Save Edits.

Tip

Attribute domains
You can use attribute domains to create a list of valid values for a feature in a geodatabase. You can also use the Validate command to ensure attribute quality. For more information, see Building a Geodatabase.

Adding an attribute value to a single feature

1. Click the primary display field of the feature to which you want to add an attribute value.

2. Click in the Value column where you want to add the attribute value.

3. Type the attribute value and press Enter.

   The attribute value is added to the feature.

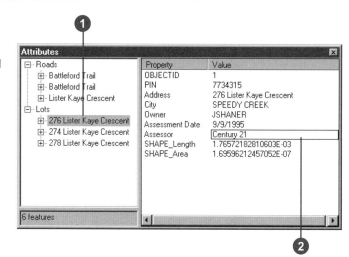

Adding an attribute value to all selected features in a layer

1. Click the layer to which you want to add an attribute value.

2. Click in the Value column where you want to add the attribute value.

3. Type the attribute value and press Enter.

   The attribute value is added to all selected features in the layer.

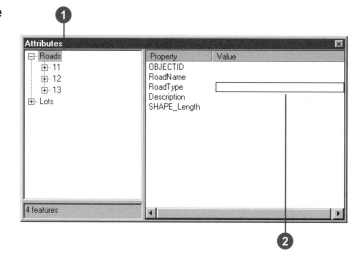

You can also add or modify an attribute value for all selected features in a layer at the same time. Simply click the layer name on the left and make your changes in the Value column on the right.

Tip

Deleting attributes

To delete an attribute value, right-click over the value and click Delete. You can also press the Delete key to delete an attribute value.

Tip

Undoing your edits

To undo any edit to feature attributes, click the Undo button on the ArcMap Standard toolbar.

Tip

Performing calculations

When editing attributes, you might need to perform calculations using the field calculator in the feature layer's attribute table dialog box. For more information, see Using ArcMap.

Tip

Adding attribute properties

You can add an attribute property for a feature by working with its attribute table in ArcCatalog. For more information, see Using ArcCatalog.

Modifying an attribute value for a feature

1. Click the primary display field of the feature for which you want to modify an attribute value.

2. Click the value you want to modify.

3. Type a new attribute value and press Enter.

   The attribute is modified for the feature.

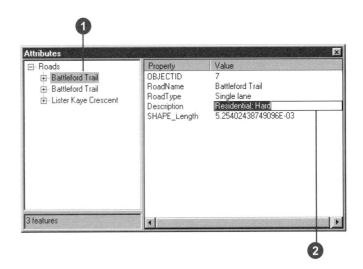

Modifying an attribute value for all selected features in a layer

1. Click the layer for which you want to modify an attribute value.

2. Click in the Value column next to the attribute property you want to modify for all selected features in the layer.

3. Type a new attribute value and press Enter.

   The attribute is modified for all selected features in the layer.

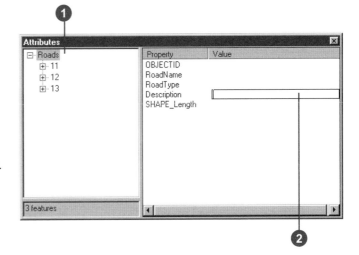

Copying and pasting attributes

Copying and pasting is an easy way to edit the attributes of features on your map. You can copy individual attribute values or all the attribute values of a feature. Attribute values can be pasted to a single feature or to all selected features in a layer.

Tip

Copying and pasting individual attribute values to an entire layer

To copy an attribute value to a layer, click the value you want to copy, right-click, and click Copy. Then, click the layer name and right-click in the Value column next to the appropriate property. Click Paste and the attribute value is copied to every selected feature in the layer.

Tip

Cutting and pasting attributes

Cutting and pasting attributes is similar to copying and pasting them. Right-click and click Cut from the context menu to remove the attribute value from its current location in the Attributes dialog box, then click Paste to paste it elsewhere.

Copying and pasting individual attribute values from feature to feature

1. Click the attribute value you want to copy.

2. Right-click the value you want to copy and click Copy.

3. Click the primary display field of the feature to which you want to paste the value.

4. Click where you want to paste the value.

5. Right-click where you want to paste the value and click Paste.

    The attribute value is pasted to the feature.

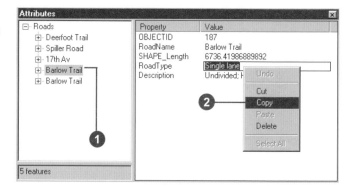

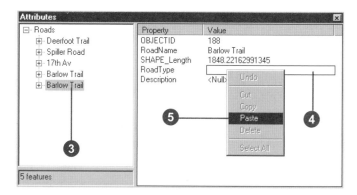

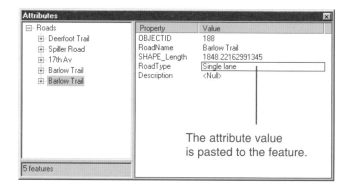

The attribute value is pasted to the feature.

Copying and pasting all attribute values from one feature to an entire layer

You can copy all attribute values from one feature to all selected features in a layer. Right-click the primary display field of the feature whose attribute values you want to copy and click Copy. Right-click the layer name to which you want to paste the attribute values. Click Paste and the attribute values are copied to every selected feature in the layer.

Copying and pasting all attribute values from feature to feature

1. Right-click the primary display field of the feature whose attribute values you want to copy and click Copy.

2. Right-click the primary display field of the feature to which you want to paste the attribute values and click Paste.

   The attribute values are pasted to the feature.

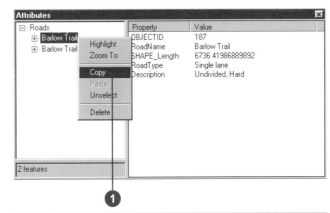

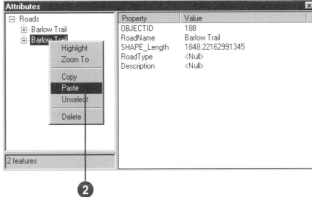

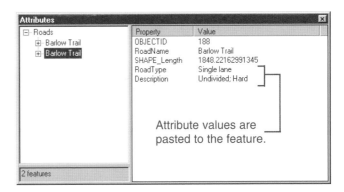

Attribute values are pasted to the feature.

Editing geodatabase attributes 10

Some features in a geodatabase are designed with subtypes, default values, and attribute domains. These can make it quicker and easier to edit feature attributes and can help prevent data entry errors.

Subtypes are logically distinct categories of a given type of feature that may have different attributes, network roles, or topology rules. When you create a new feature in a feature class with subtypes, you can choose which subtype of feature to create. For example, when creating a new building footprint, you might get the choice of residential, high-density residential, mobile home, commercial, industrial, school, and public administration building subtypes.

Because subtypes represent logical groups within a class of feature, they may typically have different attributes. In addition to a code identifying the subtypes, each subtype might have codes identifying how the data was collected. Residential buildings might get a default source description of 'digitized from plats', while mobile homes might get a default source description of 'digitized from orthophotographs'. These might be two out of a list of five permissible source descriptions.

Attributes in a geodatabase can have rules that specify that their values must fall within a particular range or be one of a list of permissible values. Building features might all have an occupancy figure for emergency planning. Residential buildings might have a valid occupancy range from 0–15, while commercial buildings might have a valid range of 0–500.

After you enter attributes for features that have domains specified in the geodatabase, you can validate your edits to check that the attributes fall in the permissible domain.

ArcInfo and ArcEditor

Editing a geodatabase with ArcMap

ArcMap editing capabilities are tightly integrated with the various aspects of the geodatabase, such as *geometric networks* and *validation rules*. While each component of the geodatabase can act independently, the true power of the geodatabase becomes evident when you bring all of these things together.

In this chapter, you will learn how editing in ArcMap takes advantage of the aspects of a geodatabase that help you maintain a valid database.

Validation rules

The geodatabase supports several broad types of validation rules: attribute validation rules, network *connectivity rules*, and relationship rules. It is important to understand that these validation rules can be broken; in certain cases, a geodatabase permits invalid *objects* to be stored in the database.

For example, if you have an attribute rule stating that the valid pressure range for a water distribution main in your water network is between 50 and 75 psi, the geodatabase won't prevent you from storing a value outside that range. However, a distribution main with a water pressure outside of this range will be an invalid object in the geodatabase. ArcMap has many editing tools that help you identify invalid features so you can correct them.

The exceptions are *edge–edge connectivity rules*, *edge–junction connectivity rules*, and coded value attribute rules. In these cases, ArcMap takes a more active role when editing features with these rules associated with them. You will learn how editing in ArcMap behaves in these contexts later in this chapter.

The general approach to the issue of validating features is that the validation process should not result in valid features being flagged as invalid (false negatives); it is, however, allowable to have features that are invalid being reported as valid (false positives). If the geodatabase did not enforce any validation, every feature would effectively be valid. When performing

validation on a particular feature, the validation occurs in five steps:

1. Validate the subtype.
2. Validate the attribute rules.
3. Validate the network connectivity rules—if network feature.
4. Perform custom validation—using optional class extension.
5. Validate the relationship rules.

This strategy means the least expensive validation is performed first. The validation process stops once a feature is found to be invalid. So, for example, if a feature fails the validity test for check number 1, then checks 2, 3, 4, and 5 are never executed.

When checking connectivity and relationship rules, all associated rules must be valid. With network connectivity rules, if you specify one rule, you must specify them all. Thus, if a type of connectivity exists that doesn't have an associated connectivity rule, the network feature is deemed invalid.

In addition to these rules, topology rules can also be established. To learn more about topology, see Chapter 4, 'Editing topology'.

To learn more about attribute validation rules, see *Building a Geodatabase*. To learn more about connectivity rules, see Chapter 12, 'Editing geometric networks' in this book, or see *Building a Geodatabase*.

Editing features with subtypes and default values

Feature classes and individual subtypes of feature classes in a geodatabase can have default values.

Default values help streamline the attribute editing process and help you maintain realistic values for the attributes of the features in your database. If most of the building features that you create in a feature class are residential, you might have a default value of residential for the building type attribute. Then when you create a new building it will automatically be given the residential attribute value. In the few cases where the building is another type, you can change the attribute.

If your feature class contains subtypes, then when you change the subtype of a feature, the feature takes on the default field values of the new subtype.

Creating new features of a subtype

1. Click the Task dropdown arrow and click Create New Feature.

2. Click the Target layer dropdown arrow and click the layer with the type of features you want to create.

3. Click the Tool Palette dropdown arrow and click the Sketch tool.

4. Click the map to digitize the feature's vertices. ►

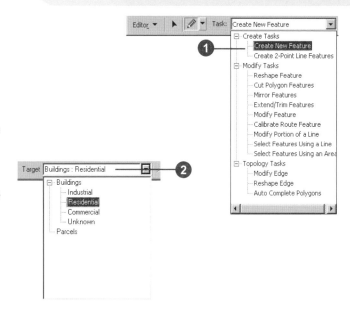

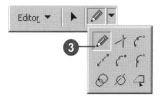

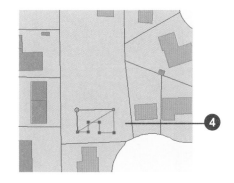

5. Double-click the last vertex to finish the feature.

6. Click the Attributes button.

   The Attributes dialog box appears. Notice that some of the fields already have values. These are the default values that were specified when this feature class was created.

7. Click the fields whose values you want to modify and type the new values.

8. Click the Close button to close the Attributes dialog box.

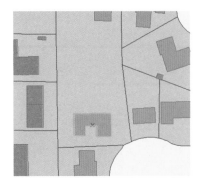

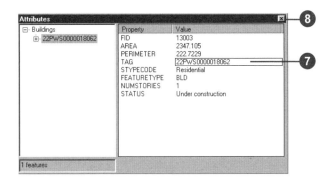

Attributes			⊗8
⊟ Buildings	Property	Value	
⊞ 22PWS0000018062	FID	13003	
	AREA	2347.105	
	PERIMETER	222.7229	
	TAG	22PWS0000018062	⊚7
	STYPECODE	Residential	
	FEATURETYPE	BLD	
	NUMSTORIES	1	
	STATUS	Under construction	
1 features			

See Also

To learn more about subtypes and attribute domains, see Building a Geodatabase.

Changing a feature's subtype

1. Click the Edit tool.
2. Click the feature whose subtype you want to change.
3. Click the Attributes button.
4. Click the value of the subtype field.

   A dropdown list with all the available subtypes appears.
5. Click the subtype you want. ▶

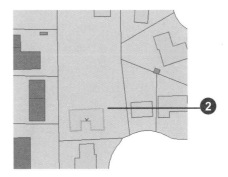

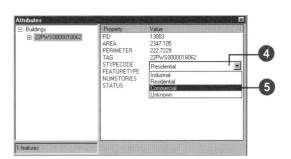

ArcInfo and ArcEditor

Tip

Default values

When you change a feature's subtype, the fields will take on the default values for the new subtype. If a field does not have a default value associated with it for the new subtype, its value remains unchanged.

The feature's symbology changes to match the new subtype. The fields with default values assume the default values for the new subtype.

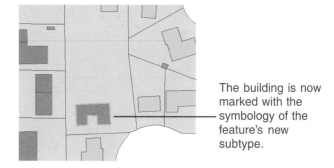

The building is now marked with the symbology of the feature's new subtype.

Editing attribute domains

Feature classes and subtypes in a geodatabase can have *attribute domains*. These are rules that control the permissible values for a feature's attributes. These help maintain the data quality and consistency of the attributes of the features in your database.

There are two types of attribute domains: *range domains* and *coded value domains*. In a water network database you may have a feature class that stores water transmission mains. Transmission mains could have a range domain that specifies that the pressure value must be within the valid pressure range of between 40 and 100 psi.

If there are only three diameters of transmission main in your water system, you could have a coded value domain that specifies that transmission mains can have a diameter of 10, 24, or 30 inches. Coded value domains can speed attribute editing because when you edit them, ArcMap gives you a dropdown list of the permissible values that you can choose from.

Modifying coded value fields

1. Click the Edit tool.

2. Click the feature whose attributes you want to edit.

3. Click the Attributes button.

4. Click the value of the coded value field you want to modify.

   A dropdown list of all the coded value descriptions in the domain appears.

5. Click the value you want for the field.

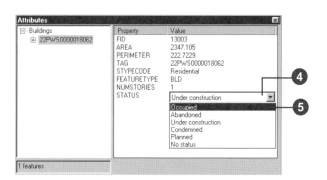

Validating features

When you edit features that have coded value or range domains, you should validate the features with the database to check that the attributes have appropriate values.

Validating features also validates any geometric network connectivity rules or relationship rules that may be defined for the feature class. For more information on relationship and connectivity rules, see Chapter 12, 'Editing geometric networks', and *Building a Geodatabase.*

Tip

Validating topology
Validating features and attributes is not the same as validating topology. For more information, see Chapter 4, 'Editing topology'.

Validating features

1. Click the Edit tool.

2. Click the features that you want to validate.

3. Click Editor and click Validate Features. ▶

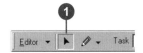

If your selection contains any invalid features, a message box appears with the number of invalid features. Only invalid features remain selected.

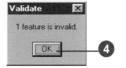

4. Click OK.

5. Click one of the invalid features.

6. Repeat step 3.

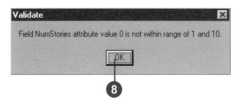

7. A message box appears telling you why the feature is invalid.

8. Click OK.

9. Click the Attributes button to view the attributes of the invalid feature.

10. Click the values that are invalid and change them.

11. Close the Attributes dialog box.

12. Repeat steps 5 through 11 for all of the invalid features.

13. Repeat steps 2 and 3. You should see a message box informing you that all the features are valid.

14. Click OK.

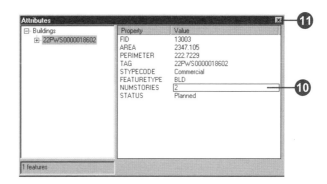

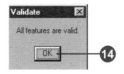

Editing relationships and related objects 11

Some feature classes and tables in a geodatabase are designed to have relationships to other feature classes or tables. When you create, modify, or delete such geodatabase objects with ArcMap, messages can be automatically sent to the geodatabase to create, modify, or delete the related objects. These types of built-in relationships are stored in *relationship classes* in the geodatabase.

If there are relationship classes between feature classes and tables in your geodatabase, you can use ArcMap editing tools to take advantage of the relationships. Using ArcMap editing tools, you can find all of the objects related to a particular object and edit them. For example, you can select a parcel and find the owner of that parcel, then edit some of the attributes of that owner without ever having to add the table that stores the owners to your ArcMap session.

You can also use ArcMap editing tools to establish a new relationship between objects or to break existing relationships between objects. For example, if a parcel changes ownership, you can delete the relationship between the parcel and its original owner, then establish a new relationship to its new owner.

After you edit related geodatabase features or tables that have relationship rules, you can validate your edits to check that the related objects still conform to the geodatabase relationship rules.

To learn more about relationship classes, see *Building a Geodatabase*.

Understanding relationships and related objects

Relationship classes allow you to maintain associations between objects in your geodatabase. These relationships can be simple and passive or they can be composite. *Composite relationships* imply parent/child relationships, or composition, and, therefore, have behavior, which is triggered through changes to objects on one side of the relationship to objects on the other side.

Relationships in a relationship class can be stored using *primary* and *foreign keys* in the object classes on either side of the relationship class. Alternatively, in the case of many-to-many relationship classes (M–N) and attributed relationship classes, the relationships are rows stored in a separate table.

You can use the Attributes dialog box or the table dialog box to find all objects related to any selected object. Once you have navigated to the related object, you can edit its attributes. You can also use the editing tools in ArcMap to break the relationship between any two objects or create new relationships between objects. When you edit objects and relationships in this way, all referential integrity is maintained.

Creating and deleting relationships

You can use the Attributes dialog box to create and delete relationships between two objects. If the relationship is managed by primary and foreign keys, the foreign key in the *destination* object is populated with the value of the primary key from the *origin* object. If a relationship between two objects is deleted, then the value for the foreign key in the destination object is replaced with a null.

If the relationship class is M–N or is attributed, then the relationships are stored in a separate table in the database. When a new relationship is created between two objects in this type of relationship class, a new row is added to that table. This new row is populated with the values from the primary keys in the origin and destination objects. If a relationship between two objects is

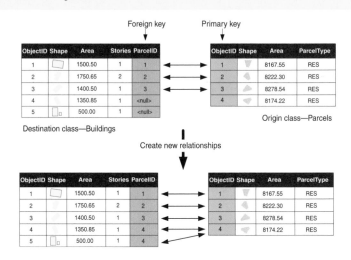

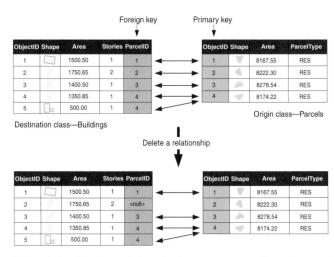

If the relationships in a relationship class are managed by primary and foreign keys (nonattributed 1–1 or 1–M relationships), creating and deleting relationships populate and null the foreign key in the destination class objects.

deleted, then the row corresponding to that relationship is deleted from the relationship table.

Deleting objects with relationships

When an object that participates in relationships with other objects is deleted from the database, all of its relationships are also deleted. If the relationships are maintained using primary and foreign keys, and the object deleted is the origin object, then the foreign key in the destination object is made null. If the object deleted is the destination object, then the origin object is not affected.

If relationships are maintained as rows in a relationship table (M–N relationships or attributed relationships) and either an origin or destination object and its relationships are deleted, then the rows corresponding to those relationships are also deleted from the relationship's table.

Creating new related objects

In ArcMap, you can select an object, then use the Attributes dialog box to create a new nonspatial object in a related class. When this new object is created, all of its attributes are populated with their appropriate default values (see *Building a Geodatabase*), and a relationship is created back to the object it was created from. You can only create nonspatial objects in this way; you cannot create new features.

If the relationships are maintained using primary and foreign keys, then the foreign key in the destination object is populated with the primary key of the origin object, regardless of whether the origin or destination object is created using the Attributes dialog box. If the relationships are maintained as rows in a relationship table (M–N relationships, attributed relationships), then a new row is added to the relationship class table.

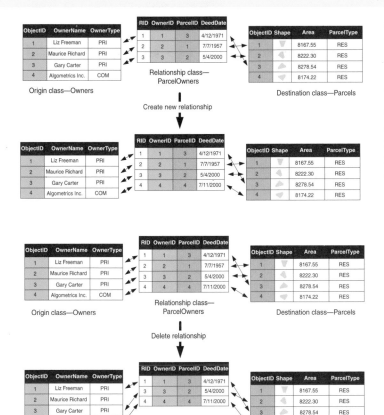

If the relationship class is M–N or is attributed, the relationships are stored as rows in the relationship class table. Creating and deleting relationships adds and removes rows in the relationship class table.

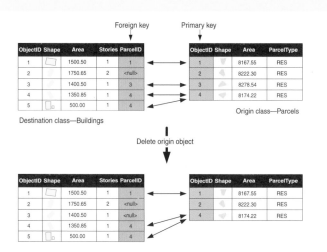

Destination class—Buildings

Origin class—Parcels

Delete origin object

When an object that participates in relationships with other objects is deleted from the database, all of its relationships are also deleted.

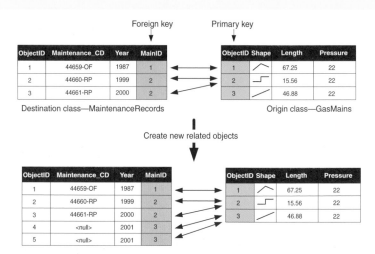

Destination class—MaintenanceRecords

Origin class—GasMains

Create new related objects

When you use the Attributes dialog box to create new related objects, a relationship is created back to the object from which it was created. If the relationships are maintained using primary and foreign keys, then the foreign key in the destination object is populated with the primary key of the origin object.

Editing composite relationships

Composite relationships have some specialized behavior. When editing the objects that participate in a composite relationship, this behavior carries over to the editing process. Edits made to the origin object in a composite relationship often directly affect its related destination objects. This behavior is partially dependent on relationship class messaging.

By default, composite relationship classes have forward messaging (see *Building a Geodatabase*)—that is, when the origin object in a composite relationship is edited, it sends messages to its related destination objects. The related objects will respond to that messaging in a standard way: if the

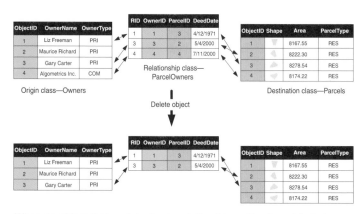

Origin class—Owners

Relationship class— ParcelOwners

Destination class—Parcels

Delete object

destination objects are nonspatial objects, then they will not change. However, if the destination objects are features when the origin object is moved, then the destination objects will also move the same distance. If the origin object is rotated, then the destination objects will also be rotated by the same angle.

Similar to *simple relationships*, composite relationships also maintain referential integrity when objects are deleted, but they do this in a different way. When the origin object in a composite relationship is deleted, all of the objects related to it through that composite relationship are also deleted. This cascade deletion will happen whether messaging is set to forward, back, both, or none.

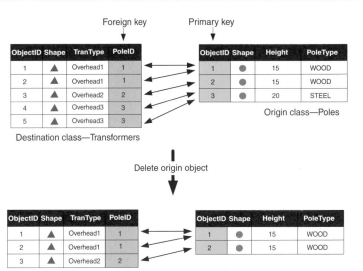

When an origin object in a composite relationship is deleted, all destination objects related to it through a composite relationship are also deleted.

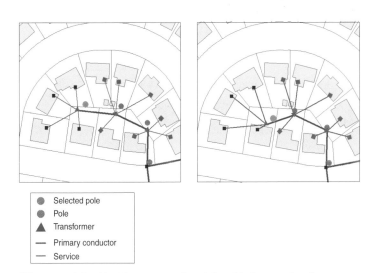

Selected pole
Pole
Transformer
Primary conductor
Service

When an origin object in a composite relationship is moved and messaging is set to forward or both, if the related objects are features, they will move the same distance to follow the feature. In this example, the selected pole is the origin object and the transformer is the destination object.

When a destination object is deleted, the relationship between it and the origin object is deleted; the origin object itself is not deleted or modified.

Splitting features that participate in relationships

Splitting a single geodatabase feature into two separate features is actually a delete and create operation—that is, the original feature is deleted and two new features are created. This has implications when the feature being split has relationships with other objects in the database.

With simple relationships, when an origin feature is split, the relationships between the original feature and its related destination objects are deleted. When the new features are created from the split operation, new relationships are created between the new feature with the larger portion of the original feature's geometry and the destination objects that were related to the original feature.

In the case of a composite relationship, the behavior is different. When an origin feature in a composite relationship is split, any objects related to it through that composite relationship are deleted before the two resulting new features are created from the split.

When splitting a destination feature in either a simple or composite relationship, the relationships between the original

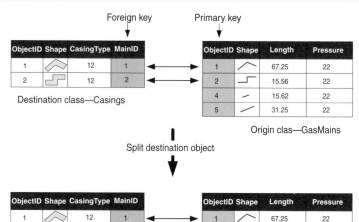

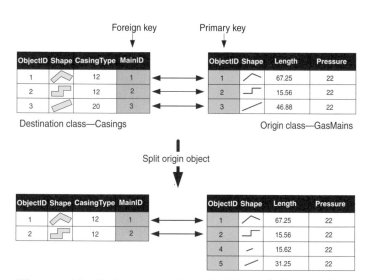

When an origin object in a composite relationship is split, its destination objects are deleted.

When splitting a destination feature in either a simple or composite relationship, the relationships between the original feature and the related origin objects are deleted, and the new relationships are created between the origin objects and both new features that result from the split.

feature and the related origin objects are deleted, and the new relationships are created between the origin objects and both new features that result from the split.

The behavior of splitting objects with relationships described here is the default behavior. You can override this behavior at the class level by writing a class extension that implements the IFeatureClassEdit interface. The IFeatureClassEdit interface has a property called CustomSplitPolicyForRelationship that allows you to specify how relationships are handled when features are split. To learn more about class extensions and how to implement them, see *Exploring ArcObjects.*

Editing relationships and related objects

The tasks presented here are all examples of editing relationships between water laterals and hydrants in a water network. The rules of this relationship class state that a hydrant lateral must have a hydrant related to it and that hydrants cannot be related to other lateral types.

Editing a related object

1. Click the Edit tool.

2. Click the hydrant lateral whose related hydrant you want to modify.

3. Click the Attributes button.

4. Double-click the lateral in the left panel of the Attributes dialog box.

5. Double-click the relationship path label.

   The related hydrant objects are listed below the path label.

6. Click the ID number of the related hydrant whose attributes you want to modify.

7. Modify the attributes of the hydrant object by clicking the value and typing a value or clicking the value and choosing the new value from the list.

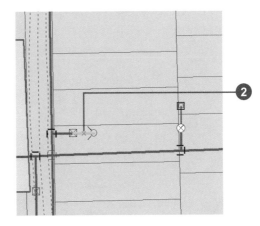

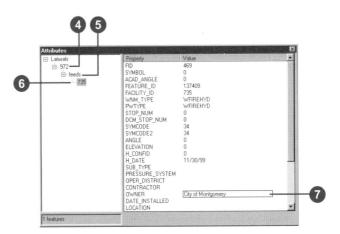

Selecting a related object

1. Click the Edit tool.

2. Click the hydrant lateral whose related hydrant you want to modify.

3. Click the Attributes button.

4. Double-click the lateral in the left panel of the Attributes dialog box.

5. Double-click the relationship path label.

   The related hydrant objects are listed below the path label.

6. Right-click the related hydrant you want to add to the map's selection and click Select. ▶

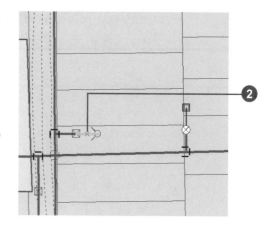

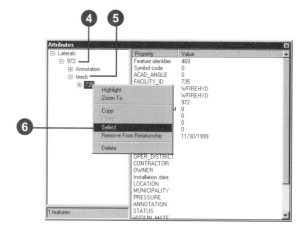

The hydrant is added to the selection.

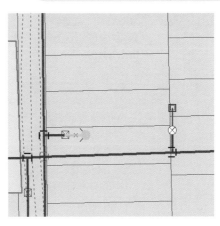

The hydrant is added to the selection.

Relating objects

Before adding a relationship between two objects, you must first create a relationship class between the feature classes or tables containing the objects you want to relate. To learn more about how to create relationship classes, see Building a Geodatabase.

Creating a new relationship between features

1. Click the Edit tool.

2. Click the features between which you want to create relationships.

3. Click the Attributes button.

4. Double-click one of the features in the left panel.

5. Right-click the relationship path label and click Add Selected. ▶

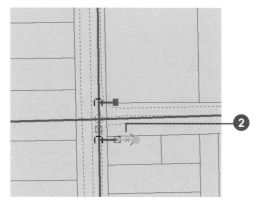

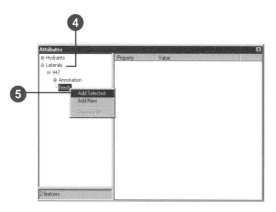

The selected object or objects are now added to the list of selected objects under the relationship class path label.

Relationships to the selected objects are added.

ArcInfo and ArcEditor

Creating a new relationship between a feature and a nonspatial object

1. Click the Edit tool.

2. Click the feature to which you want to create a relationship.

3. In the table of contents, right-click the table that contains the objects that you are relating to, then click Open. ▶

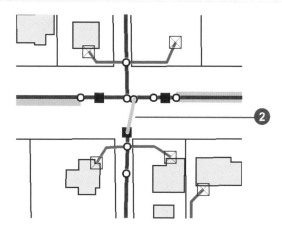

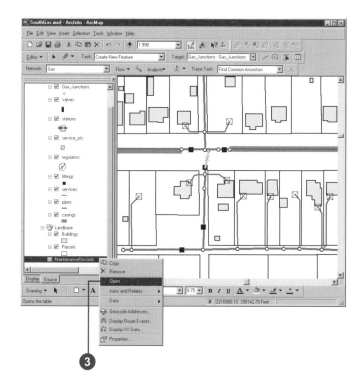

4. Click the object in the table with which you want to create a relationship to the selected feature.

5. Click the Attributes button.

6. Double-click the feature in the left panel.

7. Right-click the relationship path label and click Add Selected.

The selected object or objects are now added to the list of selected objects under the relationship class path label.

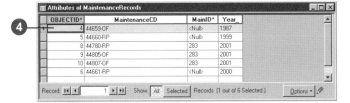

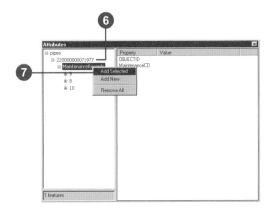

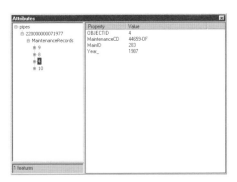

The object is listed under the relationship path label.

ArcInfo and ArcEditor

Deleting a relationship

1. Click the Edit tool.

2. Click the feature from which you want to delete a relationship.

3. Click the Attributes button.

4. Double-click the feature in the left panel.

5. Double-click the relationship path label to see a list of related objects.

6. Right-click the object from which you want to delete the relationship and click Remove From Relationship. ▶

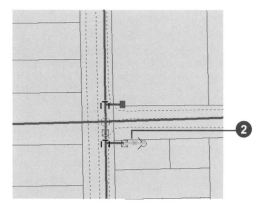

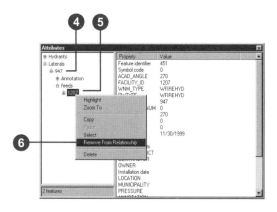

The object is no longer listed under the relationship path label.

7. Click the Close button to close the Attributes dialog box.

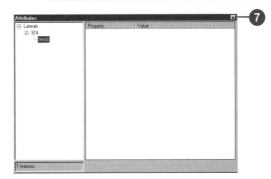

The object is no longer listed under the relationship path label.

ArcInfo and ArcEditor

See Also

You cannot use the Add New command in the Attributes dialog box to create new related features. See 'Creating new related features', later in this chapter, to learn how to create new related features.

Creating new related nonspatial objects

1. Click the Edit tool.

2. Click the feature for which you want to create a new related object.

3. Click the Attributes button.

4. Double-click the feature in the left panel. ▶

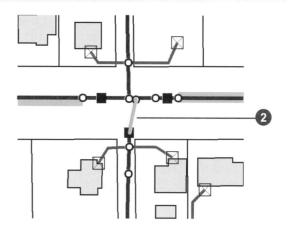

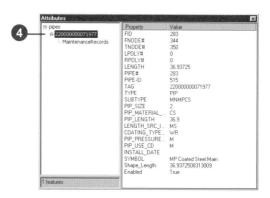

5. Right-click the relationship path label and click Add New.

   A new object is created and related to the selected feature.

6. Click the new object in the left panel to see its attributes.

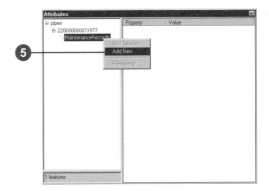

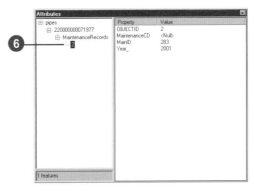

A new object is created in the related class and a relationship is created between it and the selected feature.

See Also

To learn more about ArcMap sketch tools and how to create new features, see Chapter 2, 'Editing basics', and Chapter 3, 'Creating new features'.

Creating new related features

1. Use ArcMap sketch tools to create the new feature.

2. Click the Edit tool.

3. Hold down the Shift key and click the feature for which you want to create a relationship to the new feature.

    Both the new feature and the feature you are relating it to should be selected. ▶

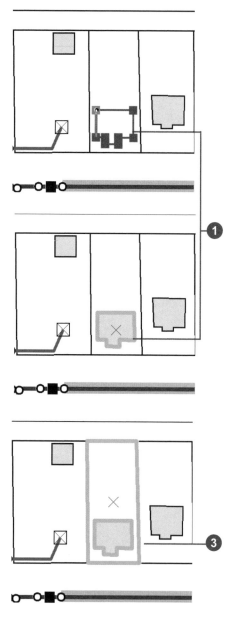

4. Click the Attributes button.

5. Double-click the feature in the left panel.

6. Right-click the relationship path label and click Add Selected.

The selected object or objects are now added to the list of selected objects under the relationship class path label.

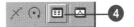

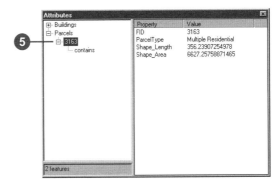

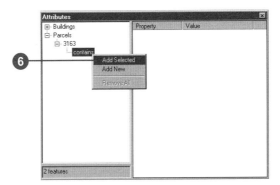

A relationship to the selected object is added.

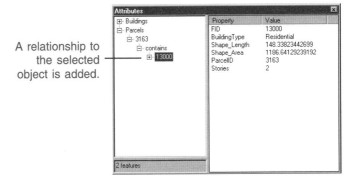

ArcInfo and ArcEditor

Tip

Deleting related features

You can also delete related features using the Delete command on the Relationship context menu in the Attributes dialog box.

Deleting related objects

1. Click the Edit tool.

2. Click the feature whose related object you want to delete.

3. Click the Attributes button.

4. Double-click the feature in the left panel.

5. Double-click the relationship path label to see a list of related objects.

6. Right-click the object you want to delete and click Delete.

   The object is deleted and no longer listed under the relationship path label.

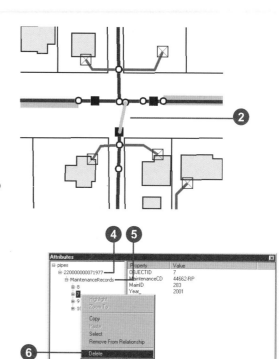

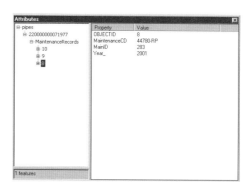

The object is no longer listed under the relationship path label.

The Attributes dialog box

The Attributes dialog box behaves the same way with composite relationships as it does with creating or deleting new features or relationships.

Editing features with composite relationships

1. Click the Edit tool.

2. Click the origin feature in the composite relationship you want to edit.

3. Click and drag the feature to a new location.

   The related features move the same x,y distance as the origin feature you moved. ▶

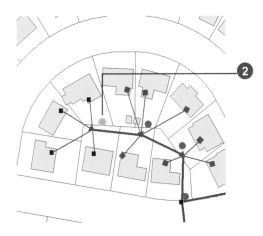

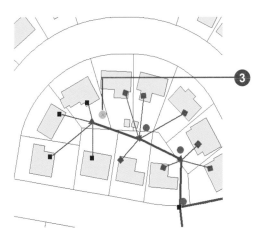

The related features move the same distance as the feature you moved.

4. Click the Rotate tool.

5. Click anywhere on the map and drag the pointer to rotate the feature to the desired location.

   The related features rotate with the feature.

6. Click the Edit tool and click a destination feature in a composite relationship.

7. Click and drag the feature to a new location.

   The origin feature in the relationship doesn't move. ▶

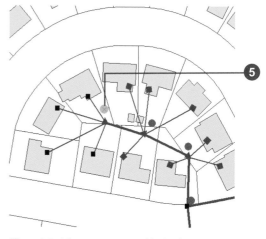

The related features rotate with the feature.

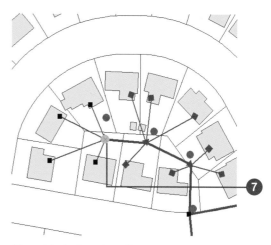

The origin feature doesn't move.

8. Click the origin feature again and click Delete.

Both the feature and its related features are deleted.

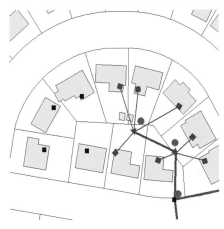

Both the origin feature and its related features are deleted.

ArcInfo and ArcEditor

Tip

Relationship rules

Relationship rules can be broken in two ways: when a feature is related to a subtype of the related class for which no valid rule applies or when a cardinality rule is broken.

To learn more about relationship rules, see Building a Geodatabase.

Validating relationships

1. Click the Edit tool and click the feature or features you want to validate.

2. Click Editor and click Validate Features.

   A message box appears telling you how many features are invalid. Only invalid features remain selected. ▶

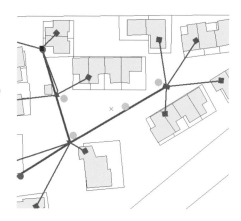

3. Click OK.

4. Click one of the invalid features.

5. Repeat step 2.

   A dialog box appears informing you why the selected feature is invalid.

6. Click OK.

7. Make the necessary edits to the relationships or the related objects to make the feature valid. This may involve adding and deleting relationships or altering the subtype of one or all of the features.

8. Repeat step 2—a message box appears informing you that all the features are valid.

9. Click OK.

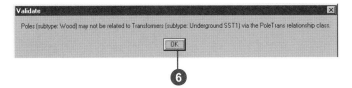

Editing geometric networks 12

IN THIS CHAPTER

- **Editing network features**

- **Creating network edges**

- **Subsuming network junctions**

- **Enabled and disabled features**

- **The Network Editing toolbar**

- **Validating network features**

In addition to simple features, ArcMap lets you edit collections of features related in a geometric network. In a geodatabase, a geometric network contains special types of network features that enable connectivity tracing, network connectivity rules, and specialized junction or switch modeling behavior.

Geometric networks are useful for modeling networks of wires, pipes, or natural water flow networks. Networks are built of edge and junction features. Edges model linear features such as pipes, wires, and streams. Junctions model nodes in the network—places where edges connect to each other—such as fittings, valves, and hydrants; switches, fuses, and transformers; or confluences, gauging stations, and water quality monitoring devices.

There are two broad categories of network features: simple and complex. Simple edge features are connected to junctions at each end. Snapping another feature along the length of a simple edge feature splits the edge into two simple edges. Complex edge features are connected to junctions at each end but may also have junctions connected to them along their length; they do not split when junctions are added. Simple junction features connect edges. Complex junctions are single custom features that can have internal networks of edges and junctions. A pump station might be modeled as a single complex junction feature in a water network, but it might be composed of a group of pipes, valves, and pumps that have complex internal network connectivity.

ArcInfo and ArcEditor

Editing network features

Geometric network features store various mechanisms and behaviors that maintain the topological connectivity between them. ArcMap editing capabilities are tightly integrated with the geodatabase when it comes to editing network features.

Creating connectivity

The connectivity of network features is based on *geometric coincidence*. If a junction is added along an edge or one edge is added along another edge, they will become connected to one another.

By using the ArcMap snapping environment, you can create new edge and junction features on the fly while maintaining network connectivity. The ArcMap snapping functionality will guarantee geometric coincidence when adding new network features along existing network features.

Simple and complex edges

An edge in a geometric network can be either simple or complex. A simple edge in a geometric network has a 1–1 relationship with edge elements in the *logical network*. A complex edge has a 1–M relationship with edge elements in the logical network. One complex edge in the geometric network can represent multiple edges in the logical network. Simple and complex edges always have junctions at their endpoints.

If you snap a junction or edge along a simple edge, then the edge being snapped to is split both in the logical network and in the geometric network, giving you two edge features. If you snap a junction or an edge along a complex edge, then that edge is split in the logical network but remains a single feature in the geometric network. It will remain a single feature; however, a new vertex is created at the point where the new junction or edge connects to it.

Default junctions

When you snap an edge to another edge where there is no junction, a junction is automatically inserted to establish connectivity. If a default junction type has been specified as part of the connectivity rules for the network, that default junction type is used. If there is no edge–edge rule between these edge types, an orphan junction is inserted, which is stored in the <network>_Junctions feature class.

Similarly, if you create a new edge in the network that is not snapped to an existing junction or edge at both ends, a junction is automatically created and connected to the free end of the new edge. If there is a connectivity rule in place that defines a default junction type for the type of edge that is being added, that default junction type is the junction that is added to the free end of the new feature. If an edge type does not have a default junction type associated with it through a connectivity rule, then an orphan junction is inserted, which is stored in the <network>_Junctions feature class.

Junction subsumption

When you snap a junction to an existing orphan junction, the orphan junction is subsumed by the new junction. That is, the orphan junction is deleted from the network, and the new junction is inserted in its place. All network connectivity is maintained. Orphan junctions cannot subsume other orphan junctions. When a junction is snapped to another junction other than an orphan junction, *subsumption* does not occur and the junction is not connected.

When you create a new edge feature in the network that has an end that does not connect to anything and there is not a connectivity rule stating what type of junction to put at its free end, a network orphan junction is inserted. This orphan junction can be subsumed by snapping another junction to it.

Moving existing network features

When a network edge or junction is moved, the network features to which it is connected respond by rubber-banding and adjusting themselves to maintain connectivity. When you move a network feature and snap it to another network feature, the features may become connected (see below).

Connectivity models

Edit operations that involve adding, deleting, moving, and subsuming network features can affect the connectivity of a geometric network. Each type of operation may or may not create connectivity, depending on the type of network features involved. The following set of diagrams illustrates various editing scenarios and their resulting connectivity or lack thereof. In these diagrams, use the key below to identify what types of features are illustrated in each scenario:

○ Orphan Junction

◉ Standard Junction

<u>SEF</u> Simple Edge

<u>CEF</u> Complex Edge

◻ Vertex

NOOP No operation completed

NOCON No connectivity established, offset features are coincident but disconnected.

Stretching and moving: When stretching or moving junctions, any edges connected to them rubber-band to remain connected. When you snap these junctions to other network features, the following illustration summarizes the network connectivity that results:

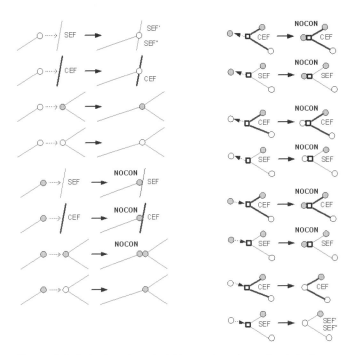

Connectivity behavior when stretching and moving network features

Deleting: Deleting network features can affect those features connected to them. When you delete an edge feature, the edge is physically deleted from the geometric network and logically deleted from the logical network; however, its connected junction features will not be deleted. When deleting junction features, if the junction being deleted is not of an orphan junction type, it will not be physically deleted from the geometric network. Rather than being deleted, the junction will become an orphan junction. When you delete an orphan junction, it is physically deleted from the geometric network. When this happens, depending on how many edges are connected to it, some edges may also be deleted. The following illustration summarizes the results of deleting network junctions:

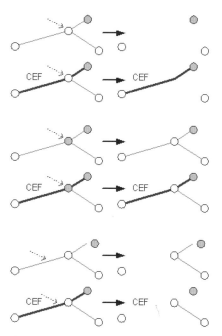

Connectivity behavior when deleting network features

Disconnecting features: The following illustration summarizes how connectivity is affected when disconnecting network edge features and junction features using the Disconnect command in ArcMap:

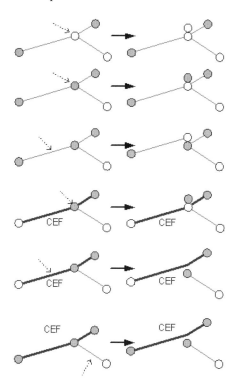

Connectivity behavior when disconnecting network features

330

Connecting features: The following illustration summarizes how connectivity is affected when connecting network features using the Connect command in ArcMap:

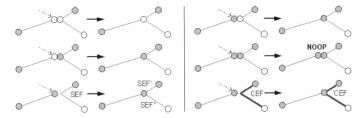

Connectivity behavior when connecting network features.

Creating new network features: When creating new network features and snapping them to other network junction and edge features, the resulting connectivity and the effects on the features you connect them to are summarized below:

Connectivity behavior when creating new network features.

ArcInfo and ArcEditor

Repairing network connectivity

Connectivity between network features is maintained on the fly as you create, delete, and modify network features. In some circumstances, the association between some network features and their logical elements may become out of sync. This can happen, for example, when using a custom tool that does not correctly handle aborting edit operations.

This kind of network inconsistency is localized to a collection of features in the network. You will be able to see what features have inconsistent connectivity in two ways: (1) when moving a network feature, if rubber-banding does not occur with other network features it is connected to and the edit operation fails, the connectivity is inconsistent, and (2) reconciling a version with inconsistent network features will result in an error (to learn more about reconciling versions, see Chapter 15, 'Working with a versioned geodatabase'). The Rebuild Connectivity tool in ArcMap rebuilds connectivity for a set of network features in an extent by re-creating their logical elements. Connectivity is established based on geometric coincidence, using the same rules as described in *Building a Geodatabase*.

The Repair Connectivity command in ArcMap repairs the connectivity within an entire geometric network or the connectivity within the currently edited version of ArcSDE. The Repair Connectivity command can be used if a large number of features have inconsistent connectivity or if the features extend across a large part of the network.

In addition to the Rebuild Connectivity tool and Repair Connectivity command, ArcMap also contains a set of tools and commands for identifying network features with either inconsistent connectivity or illegal network geometry. These are the Network Build Errors, Verify Network Connectivity, and Verify Network Geometry commands and the Verify Network

Connectivity and Verify Network Geometry tools. These tools and commands can be accessed from the Network Editing toolbar.

For more information on the Network Build Errors command, see 'Creating geometric networks: an overview' in the ArcGIS Desktop Help.

Performance considerations

Connectivity is established for new network features based on geometric coincidence. When you add or move a feature in a network, each feature class in the network must be analyzed so connectivity can be established. Performing a spatial query against each network class will determine if the new feature or moved feature is coincident with other network features at any point.

If the network is in an ArcSDE geodatabase, then analyzing for connectivity requires a number of spatial queries against the server. By using the map cache while editing the network, these spatial queries are much faster and are not as much of a load on the server. When editing network data in an ArcSDE geodatabase, always use the map cache. For more information on the map cache, see Chapter 2, 'Editing basics', or *Using ArcMap*.

Creating network edges

Through the basic editor tools in ArcMap, you can create network edges in conjunction with your preexisting features. This includes adding network edges at an existing junction, along a complex edge, or along a simple edge.

Geometric networks and topology

It is important to distinguish geometric networks and their relationships from topology and its associated rules. To learn more about topology, see Chapter 4, 'Editing topology'.

For more information on the ArcMap snapping environment, see Chapter 3, 'Creating new features'.

Creating a new network edge at an existing junction

1. Add your network feature classes to ArcMap and add the Editor toolbar.

2. Click Editor and click Start Editing.

3. Zoom to the area where you want to add the new feature.

4. Click the Tool Palette dropdown arrow and click the Sketch tool.

5. Click the Task dropdown arrow and click Create New Feature.

6. Click the Target layer dropdown arrow and click the type of edge feature you want to create. ▶

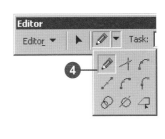

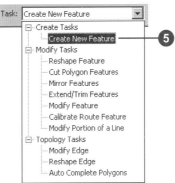

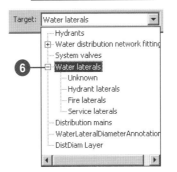

7. Check the appropriate boxes in the Snapping Environment window to set snapping to the vertex of the junction feature class to which you want to snap the new edge.

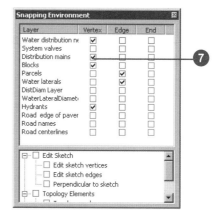

8. Move the mouse pointer near the junction until the pointer snaps to it.

9. Click the map to create the new feature's vertices.

10. Double-click the last vertex to finish the feature. ▶

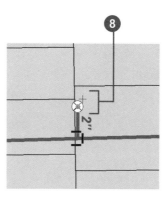

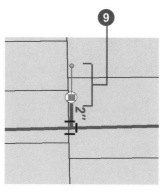

Tip

Default junction

You can specify what type of junction is placed at the free end of new edges by creating an edge–junction rule. For more information on connectivity rules, see Building a Geodatabase.

You have now created a new network edge. Since you snapped it to an existing network junction, it is automatically connected to the network.

If there is an edge–junction rule for the new edge with a default end junction type specified, this junction type will be placed at the free end of the new edge. If there is not an edge–junction rule that specifies a default junction, an orphan junction will be placed at the end of the new edge. For information on how to replace the orphan junction with another junction type, see 'Subsuming network junctions' later in this chapter.

The network junction or orphan junction is added to the end of the edge.

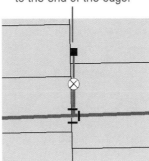

ArcInfo and ArcEditor

Tip

Adding junctions along complex edges

You can also snap a junction along a complex edge. Similar to snapping an edge, the junction is connected to the network. The complex edge is split in the logical network but remains a single feature.

Creating a new network edge along a complex edge

1. Follow steps 1–6 for 'Creating a new network edge at an existing junction' in this chapter.

2. Check the appropriate boxes in the Snapping Environment window to set snapping to the edge of the complex edge feature class to which you want to snap the new edge.

3. Move the mouse pointer over the complex edge until the pointer snaps to it.

4. Click the map to create the new feature's vertices.

5. Double-click the last vertex to finish the feature. ▶

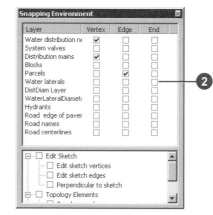

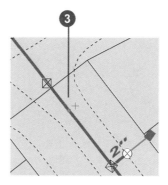

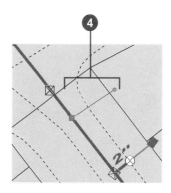

Default junction

You can specify what type of junction is placed at the free end of new edges by creating an edge–junction rule. For more information on connectivity rules, see Building a Geodatabase.

You have now created a new network edge. Since you snapped it to the edge of an existing edge, if there is an edge–edge connectivity rule between these edges, a new junction is created—the default junction type for that rule. If there is no edge–edge rule, then the new junction is an orphan network junction.

If there is an edge–junction rule for the new edge that has a default end junction type specified, this junction type will be added. If there is no edge–junction connectivity rule, an orphan junction is added.

Since the edge that was snapped to is a complex edge, it remains as a single feature but is split in the logical network.

6. Click the Edit tool.

7. Click the complex edge to which you snapped your new edge.

The entire edge is selected even though another edge and junction are connected along it. It remains a single feature.

The default junction for the edge–edge rule is added.

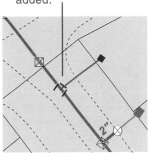

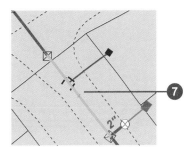

Creating a new network edge along a simple edge

1. Follow steps 1–6 for 'Creating a new network edge at an existing junction' in this chapter.

2. Check the appropriate boxes in the Snapping Environment window to set snapping to the edge of the simple edge feature class to which you want to snap the new edge.

3. Move the mouse pointer near the simple edge until the pointer snaps to it.

4. Click the map to create the new feature's vertices.

5. Double-click the last vertex to finish the feature. ▶

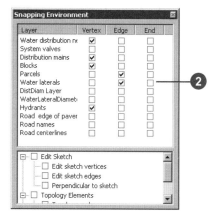

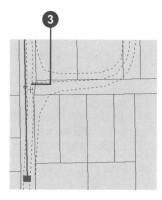

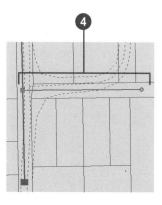

You have now created a new network edge. Since you snapped it to the edge of an existing edge, if there is an edge–edge connectivity rule between these edges, a new junction is created, which is the default junction type for that rule. If there is no edge–edge rule, then the new junction is an orphan network junction.

If there is an edge–junction rule for the new edge with a default end junction type specified, this junction type will be added. If there is no edge–junction connectivity rule, an orphan junction is added.

Because the edge that was snapped to is a simple edge, it is split into two new edge features. The value of the attributes in the new features is determined by their split policies.

6. Click the Edit tool.

7. Click the simple edge to which you snapped your new edge.

   There are now two edges split at the new junction.

The default junction for the edge–edge rule is added.

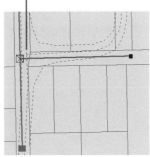

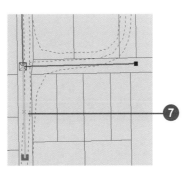

ArcInfo and ArcEditor

Subsuming network junctions

You may wish to replace network junction attributes with attributes associated with another junction type. For example, in a utilities network, a valve type or pole characteristic might change. Through basic editing functions, the properties of a junction can be subsumed by properties of another type.

1. Follow steps 1–4 for 'Creating a new network edge at an existing junction' in this chapter.

2. Click the Target layer dropdown arrow and click the type of junction feature you want to create.

3. Check the appropriate boxes in the Snapping Environment window to set snapping to the vertex of the junction feature class that you want to subsume.

4. Move the mouse pointer near the junction you want to subsume with a new junction until the pointer snaps to it. ▶

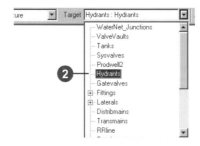

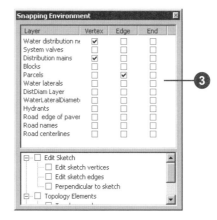

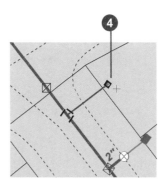

5. Click once to subsume the junction.

The original junction is deleted and replaced with the new junction; network connectivity is maintained.

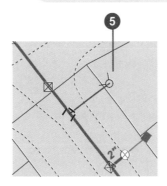

The original junction is deleted and replaced with the new junction.

ArcInfo and ArcEditor

Tip

Undoing network edits

If you move a network feature, other network features also move. Clicking the Undo button will undo the edits to all the affected features. To learn more about undoing edits, see Chapter 2, 'Editing basics'.

Tip

Cancelling the move operation

Pressing the Esc key while moving the network features will cancel the move operation.

Moving existing network features

1. Follow steps 1 and 2 for 'Creating a new network edge at an existing junction'.

2. Click the Edit tool.

3. Click the network junctions and edges that you want to move.

4. Click and drag the features to the new location.

   Other network elements that are connected to the features rubber-band. This shows how other network elements are affected by moving the selected features.

   All of the features that rubber-banded while you dragged your selected features are automatically updated to maintain network connectivity.

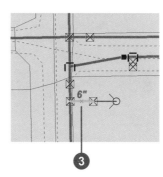

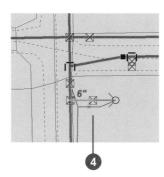

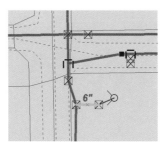

Tip

Ancillary roles

*Not all network junction features
can have ancillary roles. Those
that don't have them can't act as
sources or sinks in the network. To
learn more about network ancillary
roles, see* Building a Geodatabase.

See Also

*To learn how to set flow direction
for a network and other network
analysis tools, see* Building a
Geodatabase.

Altering a junction's ancillary network role

1. Click the Edit tool.

2. Click the network junction whose ancillary role you want to change.

3. Click the Attributes button.

4. Click the value for AncillaryRole.

5. If you want this junction feature to act as a sink in the network, click Sink.

   If you want this junction feature to act as a source in the network, click Source.

   If you don't want this junction feature to be either a source or a sink, click None.

6. Repeat steps 3–5 until all the junctions whose ancillary roles you want to change are updated.

7. Use the tools found in the Network Analysis toolbar to recalculate the flow direction of the network.

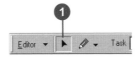

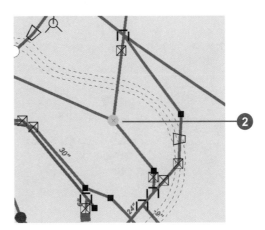

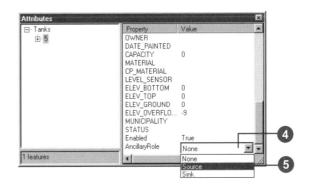

ArcInfo and ArcEditor

Enabled and disabled network features

If a feature in the network is disabled, it cannot be traced through. To learn more about network tracing, see *Building a Geodatabase*.

Tip

Enabling network features

By default, all network features have an Enabled value of True when created.

Enabling and disabling network features

1. Click the Edit tool.
2. Click the network feature you want to enable or disable.
3. Click the Attributes button.
4. Click the value for Enabled.
5. Click True if you want to enable the feature in the network.

   Click False if you want to disable the feature in the network.

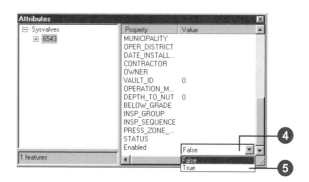

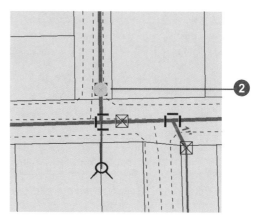

The Network Editing toolbar

The Network Editing toolbar contains tools used for managing geometric network connectivity. The connectivity between coincident network features can be explicitly changed. Instances can arise when parts of a geometric network need to be repaired; a feature having invalid geometry or connectivity between features is incorrect.

Features with invalid geometry may exist within feature classes used in building a geometric network. These features can be identified and their geometries repaired. Network connectivity ▶

Tip

About connecting and disconnecting network features

In some cases, you may wish to disconnect a feature from the network. Disconnecting a feature does not delete it from the database; it removes the topological associations it has to other features in the network. Similarly, connecting a feature to the network creates topological relationships between the feature and its coincident features.

Adding the Network Editing toolbar

1. Click Editor, point to More Editing Tools, and click Network Editing.

   The Network Editing toolbar will appear in the ArcMap window.

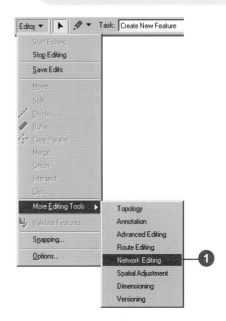

ArcInfo and ArcEditor

between features may become out of sync or inconsistent. These features can be identified and their connectivity repaired and reestablished.

Tip

Disconnecting features and tracing

Don't use the Disconnect command to remove a feature from consideration during network tracing. Instead, either change its Enabled value or place a Barrier on the feature.

Tip

Using the Network Build Errors command

The Network Build Errors command creates a selection of the features with invalid shapes using the error table generated during the network build. Invalid shapes include lines that contain multiple parts, lines that form a closed loop, lines that have zero length, and features that do not contain shapes. Once created, the selection set may be used to identify and find the features that cause the particular error. For more information on building geometric networks, see Building a Geodatabase.

 The Network Build Errors command

Disconnecting a feature from the network

1. Select the feature that you want to disconnect from the network.

2. Click the Disconnect tool on the Network Editing toolbar.

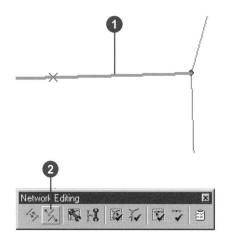

Connecting a feature to the network

1. Select the feature that you want to connect to the network.

2. Click the Connect tool on the Network Editing toolbar.

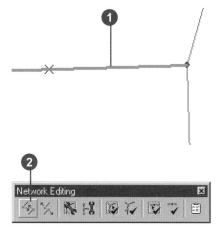

346

EDITING IN ARCMAP

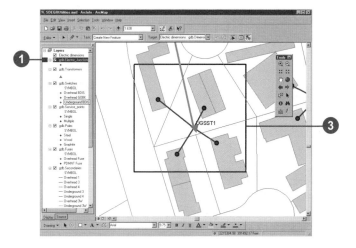

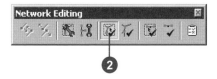

Verifying network connectivity

1. Click one of the feature classes in the geometric network in the ArcMap table of contents.

2. Click the Verify Connectivity tool on the Network Editing toolbar.

3. Click and drag a box around the network features whose connectivity you wish to verify.

   The tool will examine the features and create a selection set of the network features with inconsistent connectivity. You can then use the Rebuild Connectivity tool or the Repair Connectivity command to repair the connectivity of the features. If all connectivity is correct, a message box will appear informing you so.

Tip

Ensuring network connectivity

The Verify Connectivity tool verifies the connectivity between edges and junctions in the logical network.

The tool searches for features with no corresponding network elements, features with one or more missing network elements, features with duplicate network elements, features associated with invalid network elements, and features associated with or connected to a nonexistent network feature.

Tip

Canceling the Verify Connectivity operation

Pressing the Esc key while defining the area of interest will cancel the operation.

Tip

Verifying the entire geometric network

The Verify Connectivity command will verify the connectivity of the entire network.

The Verify Connectivity command

ArcInfo and ArcEditor

Tip

Rebuilding connectivity

During the course of editing, network connectivity is maintained on the fly. You do not need to use the Rebuild Connectivity tool unless the network connectivity has become inconsistent for some of your network features.

Tip

Repairing connectivity

The Repair Connectivity command will repair connectivity errors in the logical network.

During the process of repairing network connectivity, actions may occur that require review by the user. A message box will appear at the end of the process listing the type of warning, the feature class, and the object ID of the feature.

The warning types can be for the creation of new orphan junctions, invalid geometries, coincident junctions, or coincident vertices.

  The Repair Connectivity command

Rebuilding network connectivity

1. Click one of the feature classes in the geometric network in the ArcMap table of contents.

2. Click the Rebuild Connectivity tool on the Network Editing toolbar.

3. Click and drag a box around the network features whose network connectivity you want to rebuild.

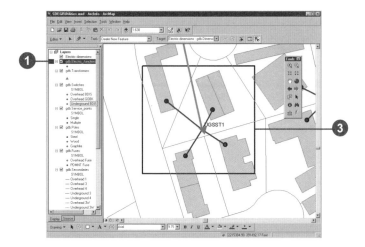

Tip

Ensuring network feature geometry

The Verify Network Feature Geometry tool verifies that the geometry of features that participate in the geometric network are valid shapes. Invalid shapes include features that have empty geometry, edge features that contain multiple parts, edge features that form a closed loop, and edge features that have zero length.

Tip

Canceling the Verify Network Feature Geometry operation

Pressing the Esc key while defining the area of interest will cancel the operation.

Tip

Verifying the entire geometric network

The Verify Network Feature Geometry command will verify the feature geometry of the entire network or any subset of selected features.

 The Verify Network Feature Geometry command

Verifying network feature geometry

1. Click one of the feature classes in the geometric network in the ArcMap table of contents.

2. Click the Verify Network Feature Geometry tool on the Network Editing toolbar.

3. Click and drag a box around the network features whose geometry you wish to verify.

   The tool will examine the features and create a selection set of the network features whose feature geometry is invalid. You can then use the basic editing tools to correct the geometry of the features. If all feature geometry is correct, a message box will appear informing you so.

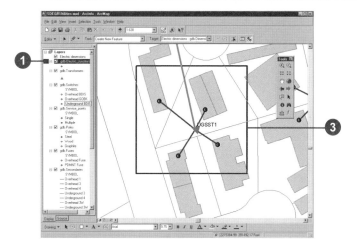

ArcInfo and ArcEditor

Validating network features

The validation process ensures that the network features follow the connectivity rules. This enables you to find those features that were modified and are in conflict with the predetermined network connectivity rules.

For more information on how to create and modify connectivity rules, see *Building a Geodatabase*.

1. Click the Edit tool.

2. Click the network features you want to validate.

3. Click Editor and click Validate Features. ▶

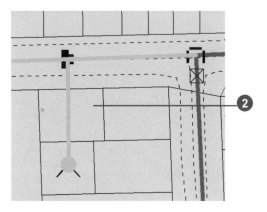

Tip

Validation rules

Network features may have connectivity rules as well as attribute and relationship validation rules associated with them. To learn more about validating attribute and relationship rules, see the tasks outlined earlier in this chapter.

Tip

Validating connectivity rules

Connectivity rules are validated following subtype and attribute validation.

If there are any invalid features, a message box appears telling you how many of the features are invalid. Only those features that are invalid remain selected.

4. Click OK.

5. Click one of the invalid network features.

6. Repeat step 3.

   A dialog box appears informing you why the selected feature is invalid.

7. Click OK.

8. Make the necessary edits to the network to make the feature valid. This may involve performing some of the network editing tasks described earlier in this chapter.

9. Repeat step 3—you should see a message box informing you that all the features are valid.

10. Click OK.

Editing annotation

13

Adding text to a map can often enhance the display of geographic features and improve your map's overall presentation. Text adds information and provides a context for the map and can help clarify features or the message of a map. You can also use text to add emphasis or focus to a particular area, feature, or trend, for example.

Using *annotation* is one option in ArcGIS for storing text to place on your maps. Annotation can be used to describe particular features or add general information to the map. You can use annotation, much like labels, to add descriptive text for many map features, or you can manually annotate just a few features. With annotation, the position, text string, and display properties are all stored together and are all individually editable. Annotation provides flexibility in the appearance and placement of your text because you can select individual pieces of text and edit them.

Annotation can be linked directly to the feature that is being described. For example, a feature class that contains streets may have the street's name associated with each street feature. Annotation can also be a piece of text that exists independently of any other feature, such as the name of a mountain range on a map.

This chapter describes the tools used to edit annotation stored in a geodatabase. You'll learn about creating annotation features using different construction methods, modifying where your annotation is placed and how it looks, and creating and working with feature-linked annotation.

Working with annotation in the geodatabase

Annotation in the geodatabase

When creating new annotation or when converting from existing annotation or labels, you can choose to store your new annotation in a geodatabase or in a particular *map document*. If you have many pieces of annotation, annotation that needs to be used outside a single map document, or several people who are concurrently editing the annotation, you will want to store your annotation in a geodatabase. The specialized tools for creating and editing annotation that are presented in this chapter can only be used with annotation that is stored in a geodatabase.

Working with geodatabase annotation

Storing annotation in a geodatabase is similar to storing geographic features—lines, points, and polygons—in a geodatabase. Annotation in the geodatabase is stored in special feature classes called *annotation classes*. Geographic features are stored as ESRI Simple Features, while annotation is stored as ESRI Annotation Features.

You can add annotation stored in a geodatabase to any map, and it appears as an annotation layer in the ArcMap table of contents. Like other feature classes in the geodatabase, all features in an annotation class have a geographic location, an extent, and attributes and can either be inside a feature dataset or be standalone feature classes in a geodatabase. However, annotation is unique because, unlike simple features, each annotation feature has its own symbology, including font, color, and so on. Annotation is often text, but it can also include shapes and graphics, such as boxes and arrows.

Geodatabase annotation can be *standard annotation* or *feature-linked annotation*. Standard annotation elements are pieces of geographically placed text that are not formally associated with features in the geodatabase. For example, you might have a piece of standard annotation that represents a mountain range—the annotation simply marks the general area on the map. Feature-linked annotation is a special type of geodatabase annotation that is linked by a geodatabase relationship class to the features that are being annotated. If you have an ArcEditor or ArcInfo license, you can create and edit feature-linked annotation; if you have an ArcView license, you can view feature-linked annotation but not create or edit it.

If you want to use the Annotation toolbar construction tools or the Convert Labels to Annotation command with geodatabases and annotation created in ArcGIS 8, you'll need to upgrade your geodatabase to ArcGIS 9 and use the Update Annotation Feature Class tool in ArcToolbox™. To learn how to upgrade a geodatabase, see Chapter 2, 'Editing basics'. To learn how to use the Update Annotation Feature Class tool, see 'Updating annotation created in ArcGIS 8' in this chapter.

If you have annotation in other formats, such as coverage or CAD, you can also use ArcToolbox to convert these formats into geodatabase annotation. To learn more, see *Building a Geodatabase* or the ArcGIS Desktop Help.

Feature-linked annotation

The text in feature-linked annotation reflects the value of a *field* or fields from the feature to which it is linked. For example, a hydrant in a water network may be annotated with its pressure, which is stored in a field in the feature class. In the same network, the water transmission mains may be annotated with their names.

Annotation links to features through a composite relationship with messaging. The feature class being annotated is the origin class in the relationship, while the annotation feature class is the destination class. As with other composite relationships, the origin feature controls the destination feature—meaning the location and lifetime of the annotation. When the origin feature is moved or rotated, the linked annotation also moves or rotates with it. And when an origin feature is deleted from the geodatabase, the linked annotation feature is also deleted. In addition, if an attribute value for the origin feature changes, feature-linked annotation has special behavior to automatically update the linked annotation that is based on this attribute. An annotation feature class can link to only one feature class, but a feature class can have any number of linked annotation feature classes.

For example, a hydrant in the water network is moved by 50 feet. When the hydrant is moved, its linked annotation moves with it. In the same network, the name of a transmission main may change. When the value in its name field is modified, the text stored in its linked annotation feature is automatically changed as well.

To learn more about working with labels and annotation, see *Using ArcMap*. To learn more about working with feature-linked annotation and converting annotation formats to geodatabase annotation, see *Building a Geodatabase*.

Updating annotation created in ArcGIS 8

If you have a geodatabase created in ArcGIS 8, you'll need to do two things before you can use some of the ArcGIS 9 labeling and annotation tools with your data.

You'll first need to upgrade your geodatabase. To learn how, see Chapter 2, 'Editing basics'.

After you've upgraded your geodatabase, you'll need to run the Update Annotation Feature Class tool on your ArcGIS 8 annotation feature classes. Once you've done this, you can append annotation into these feature classes with the Convert Labels to Annotation command or use the Annotation toolbar construction and editing tools with them.

It is important to note that you won't be able to view updated annotation in ArcGIS 8. You can always view earlier versions of annotation in later versions of ArcGIS.

Geodatabases and annotation feature classes created in ArcGIS 9 do not need to be updated.

1. Upgrade your ArcGIS 8 geodatabase. To learn how, see Chapter 2, 'Editing basics'.

2. Click the ArcToolbox button.

3. Double-click the Data Management Tools toolbox.

4. Double-click the Feature Class toolset.

5. Double-click the Update Annotation Feature Class tool.

6. Click the Browse button and navigate to the ArcGIS 8 annotation feature class you want to update.

7. Click the annotation feature class and click Add.

8. Click OK to execute the tool.

9. Add the updated annotation feature class to ArcMap.

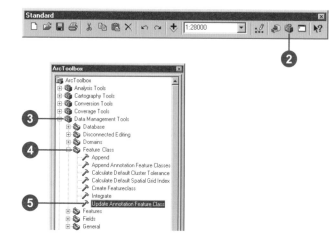

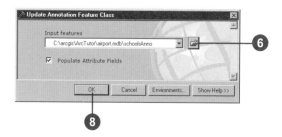

Converting labels to annotation

Labeling is the process of automatically generating text derived from feature attributes and placing it near features on a map. Because *labels* are not selectable and you cannot edit the properties of individual labels, you may want to convert your labels to annotation. Annotation can be stored in a map document or a geodatabase.

When converting to geodatabase annotation, ArcMap can create annotation feature classes or append to existing ones. When converting to feature-linked annotation, ArcMap also creates a relationship class to maintain the link between the features and the annotation.

The annotation feature class and relationship class are created inside the same feature dataset in which the feature class is stored or at the geodatabase level for a standalone feature class.

To convert labels in an ArcGIS 8 geodatabase, you need to upgrade your geodatabase first. See Chapter 2, 'Editing basics', for more information. ▶

Converting labels to geodatabase annotation

1. Click the Add Data button in ArcMap to add the feature class for which you want to create annotation in your map.

2. Label the features in your map as described in *Using ArcMap*, including setting a reference scale and data frame extent.

3. Right-click the layer in the table of contents. To convert labels from more than one layer, right-click the data frame.

4. Click Convert Labels to Annotation.

5. For Store Annotation, click In a database.

6. Specify the features you want to create annotation for.

7. To create feature-linked annotation, check the Feature Linked box. To create standard annotation, leave the box unchecked.

8. If you're creating standard annotation and want to add the annotation to an existing standard annotation feature class, check the Append box.

9. If you're creating feature-linked annotation, click the name of the new annotation feature class to change it. ▶

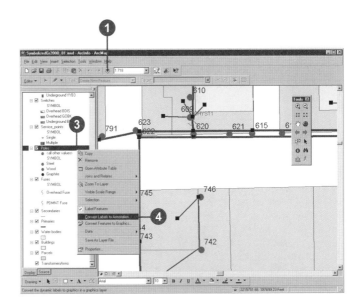

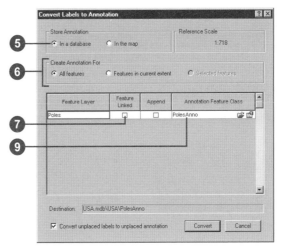

To learn more about preparing labels for conversion and converting labels to annotation that is stored in a map document, see *Using ArcMap* or the ArcGIS Desktop Help.

Tip

Converting label classes to annotation with ArcEditor, ArcInfo, and ArcView

Annotation classes are to a geodatabase annotation feature class as label classes are to a layer's labels. With an ArcEditor or ArcInfo license, the label classes will be converted into separate annotation classes within the annotation feature class. With ArcView, you cannot create multiple annotation classes, so all of your label classes will be combined into a single annotation class.

Tip

Adding annotation

When all of the labels have been converted to annotation, the new annotation feature class is automatically added to the map.

Tip

Using versions

If you're appending to an existing annotation feature class, convert your labels to annotation before you version your data when possible.

10. If you're creating standard annotation, click the Open Folder button and specify the path and name of the new annotation feature class you will create or, if you're appending, the existing standard annotation feature class you're appending to.

11. If you're appending to an existing feature class, skip to step 17.

12. Click the Properties button.

13. Check the box to require edited annotation features to maintain reference to their associated text symbols stored in the feature class.

14. Specify additional editing behavior for the new annotation feature class.

15. If you are creating the new annotation feature class in an ArcSDE geodatabase and want to use a custom storage keyword, check the Use configuration keyword box, then choose the keyword you want to use (ArcInfo and ArcEditor only).

16. Click OK. ▶

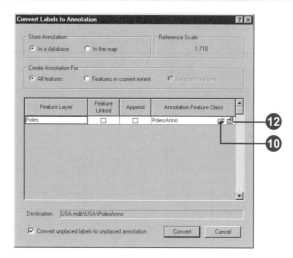

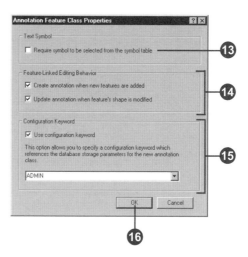

17. Some labels may not currently display on the map because there is no room for them.

To convert these labels, check the Convert unplaced labels box. This saves the unplaced labels in the annotation feature class, allowing you to later position them one at a time in an ArcMap edit session.

18. Click Convert.

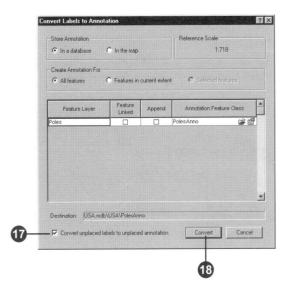

Why is the Unplaced Annotation button unavailable?

You need to be in an edit session first. Click Editor, then Start Editing.

Drawing unplaced annotation

You can check the Draw box on to show unplaced annotation on the map. Unplaced annotation features are drawn in red.

After you've placed an annotation feature on your map, the feature is selected and the Edit Annotation tool becomes active. To learn how to move or resize the annotation feature, see 'Editing the size and position of annotation features' in this chapter.

To learn more about converting labels to feature-linked annotation and importing annotation into a geodatabase, see Building a Geodatabase.

Adding unplaced annotation to a map

1. Click the Unplaced Annotation button on the Annotation toolbar.

   If the button is unavailable, make sure you are in an edit session.

2. Click the Show dropdown arrow on the Unplaced Annotation dialog box to search in a particular annotation layer or in all visible annotation layers.

3. Check Visible Extent if you only want to search for unplaced annotation in the current map extent.

4. Click Search Now.

   Any unplaced annotation features are listed.

5. Select the annotation feature you want to place on your map.

6. Right-click and click Place Annotation or press the spacebar.

   Once placed, the feature is selected and the Edit Annotation tool becomes active so you can move or resize the feature.

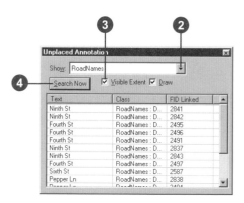

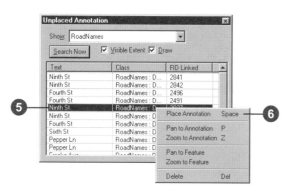

Creating new annotation features

The Editor and Annotation toolbars provide the tools you need to create new geodatabase annotation features. The Annotation toolbar allows you to choose the construction method—horizontal, curved, and so on—and the symbol of your new annotation. You'll enter the text of your annotation in the Text box on the Annotation toolbar, but you can press a shortcut key to change the text for constructing new annotation.

To use the tools on the Annotation toolbar, you need to be in an edit session and have an annotation feature class as the target. Your annotation feature class also needs to have a symbol collection: see *Building a Geodatabase*. To use the construction tools with ArcGIS 8 annotation, you need to upgrade your geodatabase and update your annotation feature class.

The tools on the Annotation toolbar work with annotation stored in a geodatabase. Annotation stored in a map document is created and edited with the Draw toolbar. To learn more, see *Using ArcMap*.

Starting an edit session and setting the target annotation feature class

1. Add an annotation feature class to your map.

2. Click Editor and click Start Editing.

3. Click the Target dropdown arrow and click the annotation feature class you want to edit.

You need to set the target annotation feature class when constructing or copying and pasting annotation features.

Adding the Annotation toolbar

1. Click Editor, point to More Editing Tools, and click Annotation.

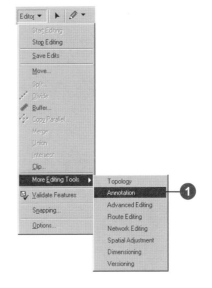

You can also add the Annotation toolbar from the list of toolbars on the View menu.

The Annotation toolbar

Construct straight annotation.

Construct horizontal annotation.

Construct annotation with a leader line.

Text box: Use to enter the text of new annotation.

Unplaced Annotation: View the annotation that was not placed when converting labels to annotation.

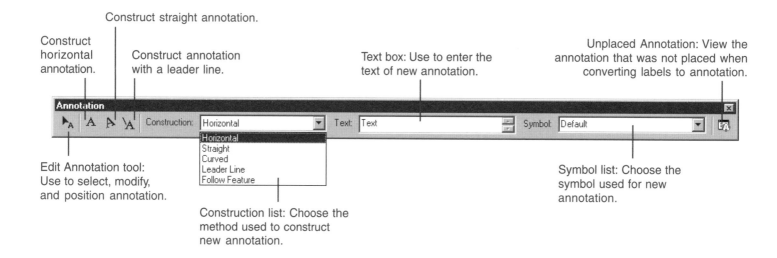

Edit Annotation tool: Use to select, modify, and position annotation.

Construction list: Choose the method used to construct new annotation.

Symbol list: Choose the symbol used for new annotation.

You use the Sketch tool with the Construction dropdown list to create annotation. The one-click buttons are simply shortcuts that activate the Sketch tool and a particular construction method.

Tip

Snapping to features

The Snap To Feature command enables snapping when you're constructing a new annotation feature. You can use Snap To Feature by right-clicking when constructing annotation.

Tip

Using annotation from ArcGIS 8

If you want to use the Annotation toolbar construction tools with annotation created in ArcGIS 8, you'll first need to upgrade your geodatabase to ArcGIS 9 and use the Update Annotation Feature Class tool in ArcToolbox.

See Also

To learn how to define annotation classes and symbols, see Building a Geodatabase.

Constructing horizontal annotation

1. Click the Horizontal Annotation button on the Annotation toolbar.

   The Sketch tool and Horizontal method are activated.

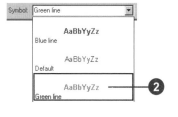

2. Optionally, use the Default symbol or choose another symbol from the Symbol dropdown list.

3. Type the text you want to place on your map in the Text box.

4. Click where you want to place the annotation on the map.

Horizontal annotation is created.

Tip

Placing annotation at a specific location

You can enter coordinates at which to place your annotation using the Absolute X,Y dialog box. To use Absolute X,Y, press F6 or right-click when constructing annotation.

Tip

Using a shortcut to change the annotation symbol

With the Sketch tool active, press the S key to activate the Symbol box on the Annotation toolbar.

Tip

Using the Find Text command on the Sketch tool context menu

Find Text populates the Text box on the Annotation toolbar with a text expression from a feature under the cursor position. If the target is a feature-linked annotation feature class, text is derived only from a feature in the origin feature class. With a standard annotation feature class as the target, the text is based on the label expression of the layer containing the first visible and selectable feature. You can also use Ctrl + W as a shortcut to Find Text.

Constructing straight annotation

1. Click the Straight Annotation button on the Annotation toolbar.

   The Sketch tool and Straight method are activated.

2. Optionally, use the Default symbol or choose another symbol from the Symbol dropdown list.

3. Type the text you want to place on your map in the Text box.

4. Click where you want to place the annotation on the map.

   As you move your mouse, the text will rotate about the anchor point.

5. Click again to finish placing the annotation.

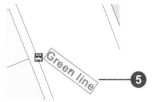

Straight annotation is created.

Working with leader lines

In many cases, you'll just want to add a leader line or callout to a regular annotation class, such as the Default class in the Symbol dropdown list. This method is flexible because you can set a different leader for each annotation feature or use the same one for all features. You can modify the appearance of the leader and callout by following the steps in 'Setting leader line symbol properties'.

If you want to use the same leader line symbol every time you create a new annotation feature, you can also use ArcCatalog to create an annotation class that has a predefined leader symbol. Then, when you are creating new annotation features in ArcMap, choose it from the Symbol dropdown list. To learn how to modify the symbology of a predefined leader symbol, see Building a Geodatabase.

See Also

To learn how to define annotation classes that include leader line symbols, see Building a Geodatabase.

Constructing annotation that has a leader line

1. Click the Leader Line Annotation button on the Annotation toolbar.

   The Sketch tool and Leader Line method are activated.

2. Optionally, use the Default symbol or choose another symbol from the Symbol dropdown list.

   If you defined an annotation class that has a leader symbol in ArcCatalog, you can use it. The cursor changes to the leader line symbol.

3. Type the text you want to place on your map in the Text box.

4. Click where you want to start the annotation feature's leader line.

5. Drag the annotation feature where you want to place it.

6. Click again to finish placing the annotation.

To modify the leader added to these symbols, see 'Setting leader line symbol properties' in this chapter.

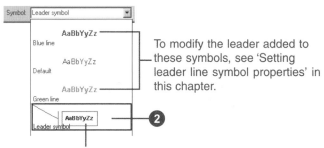

Use ArcCatalog to modify this symbol, which is a predefined annotation class (see *Building a Geodatabase*).

Annotation with a leader line is created.

Setting leader line symbol properties

1. Click Editor on the Editor toolbar and click Options.

2. Click the Annotation tab.

3. Click the Leader button.

4. Click the Type dropdown arrow and click the type of callout you want to use. Steps 5–10 apply to line callouts.

5. Click one of the Style buttons to set the style of the leader line.

6. Check Leader.

7. Click Symbol underneath the Leader check box to change the color and width of the leader line. Click OK on the Symbol Selector dialog box.

8. Optionally, check the Accent Bar and Border boxes to add them to your leader line symbol. Click Symbol to change the Accent Bar or Border symbol properties.

9. Optionally, change the Gap and Leader Tolerance.

10. Optionally, change the margins.

11. Click OK on the Editor dialog box.

12. Click OK on the Editing Options dialog box.

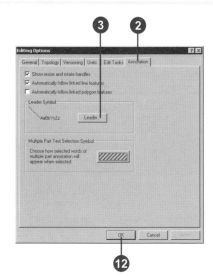

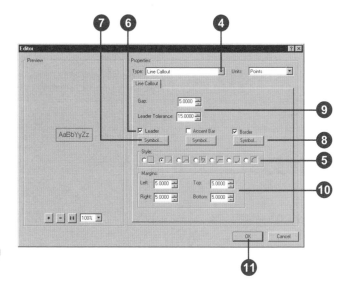

Using the Sketch tool to construct annotation

You can use the Sketch tool with any of the methods in the Construction dropdown menu to construct new annotation.

Adding a one-click button for curved construction

Instead of using the Sketch tool and the Construction dropdown menu, you can add a button to construct curved annotation with a single click. You can add the command from the Advanced Edit tools list in the Customize dialog box.

Snapping to features

The Snap To Feature command enables snapping when you're constructing a new annotation feature. You can use Snap To Feature by right-clicking when constructing annotation.

Constructing curved annotation

1. Click the Construction dropdown arrow and click Curved.

2. Optionally, use the Default symbol or choose another symbol from the Symbol dropdown list.

3. Click the Sketch tool.

4. Type the text you want to place on your map in the Text box.

5. Click where you want to start the curved annotation.

6. Click to add vertices to define the baseline of the curved annotation feature.

7. Double-click to finish the sketch and place the annotation.

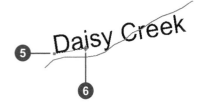

The annotation is placed along the baseline. To learn how to edit the baseline sketch, see 'Editing the size and position of annotation features' in this chapter.

Tip

Adding a one-click button for follow feature construction

Instead of using the Sketch tool and the Construction dropdown menu, you can add a button to construct follow feature annotation with a single click. You can add the command from the Advanced Edit tools list in the Customize dialog box.

Tip

Switching sides

When the constraint option is Left side or Right side, you can use the Tab key to switch between the sides.

Tip

Flipping annotation

You can press the L key to flip the annotation 180 degrees.

Tip

Switching between parallel and perpendicular

You can press the P key to toggle the annotation placement angle between parallel and perpendicular.

Tip

Using a shortcut to Follow Feature Options

You can press the O key to open the Follow Feature Options dialog box.

Constructing annotation in follow feature mode

1. Click the Construction dropdown arrow and click Follow Feature.

2. Optionally, click an annotation symbol from the Symbol dropdown list.

3. Click the Sketch tool.

4. Type the text you want to place on your map in the Text box.

5. Click the feature you want your annotation to follow.

6. Drag the annotation feature where you want to place it.

   If you want to change how the annotation follows the feature, see 'Setting follow feature mode options' in this chapter.

7. Click again to place the annotation in the position you want along the feature.

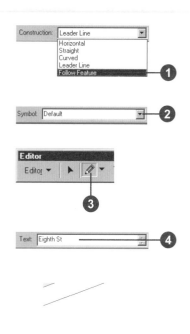

Setting follow feature mode options

1. Click the Sketch tool.

2. Click the Construction dropdown arrow and click Follow Feature.

3. Press the O key to open the Follow Feature Options dialog box.

   If the dialog box does not open, you may need to click the map first to give it focus.

4. Click Straight or Curved to set whether the annotation will follow the feature as a straight line through the end points of the text string or as a curve.

5. Click Parallel or Perpendicular to set the annotation to follow parallel along the feature or perpendicular to the feature.

6. Click one of the Constrain Placement buttons to constrain the annotation when you drag it along the feature.

7. Optionally, type a value to offset the annotation from the feature.

8. Click OK.

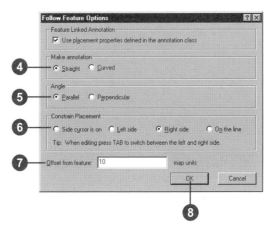

Tip

Shortcuts to copying and pasting

You can also cut, copy, and paste using the standard Windows shortcuts, which are listed on the Edit menu of the ArcMap Main menu.

Tip

Copying and pasting annotation

The new annotation feature is pasted exactly on top of the existing feature and is selected. You can drag the new, selected feature a short distance and see that you do, in fact, have both features.

Tip

Using the Edit and Edit Annotation tools' context menus

The commands on the Edit tool context menu are also found on the Edit Annotation tool's context menu. However, the Edit Annotation tool has additional commands on its context menu.

Tip

Switching between the Sketch, Edit, and Edit Annotation tools

With any of these tools active, press the E key to cycle among them.

Copying and pasting annotation

1. Using the Edit Annotation tool or the Edit tool, select the annotation feature you want to copy and paste.

2. Set the Target to the annotation feature class into which you want to paste.

3. Right-click and click Copy.

4. Right-click and click Paste.

   The annotation feature is added to the feature class and is pasted on top of the feature copied. You can use the Edit or Edit Annotation tools to position the pasted text.

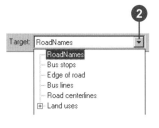

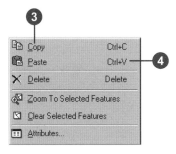

Deleting annotation

1. Using the Edit Annotation tool or the Edit tool, select the annotation feature you want to delete.

2. Press the Delete key.

   The annotation feature is removed from the feature class.

Editing the size and position of annotation features

You can use the editing tools in ArcMap to edit both feature-linked annotation and standard annotation. Some of the editing tasks you can complete include resizing, moving, rotating, and applying various follow feature options to your annotation.

The Edit Annotation tool, which is located on the Annotation toolbar in ArcMap, is especially useful for modifying annotation. The Edit Annotation tool's context menu, which you can open by selecting an annotation feature and right-clicking it, provides you with a list of many annotation editing functions.

To learn about using the Edit Annotation tool to change the way your annotation looks, see 'Editing the appearance of annotation features' in this chapter.

Tip

Using the resize handle
The resize handle's location is determined by the alignment of the text. For example, an annotation feature with text that is left-aligned will have its resize handle located on the right.

Resizing annotation

1. Click the Edit Annotation tool on the Annotation toolbar.

2. Click to select the annotation feature you want to resize.

3. Move the mouse pointer over the red resize handle.

   The pointer becomes a line with arrows at both ends while it's over the resize handle.

4. Drag the text to make it larger or smaller.

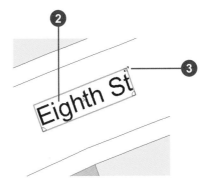

The annotation feature is resized.

Moving annotation

1. Click the Edit Annotation tool or the Edit tool.

2. Select the annotation feature you want to move.

3. Drag the annotation where you want it to be placed.

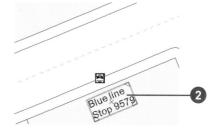

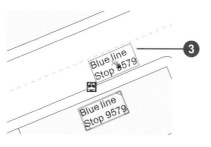

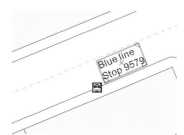

The annotation feature is moved.

Tip

Turning off the rotate and resize handles

You can turn off the rotate and resize handles. Click Editor, Options, then click the Annotation tab and uncheck the Show resize and rotate handles box.

Tip

Editing multiple annotation classes in ArcView

With an ArcView license, you cannot edit an annotation feature class that has more than one annotation class in it.

Tip

Changing the pivot point

If you want to rotate about a pivot point other than a rotate handle, use rotate mode. See 'Rotating annotation in rotate mode' in this chapter.

Rotating annotation using the rotate handles

1. Click the Edit Annotation tool on the Annotation toolbar.

2. Select the annotation you want to rotate.

3. Move the pointer over a rotate handle.

   The cursor changes to the rotate symbol while it's over the rotate handle.

4. Click a rotate handle and drag the annotation to where you want it placed.

   The other rotate handle is the pivot point.

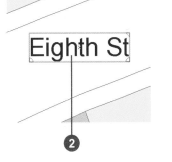

The annotation feature is rotated.

Rotating annotation in rotate mode

1. Click the Edit Annotation tool on the Annotation toolbar.

2. Select the annotation that you want to move.

3. Right-click the text to open the context menu.

4. Click Rotate Mode.

   The mouse pointer changes to a rotate symbol.

5. Click and drag the text to where you want it placed. The text rotates freely about the selection anchor.

   You can also press the A key to enter a specific angle for the rotation.

6. When you've positioned the text where you want it, right-click and click Finish Rotate Mode.

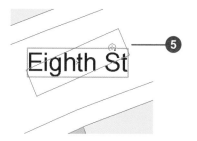

The annotation feature is rotated.

Moving annotation using follow feature mode

1. Click the Edit Annotation tool on the Annotation toolbar.

2. Select the annotation you want to move.

3. Right-click over the feature you want the annotation to follow.

   The feature the annotation follows is determined by the position of the cursor when you right-click. The first selectable and visible feature under your cursor is followed.

4. Click Follow This Feature.

   The feature the annotation is going to follow flashes on the screen and the annotation moves to align to the feature.

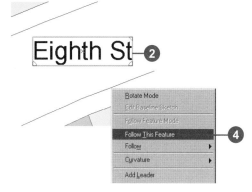

The annotation feature is now following this line feature.

Editing the appearance of annotation features

You can use the editing tools, including the Edit Annotation tool, to change how your annotation looks. The primary ways of modifying annotation appearance are with the Attributes dialog box and the Edit Annotation tool.

You can use the Attributes dialog box to modify the appearance of your annotation. In it, you can change symbolization properties, such as changing the annotation symbol or adding formatting to text. You can also update your annotation's attributes and change the text string that is displayed.

The Edit Annotation tool's context menu has commands to modify the appearance of annotation. Some of the tasks that you can use it for include to stack or flip annotation and to modify the annotation construction method—for example, to make horizontal annotation curved.

Changing annotation symbology

1. Using the Edit Annotation tool or the Edit tool, select the annotation for which you want to change symbols.

2. Click the Attributes button on the Editor toolbar.

3. Click the Annotation tab.

4. Click the dropdown arrow and click a new annotation symbol.

    You can only change the symbol if you have defined more than one annotation symbol.

5. Click the symbol you want to use.

6. Click Apply.

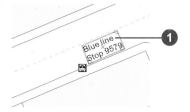

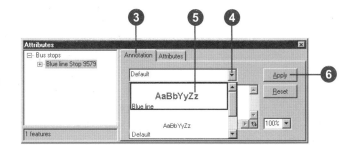

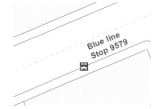

The annotation feature's symbol is updated.

Tip

Changing the symbol for multiple annotation features

To update the annotation symbol for more than one feature at a time, select all the annotation features you want to change, click the annotation feature class name on the left side of the Attributes dialog box, and choose the new symbol from the dropdown list on the Annotation tab.

Tip

Switching between Formatted and Unformatted views

If the zoom box is present in the lower right corner of the Attributes dialog box, you are working in Formatted view. If you want to type in text formatting tags, you can switch to Unformatted view.

See Also

To learn how to define annotation classes and symbols, see Building a Geodatabase.

See Also

You can use the tools on the Draw toolbar to change the symbology of map document annotation. To learn more, see Using ArcMap.

Modifying annotation formatting

1. Using the Edit Annotation tool or the Edit tool, select the annotation you want to format.

2. Click the Attributes button on the Editor toolbar.

3. Click the Annotation tab.

4. If you don't see the zoom box located below the Reset button on the right side of the Attributes dialog box, click the button to switch to Formatted view.

5. Select the text you want to modify.

6. Click the formatting buttons at the bottom of the Attributes dialog box or right-click and choose the formatting you want to apply from the context menu.

   The formatting context menu is only available in Formatted view.

7. Click Apply.

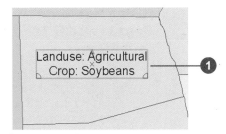

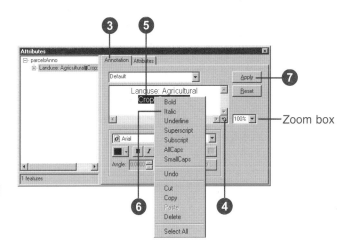

Zoom box

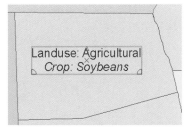

The text that was selected on the Annotation tab is formatted.

Using text formatting tags to modify annotation symbology

1. Using the Edit Annotation tool or the Edit tool, select the annotation to which you want to apply text formatting tags.

2. Click the Attributes button on the Editor toolbar.

3. Click the Annotation tab.

4. If you see the zoom box below the Reset button on the right side of the Attributes dialog box, click the button to switch to Unformatted view.

5. Type the formatting tags you want to apply to your text.

6. Click Apply.

The formatting tags are displayed as plain text in Unformatted view. You can switch to Formatted view to see your text as it will appear on the map.

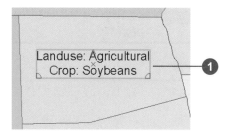

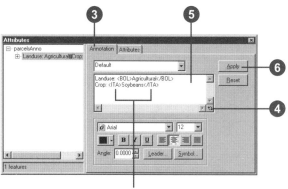

Text formatting tags

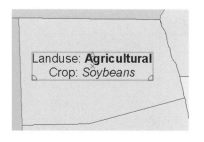

The text between the formatting tags is bolded and italicized.

Modifying the attributes of annotation

1. Using the Edit Annotation tool or the Edit tool, select the annotation containing the attributes you want to modify.

2. Click the Attributes button on the Editor toolbar.

3. Click the Attributes tab.

4. Click the Value column for the entry you want to change—TextString in this example.

5. Type the new value for the attribute.

6. Optionally, modify other attributes, such as the font or font size.

7. Close the Attributes dialog box.

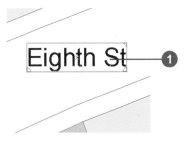

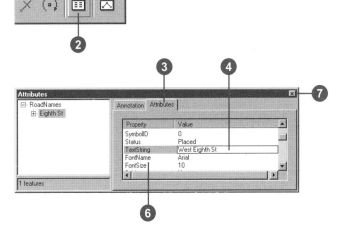

As soon as you click away from the modified attribute value, the text is updated on the map and in the list of features in the Attributes dialog box.

Making annotation horizontal

1. Click the Edit Annotation tool on the Annotation toolbar.

2. Select the straight or curved annotation that you want to make horizontal.

3. Right-click, point to Curvature, and click Horizontal.

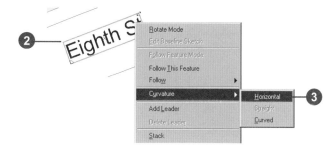

The annotation feature is placed horizontally.

Making annotation curved

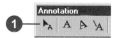

1. Click the Edit Annotation tool on the Annotation toolbar.

2. Select the annotation that you want to curve.

3. Right-click, point to Curvature, and click Curved.

The annotation feature becomes curved.

When are the Straight and Curved commands available?

Straight is only enabled if the selected annotation is curved or horizontal.

Curved is only enabled if the selected annotation is horizontal or straight and is not stacked.

Making curved annotation straight

1. Click the Edit Annotation tool on the Annotation toolbar.

2. Select the curved annotation that you want to make straight.

3. Right-click, point to Curvature, and click Straight.

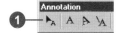

The annotation feature is straightened.

Tip

What are the green and purple vertices?

Move the green inflection point vertices to change the shape of the baseline. Move the purple vertices to change part of the baseline curvature.

Tip

Using a shortcut to Edit Baseline Sketch

Double-click a selected annotation feature to enter and exit baseline edit mode.

Tip

Why isn't Edit Baseline Sketch available?

This command is only enabled if a single curved annotation feature is selected. To make an annotation curved, use the Curved command on the Edit Annotation tool context menu.

Modifying the shape of curved annotation

1. Click the Edit Annotation tool on the Annotation toolbar.

2. Select the curved annotation that you want to change shape.

3. Right-click and click Edit Baseline Sketch.

4. To move a vertex, position the cursor over the vertex until the cursor's shape changes, then click and drag.

5. Optionally, add a vertex by right-clicking the baseline sketch and clicking Insert Vertex.

   To delete a vertex you've added, right-click and click Delete Vertex.

6. When you're finished, right-click and click Finish Baseline Sketch.

Removing a leader line

To remove the leader line from your annotation, select the annotation using the Edit Annotation tool, right-click, and click Delete Leader.

For more information on setting symbol properties and using leader line symbols, see Using ArcMap.

To learn how to set the default leader symbol properties, see 'Setting leader line symbol properties' in this chapter.

Adding a leader line to annotation

1. Click the Edit Annotation tool on the Annotation toolbar.

2. Select the annotation to which you want to add a leader line.

3. Right-click and click Add Leader.

4. Optionally, change the position of the start of the leader line. Move your cursor over the vertex until the cursor's shape changes, then click and drag.

5. Click the annotation and drag it to the desired position.

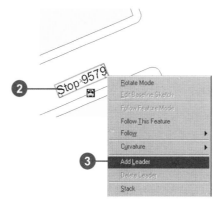

Stacking annotation

1. Click the Edit Annotation tool on the Annotation toolbar.

2. Select the text that you want to stack.

   If you are stacking a single annotation feature, it must have more than one word in it.

3. Right-click and click Stack.

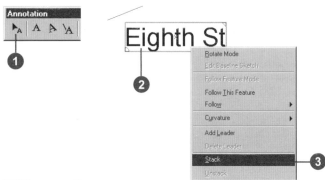

The text is placed on multiple lines.

Unstacking annotation

1. Click the Edit Annotation tool on the Annotation toolbar.

2. Select the stacked text that you want to unstack.

3. Right-click and click Unstack.

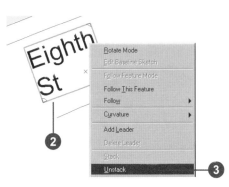

The text is placed on a single line.

Flipping annotation by 180 degrees

1. Click the Edit Annotation tool on the Annotation toolbar.

2. Select the annotation that you want to flip.

3. Right-click and click Flip Annotation.

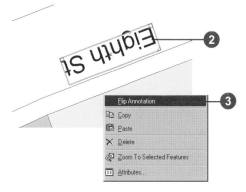

The annotation feature is flipped by 180 degrees.

Converting annotation to multiple parts

1. Click the Edit Annotation tool on the Annotation toolbar.

2. Select the annotation you want to convert to multiple parts.

3. Right-click and click Convert to Multiple Parts.

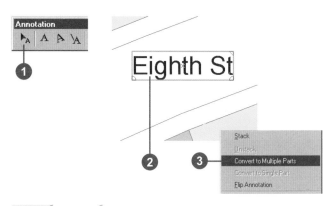

The annotation feature is converted into multiple parts.

Editing a part of multiple part annotation

1. Click the Edit Annotation tool on the Annotation toolbar.

2. Select the multiple part annotation feature.

3. Double-click the part you want to edit. By default, the part is highlighted in magenta stripes.

   You can drag the part to a new location or right-click to access other commands.

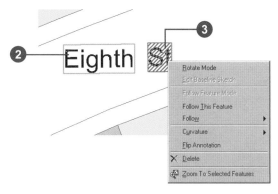

Working with feature-linked annotation

Feature-linked annotation is related to another feature class in the geodatabase. When you create new features, you can have new annotation be created automatically. When the origin feature is moved or rotated, the linked annotation also moves or rotates with it. And when an origin feature is deleted from the geodatabase, the linked annotation feature is also deleted. The annotation is also updated when you change an attribute of the feature that the annotation text is based on.

There are several ways to create feature-linked annotation. If you have defined a feature-linked annotation feature class, annotation will be created automatically as you create new features using the editing tools in ArcMap. To learn how to create new feature classes, see *Building a Geodatabase*.

You can also use the Annotate selected features command in ArcMap to add linked annotation to existing features.

Another way to create new feature-linked annotation is to convert labels or other annotation formats to feature-linked ▶

Creating new features with linked annotation

1. Zoom to the area where you want to add the new feature.

2. Click the Sketch tool.

3. Click the Task dropdown arrow and click Create New Feature.

4. Click the Target layer dropdown arrow and click the type of feature you want to create.

5. Click the map to create the new feature's vertices.

6. Double-click the last vertex to finish the feature.

An annotation feature is automatically created and linked to the new feature.

If your feature has default values for the field from which the annotation is derived, the annotation appears and reflects the values from those fields.

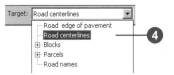

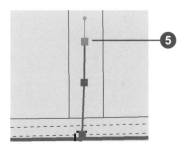

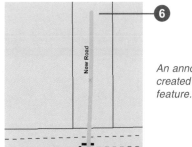

An annotation feature is created along with the new feature.

annotation. See *Building a Geodatabase* to learn how to convert labels to feature-linked annotation or how to use the ArcToolbox annotation conversion tools to create feature-linked annotation from coverage or CAD annotation.

Modifying features with linked annotation

1. Click the Edit tool.

2. Click the feature you want to edit.

3. Click the Attributes button.

4. Optionally, click the value from which the annotation is derived and modify the attribute value.

   The annotation is automatically updated to reflect the change.

5. Click the Close button to close the Attributes dialog box. ▶

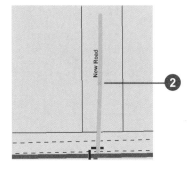

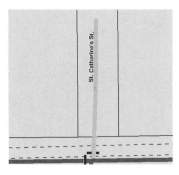

The linked annotation is automatically updated with the new attribute information.

Editing the shape of a feature that has linked annotation

If you change the shape of a feature that has feature-linked annotation, the annotation is automatically repositioned if it needs to be moved in order to accommodate the feature's new geometry.

6. Optionally, click and drag the feature to a new location.

   The linked annotation feature moves with the feature.

7. Optionally, click the Rotate tool.

8. Optionally, click anywhere on the map and drag the pointer to rotate the feature to the desired location.

   The annotation rotates with the feature.

9. Optionally, click the Delete button on the Standard toolbar.

   The feature you selected, along with its linked annotation, is deleted from the database.

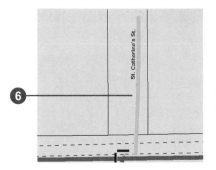

The linked annotation and the feature move together to the new location.

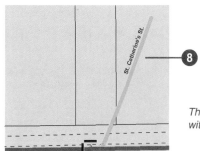

The feature is rotated along with its linked annotation.

ArcInfo and ArcEditor

Tip

Placing annotation from the Unplaced Annotation dialog box

Sometimes some of the generated annotation cannot automatically be placed on the map. To place these annotation features, click the Unplaced Annotation button on the Annotation toolbar. To learn more, see 'Adding unplaced annotation to a map' in this chapter.

Tip

Using versions

When possible, avoid conflicts by generating your annotation before you version your data.

Generating feature-linked annotation

1. Click the Add Data button to add a feature class and its linked annotation class to your map.

2. Click the Select Features button to select the features for which you want to generate annotation. To create annotation for all of the features, select all of the features.

3. Right-click the feature class in the table of contents.

4. Point to Selection.

5. Click Annotate Selected Features.

6. Check the related annotation classes in which you want to store the annotation.

7. Check the check box to add unplaced labels to the overflow window.

8. Click OK.

   If any annotation features could not be placed on the map, they are listed in the Unplaced Annotation dialog box.

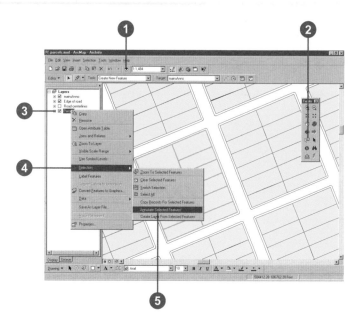

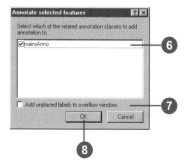

Editing dimension features

14

Dimension features are used to communicate information about the dimensions of geographic features, or distances between them, on a map. In this respect, they are similar to annotation. However, dimension features exclusively express distance measurements. Dimension features can be used to show the length of a property line, the distance between bridge spans, or the length of a feature along one axis.

Dimension features are stored in *dimension feature classes* in a geodatabase. Dimension feature classes can have one or more styles to ensure that the dimension features you create are consistent with your mapping standards.

Editing dimension features

Dimension features, unlike simple features, know how they are created. A dimension feature requires a specific number of points to be entered into the edit sketch to describe its geometry. The standard edit tools can be used to manually input the points required for these *construction methods*. In addition to the manual construction methods, there are several tools that allow you to create new dimension features from existing dimension features and other features. These tools are collectively called the Autodimension tools.

You can assign a style to a dimension feature when you create it or change an existing dimension feature's style. Dimension features draw and symbolize themselves based on the properties of their assigned style.

Construction methods

The type of dimension feature you are creating will dictate the number of points that are required as input.

The following is a list of dimension types and the number of points required for their construction:

- Simple aligned: two points

- Aligned: three points

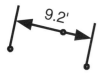

- Linear (horizontal and vertical): three points

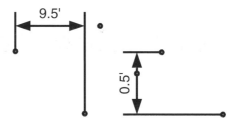

- Rotated linear: four points

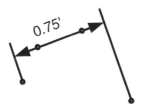

You can specify what type of construction method to use to create your dimension feature. The construction method dictates the type of dimension that is created. Each construction method knows how many points are required to create a specific kind of dimension feature. When using these methods, Finish Sketch is automatically called once you have inputted the correct number of points. The exceptions are the free construction methods.

The free construction methods also know how many points are required for input; however, they do not call Finish Sketch automatically. With the free construction methods, you can add as many points into the edit sketch as you need to construct your dimension feature. When you call Finish Sketch, the type of dimension feature that is created will depend on the number of points in your sketch.

The following summarizes the different construction methods:

- **Simple aligned:** creates simple aligned dimension features. It requires two points as input: the beginning dimension point and the end dimension point. Finish Sketch is automatically called after the second point is inputted.

- **Aligned:** creates aligned dimension features. It requires three points as input: the beginning dimension point, the end dimension point, and a third point describing the height of the dimension line. Finish Sketch is automatically called after the third point is inputted.

- **Linear:** creates horizontal and vertical dimension features. It requires three points as input: the beginning dimension point, the end dimension point, and a third point describing the height of the dimension line. The location of the third point relative to the beginning and ending dimension points will dictate whether the dimension feature is horizontal or vertical. Finish Sketch is automatically called after the third point is inputted.

- **Rotated linear:** creates rotated linear dimension features. It requires four points as input: the beginning dimension point, the end dimension point, a third point describing the height of the dimension line, and a fourth point describing the extension line angle. Finish Sketch is automatically called after the fourth point is inputted.

- **Free aligned:** creates simple aligned and aligned dimension features. It requires either two or three points as input. If you call Finish Sketch with two points in the edit sketch, a simple aligned dimension feature is created. If you call Finish Sketch with three points in the edit sketch, an aligned dimension feature is created. If you call Finish Sketch with less than two or more than three points in the edit sketch, the edit operation will fail.

- **Free linear:** creates horizontal linear, vertical linear, and rotated linear dimension features. It requires either three or four points as input. If you call Finish Sketch with three points in the edit sketch, a horizontal or vertical linear dimension feature is created. If you call Finish Sketch with four points in the edit sketch, a rotated linear dimension feature is created. If you call Finish Sketch with less than three or more than four points in the edit sketch, the edit operation will fail.

Autodimension tools

The Autodimension tool palette contains four tools for automatically creating dimension features: Dimension Edge, Perpendicular Dimensions, Baseline Dimension, and Continue Dimension. Using these tools, you can create new dimension features based on existing dimension features or other features on your map.

Dimension Edge works on any type of feature. The Dimension Edge tool will automatically create a dimension whose baseline is defined by a line segment of an existing feature.

Perpendicular Dimensions simultaneously creates two dimension features that are perpendicular to one another.

Baseline Dimension and Continue Dimension are both used only on existing dimension features. Baseline Dimension creates a new dimension feature whose beginning dimension point is based on the same beginning point of a previous dimension feature. The Continue Dimension tool creates a new dimension feature whose beginning dimension point is the same as the end dimension point of the existing dimension feature being continued. The Baseline Dimension and Continue Dimension tools create the same type of dimension as the existing dimension they are applied to and assign it the style selected in the Style dropdown list in the Dimensioning toolbar.

ArcInfo and ArcEditor

Dimension styles

All dimension features are associated with a *dimension style*. When you create a new dimension feature, you must assign it a dimension style. This dimension style must exist in the dimension feature class in which you are creating your new dimension feature. Once a dimension feature is created, it assumes all of the properties of its style. You can use the Attributes dialog box to modify some of those properties; however, some properties, such as the symbology of the dimension feature elements, cannot be modified.

To learn more about dimension styles and how to create them, see *Building a Geodatabase*.

The Dimensioning toolbar

The Autodimension tools and the controls for setting the construction method and assigning a dimension style are located on the *Dimensioning toolbar*. The controls on the Dimensioning toolbar are only active when you are editing, and the feature class selected in the Editor toolbar's Target dropdown list is a dimension feature class.

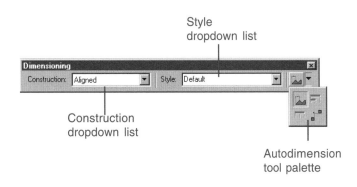

Style dropdown list

Construction dropdown list

Autodimension tool palette

The Construction dropdown list contains all of the methods for constructing dimension features. The construction method dictates the number of points required to construct a dimension feature and the type of dimension feature that is created.

The Styles dropdown list contains all of the styles in the dimension feature class that are selected in the Target dropdown list in the Editor toolbar. New dimension features are created and assigned the style that is selected in the Style dropdown list.

It is important to remember that the Baseline Dimension and Continue Dimension tools will only be active if a dimension feature is selected. The Dimension Edge tool will be active when any feature is selected.

Modifying a dimension feature's geometry

Dimension features not only draw and symbolize themselves based on their assigned style but are also able to regulate the modification of their geometry. By using the editing tools in ArcMap that you use to modify the geometry of other types of features, you can modify a dimension feature's geometry while maintaining the correct configuration of points for a valid dimension feature.

When you are modifying a dimension feature, there are a series of vertices you can pick up and move with the Edit tool and move to alter the dimension feature's geometry. You can't add additional vertices or delete any of the existing vertices. The following diagram illustrates what aspect of a dimension feature is modified when one of these vertices is moved:

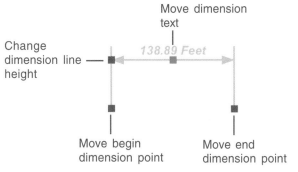

A dimension feature's geometry can be modified by moving a set of vertices while maintaining a valid dimension feature.

You can move a dimension feature's text away from its dimension line. The way the text is shown is dependent on the style chosen for the dimension feature. Some styles have line decoration including a leader line. For these styles, if you move the dimension feature's text far enough from the dimension line that it surpasses the leader line tolerance, then that leader line will automatically be displayed.

If a dimension feature's style has a text symbol with a leader line, that leader line is drawn when the text is moved farther away from the dimension line than the leader tolerance for the text symbol.

The extension line angle and the other properties of a dimension feature's geometry can be modified by altering the values of some of its fields. The following is a list of the fields you can modify for a dimension feature and how they correspond to its geometry:

Field	Property
BEGINX	x-coordinate of the beginning dimension point
BEGINY	y-coordinate of the beginning dimension point
ENDX	x-coordinate of the end dimension point
ENDY	y-coordinate of the end dimension point
DIMX	x-coordinate of the dimension line height
DIMY	y-coordinate of the dimension line height
TEXTX	x-coordinate of the text point (null if the text hasn't been moved relative to the dimension feature)
TEXTY	y-coordinate of the text point (null if the text hasn't been moved relative to the dimension feature)
EXTANGLE	Extension line angle

For more information on editing a feature's geometry, see Chapter 7, 'Editing existing features'. For more information on text symbols and text decoration, see *Using ArcMap*.

Modifying a dimension feature's properties

A dimension feature gets most of its properties from its style.
However, you can override some aspects of a dimension feature's
style. The following are the properties that can differ between a
dimension feature and its style:

• Dimension line display

• Dimension line arrow symbol display

• Extension line display

For more information about dimension styles, see *Building a
Geodatabase*.

In addition to overriding these style properties, you can also
change a dimension feature's style, specify a custom value to use
for the dimension text instead of the length of the dimension
feature and change the extension line angle.

Dimension features can be modified using the Attributes dialog
box. Dimension features have a special Attributes dialog box to
allow you to easily modify their various properties. However, you
can also use the standard Attributes dialog box to modify the
properties of a dimension feature or to modify the values of fields
that you have added to your dimension feature class.

Switch to standard
Attributes dialog box

Change between custom
value and system value

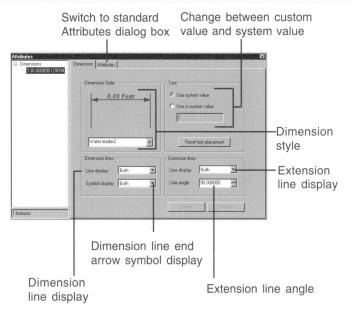

Dimension
style

Extension
line display

Extension line angle

Dimension line end
arrow symbol display

Dimension
line display

*A dimension feature's properties can be modified by a Dimension
Attributes dialog box or by using the standard Attributes dialog box.*

Each property of a dimension feature that you can change in the
dimensioning Attributes dialog box can also be changed by
altering the values of some of its fields. A list of the fields that
you can modify for a dimension feature and how they correspond
to its properties are illustrated on the following page:

Field	Property
STYLEID	ID of the dimension style.
USECUSTOMLENGTH	0 indicates that the feature's length is used for the dimension text; 1 indicates a custom value is used for the dimension text.
CUSTOMLENGTH	Value used for the dimension text if USECUSTOMLENGTH is 1.
DIMDISPLAY	Null indicates both dimension lines are displayed; 1 indicates only the beginning dimension line is displayed; 2 indicates only the end dimension line is displayed; 3 indicates none of the dimension lines are displayed.
EXTDISPLAY	Null indicates both extension lines are displayed; 1 indicates only the beginning extension line is displayed; 2 indicates only the end extension line is displayed; 3 indicates none of the extension lines are displayed.
MARKERDISPLAY	Null indicates both dimension line end arrow markers are displayed; 1 indicates only the beginning dimension line end arrow marker is displayed; 2 indicates only the end dimension line end arrow marker is displayed; 3 indicates none of the dimension line end arrow markers are displayed.

For more information on using the Attributes dialog box in ArcMap, see Chapter 9, 'Editing attributes'.

Adding the Dimensioning toolbar

The Autodimension tools and the controls for setting the construction method and assigning a dimension style are located on the Dimensioning toolbar. The controls on the Dimensioning toolbar are only active when you are editing, and the feature class selected in the Editor toolbar's Target dropdown list is a dimension feature class.

Tip

Adding the toolbar
You can also add the toolbar by clicking the View menu, pointing to Toolbars, then clicking Dimensioning.

1. Right-click the Main menu.

2. Click Dimensioning.

3. Dock the toolbar to the ArcMap window. Now each time you start ArcMap the toolbar will be displayed.

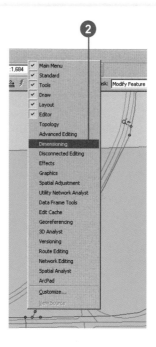

Creating dimension features

By using the tools provided on the basic Editor toolbar and those provided on the Dimensioning toolbar, you can create many types of dimension features.

The edit sketch

ArcMap contains many tools to help you enter points into your edit sketch. All of the same tools can be used to enter the points required for the various dimension feature construction methods.

Creating a simple aligned dimension feature

1. Add your dimension feature class to ArcMap, then add the Editor toolbar and the Dimensioning toolbar.

2. Click Editor and click Start Editing.

3. Zoom to the area where you want to add the new feature.

4. Click the Tool palette dropdown arrow and click the Sketch tool.

5. Click the Task dropdown arrow and click Create New Feature.

6. Click the Target layer dropdown arrow and click the dimension feature class. ►

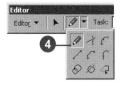

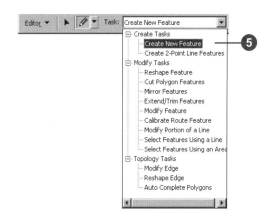

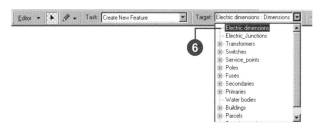

ArcInfo and ArcEditor

Tip

Edit sketch display

When creating dimension features, the edit sketch will actually show you how the resulting dimension feature will look as you move your mouse.

The exceptions are the free dimension construction methods. With these construction methods, the edit sketch display is the same as that for creating simple features.

Tip

Using the Magnifier Window

To more accurately place your vertices, use the Magnifier Window found under Window on the Main menu. To learn more about the Magnifier Window, see Using ArcMap.

Tip

Adjusting the Snapping Environment

By adjusting the settings in the Snapping Environment dialog box, you can more accurately place your vertices. To learn more about the Snapping Environment, see Chapter 3, 'Creating new features'.

7. Click the Style dropdown arrow and click the style you want your new dimension feature to have.

8. Click the Construction dropdown arrow and click Simple Aligned.

9. Click the map at the beginning dimension point to start the edit sketch.

   As you move the mouse, you will see that the new dimension dynamically draws itself with your mouse location as the end dimension point. ▶

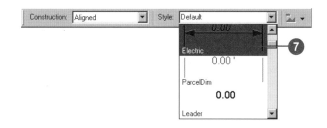

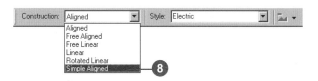

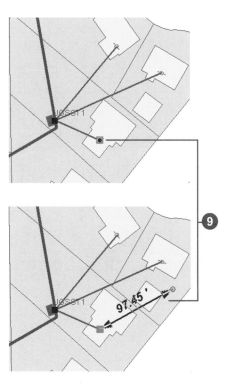

10. Click the map at the end dimension point.

    The sketch is automatically finished and the new simple aligned dimension feature is created with the style you selected.

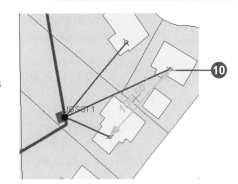

ArcInfo and ArcEditor

Tip

Aligned dimension features

An aligned dimension feature's dimension line is always parallel to its baseline.

To learn more about the different types of dimension features, see Building a Geodatabase.

Creating an aligned dimension feature

1. Follow steps 1–7 for 'Creating a simple aligned dimension feature' in this chapter.

2. Click the Construction dropdown arrow and click Aligned.

3. Click the map at the beginning dimension point to start the edit sketch.

   As you move the mouse, you will see that the new dimension dynamically draws itself with your mouse location as the end dimension point. ►

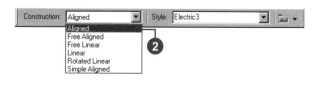

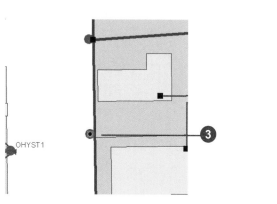

4. Click the map at the end dimension point.

   The new dimension continues to dynamically draw itself; now, however, the beginning and end dimension points are fixed, and the height of the dimension line changes as you move your mouse.

5. Click the map where you want the dimension line to be.

   The sketch is automatically finished, and the new aligned dimension feature is created with the style you selected.

   Since you selected Aligned as your construction method, the dimension line is parallel to the baseline.

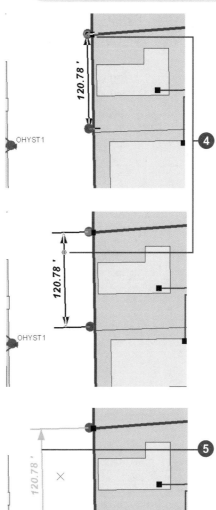

ArcInfo and ArcEditor

Tip

Linear dimension features

A linear dimension feature's dimension line is generally not parallel to its baseline. Therefore, the distance represented by a linear feature is not the length of the baseline.

To learn more about the different types of dimension features, see Building a Geodatabase.

Creating a linear dimension feature

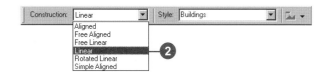

1. Follow steps 1–7 for 'Creating a simple aligned dimension feature' in this chapter.

2. Click the Construction dropdown arrow and click Linear.

3. Click the map at the beginning dimension point to start the edit sketch.

   As you move the mouse, you will see that the new dimension dynamically draws itself with your mouse location as the end dimension point. ▶

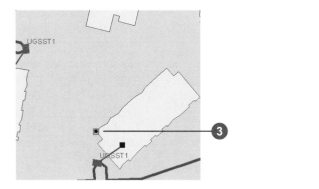

4. Click the map at the end dimension point.

The new dimension continues to dynamically draw itself; now, however, the beginning and end dimension points are fixed, and the height of the dimension line changes as you move your mouse.

If you move your mouse to the left or right of the baseline, you will see a vertical linear dimension feature. If you move your mouse above or below the baseline, you will see a horizontal linear dimension feature. ▶

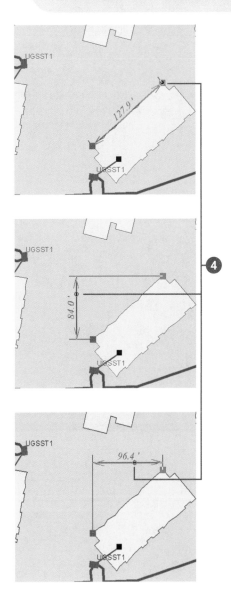

5. Click the map where you want the dimension line to be.

The sketch is automatically finished, and the new linear dimension feature is created with the style you selected.

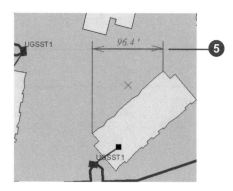

Creating a rotated linear dimension feature

1. Follow steps 1–7 for 'Creating a simple aligned dimension feature' in this chapter.

2. Click the Construction dropdown arrow and click Rotated Linear.

3. Click the map at the beginning dimension point to start the edit sketch.

   As you move the mouse, you will see that the new dimension dynamically draws itself with your mouse location as the end dimension point. ▶

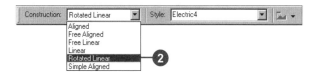

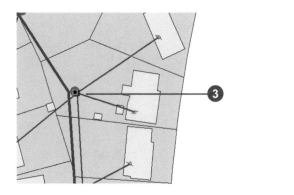

4. Click the map at the end dimension point.

The new dimension continues to dynamically draw itself; now, however, the beginning and end dimension points are fixed, and the height of the dimension line changes as you move your mouse.

If you move your mouse above or below the baseline, you will see a horizontal linear dimension feature. If you move your mouse to the left or right of the baseline, you will see a vertical linear dimension feature. ▶

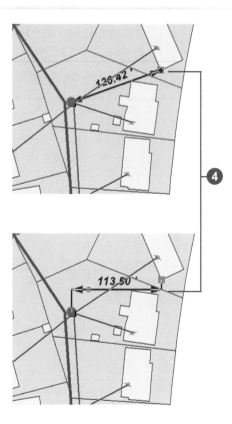

5. Click the map where you want the dimension line to be.

The new dimension continues to dynamically draw itself; now, however, the beginning and end dimension points and dimension line height are fixed, and the angle of the extension lines changes as you move your mouse.

6. Click the map at the angle you want the extension lines to be.

The sketch is automatically finished, and the new rotated linear dimension feature is created with the style you selected.

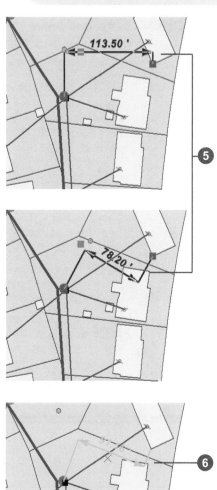

ArcInfo and ArcEditor

Creating a dimension feature with the free aligned construction method

1. Follow steps 1–7 for 'Creating a simple aligned dimension feature' in this chapter.

2. Click the Construction dropdown arrow and click Free Aligned.

3. Click the map at the beginning dimension point to start the edit sketch.

   As you move the cursor, the dimension feature won't dynamically draw itself.

4. Use ArcMap sketch tools and construction methods to enter the end dimension point.

   If you are creating a simple aligned dimension feature, skip to step 6. ►

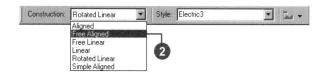

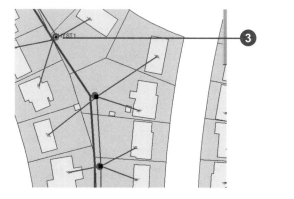

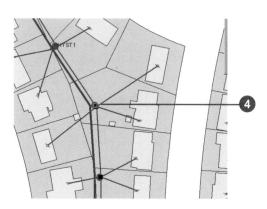

5. Use ArcMap sketch tools and construction methods to enter the point where you want the dimension line to be.

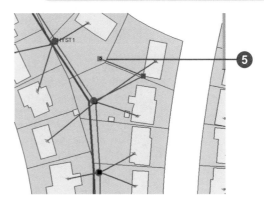

6. If your sketch has more than three vertices or has any vertices that do not represent the beginning or end dimension point or dimension line height, right-click and click Delete Vertex to delete them before continuing to step 7. ▶

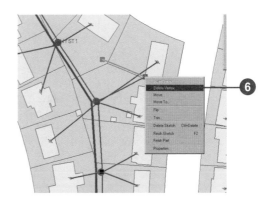

7. Right-click the sketch and click Finish Sketch.

The new dimension feature is created with the style you selected. If the edit sketch has two points, then a simple aligned feature is created. If the sketch has three points, then an aligned dimension feature is created.

The dimension feature points that the vertices represent will be determined by the order in which you entered them into the edit sketch. The vertex first entered will be used as the beginning dimension point. The second vertex entered will be used as the end dimension point. If the edit sketch has three vertices, the third vertex will be used as the dimension line height point.

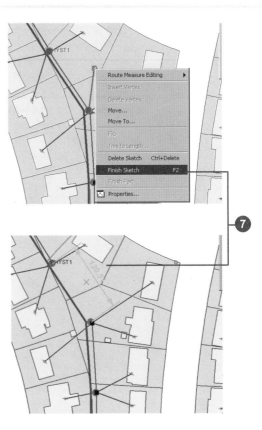

Creating a dimension feature with the free linear construction method

1. Follow steps 1–7 for 'Creating a simple aligned dimension feature' in this chapter.

2. Click the Construction dropdown arrow and click Free Linear.

3. Click the map at the beginning dimension point to start the edit sketch.

   As you move the cursor, the dimension feature won't dynamically draw itself.

4. Use ArcMap sketch tools and construction methods to enter the end dimension point. ▶

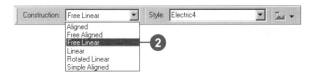

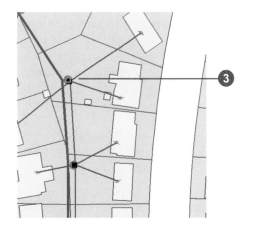

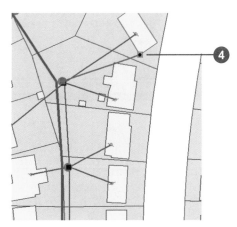

ArcInfo and ArcEditor

Tip

Extension line angle

When creating rotated linear dimensions, the extension line angle is calculated such that the dimension line is parallel to the line between the third and fourth construction points.

5. Use ArcMap sketch tools and construction methods to enter the point where you want the dimension line to be.

   If you are creating a horizontal or vertical linear dimension feature, skip to step 7.

6. Use ArcMap sketch tools and construction methods to enter the point that describes the extension line angle. ▶

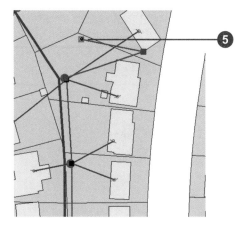

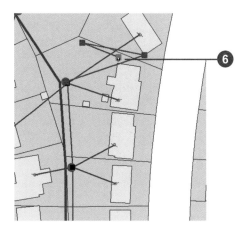

7. If your sketch has more than four vertices or has any vertices that do not represent the beginning or end dimension point, dimension line height, or extension line angle, you must delete them before continuing to step 8.

8. Right-click the sketch and click Finish Sketch.

The new dimension feature is created with the style you selected. If the edit sketch has three points, then a vertical or horizontal linear dimension feature is created. If the sketch has four points, then a rotated linear dimension feature is created.

The dimension feature points that the vertices represented will be determined by the order in which you entered them into the edit sketch. The vertex first entered will be used as the beginning dimension point. The second vertex entered will be used as the end dimension point. The third vertex will be used as the dimension line height point. If the edit sketch has four vertices, the fourth vertex will be used to describe the extension line angle.

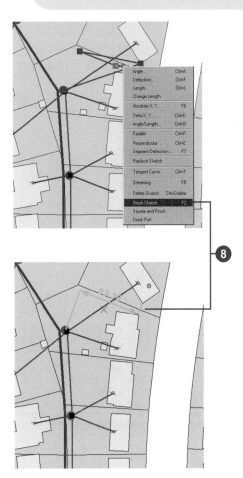

Tip

Autodimension tools

The Dimension Edge tool only creates linear dimension features by automatically using vertices on existing features for their beginning and end dimension points.

Tip

The Dimension Edge tool and diagonal features

To use the Dimension Edge tool to obtain diagonal measurements, after clicking on the line, position the cursor over the beginning vertex of the line segment. The diagonal measurement will appear.

Creating a dimension feature with the Dimension Edge tool

1. Follow steps 1–7 for 'Creating a simple aligned dimension feature' in this chapter.

2. Select the feature whose edge you want to use as the baseline for your new dimension feature.

3. Click the Tool Palette dropdown arrow and click the Dimension Edge tool.

4. Click the edge you want to use as the baseline for your dimension feature.

   As you move your mouse, the new dimension dynamically draws itself with the beginning and end dimension points fixed at the ends of the edge you clicked; the height of the dimension line changes.

   If you move your mouse to the left or right of the baseline, a vertical linear dimension feature is shown. If you move your mouse above or below the baseline, a horizontal linear dimension feature is shown.

5. Click the map where you want the dimension line to be.

   The sketch is automatically finished and a new linear dimension feature is created with the style you selected.

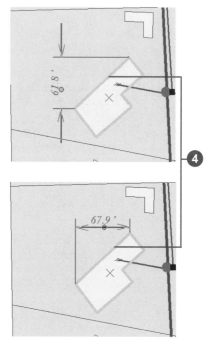

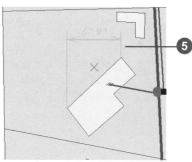

Creating two dimension features with the Perpendicular Dimensions tool

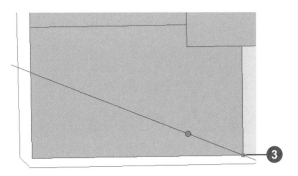

1. Follow steps 1–7 for 'Creating a simple aligned dimension feature' in this chapter.

2. Click the Tool Palette dropdown arrow and click the Perpendicular Dimensions tool.

3. Click the map at the beginning dimension point to start the edit sketch.

   A line will appear on the map that runs through the first vertex placed and the location of the mouse pointer.

4. Click the map again to establish the angle of the first dimension feature.

   As the mouse pointer is moved away from the first line, two dimension features will appear. The first will be along the established line and the second will run perpendicular from the line to the location of the mouse pointer. ▶

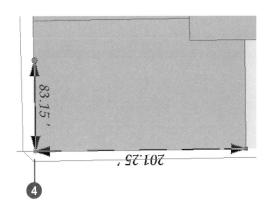

5. Click the map once again to establish the length of the perpendicular measurement.

This will complete the two dimension features.

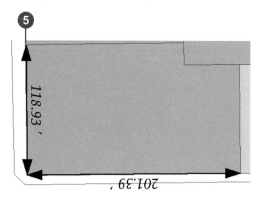

Creating a dimension feature with the Baseline Dimension tool

1. Follow steps 1–7 for 'Creating a simple aligned dimension feature' in this chapter.

2. Select the dimension feature whose beginning dimension point you want to use as the beginning dimension point for your new dimension feature.

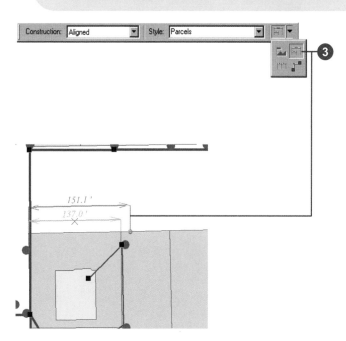

3. Click the Autodimension tool palette dropdown arrow and click the Baseline Dimension tool.

   As you move your mouse, the new dimension feature dynamically draws itself with the beginning dimension point fixed at the beginning dimension point of the dimension feature you selected in step 2. The height is fixed at the height of the dimension feature you selected, plus the baseline height for the style you selected in step 2.

   The end dimension point changes as you move your mouse, keeping the baseline for the new dimension feature parallel to the baseline of the dimension feature you selected in step 2. ▶

Baseline height

For a dimension feature created with the Baseline Dimension tool, the height of the dimension line will be controlled by the baseline height property of its style.

The baseline height is only used for creating dimension features. If you change an existing dimension feature's style to a style with a different baseline height, the height of the dimension line will not change.

For more information about styles and how to set the baseline height property, see Building a Geodatabase.

4. Click the map where you want the end dimension point to be.

The sketch is automatically finished, and a new dimension feature is created with the style you selected. The dimension type will be the same as the dimension feature you selected in step 2.

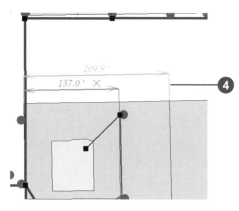

Creating a dimension feature with the Continue Dimension tool

1. Follow steps 1–7 for 'Creating a simple aligned dimension feature' in this chapter.

2. Select the dimension feature whose end dimension point you want to use as the beginning dimension point for your new dimension feature.

3. Click the Tool Palette dropdown arrow and click the Continue Dimension tool.

   As you move your mouse, the new dimension feature dynamically draws itself with the beginning dimension point fixed at the end dimension point of the dimension feature you selected in step 2. The height is also fixed at the height of the dimension feature you selected in step 2.

   The end dimension point changes as you move your mouse, keeping the baseline for the new dimension feature parallel to the baseline of the dimension feature you selected in step 2. ▶

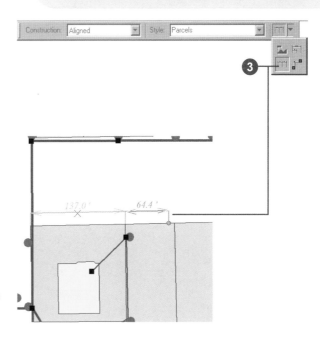

4. Click the map where you want the end dimension point to be.

The sketch is automatically finished, and a new dimension feature is created with the style you selected. The dimension type will be the same as the dimension feature you selected in step 2.

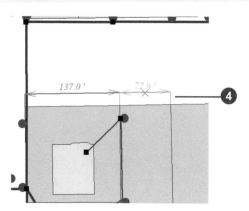

Modifying dimension features

Modifying the dimension feature geometry goes beyond modifying the dimension line height. You can also modify the beginning dimension point, the end dimension point, and the dimension text placement. You can use the Edit tool with the Modify Feature task or the Attributes dialog box to modify dimension feature geometry.

The Attributes dialog box can be used to modify geometry and style. From the Attributes dialog box, you can modify:

- Dimension line display
- Dimension line arrow symbol display
- Extension line display
- Extension line angle
- Dimension text value

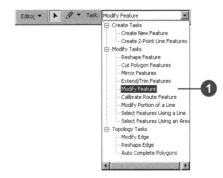

Tip

Modifying perpendicular dimensions

Once the perpendicular dimensions have been created, they act independently of one another and can be selected and modified as described in this chapter.

Modifying a dimension feature's geometry

1. Click the Task dropdown arrow and click Modify Feature.

2. Click the Edit tool and click the dimension feature whose geometry you want to modify.

3. Position the pointer over the vertex that corresponds to the aspect of the dimension's geometry you want to modify.

4. Click and drag the vertex to the desired location.

   As you move your mouse, the dimension feature dynamically updates itself so you can see how the feature will look after you have modified its geometry. ▶

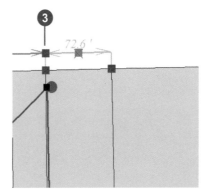

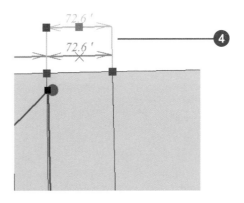

Modifying a dimension feature's geometry attributes

In addition to using the Edit tool with the Modify Feature task, you can also use the Attributes dialog box to modify the dimension feature's geometry.

5. Right-click over any part of the sketch and click Finish Sketch.

   The dimension feature's geometry is updated.

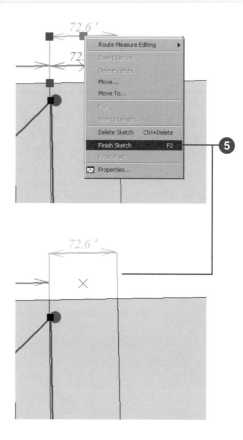

Modifying a dimension feature's style

1. Click the Edit tool and click the dimension feature whose style you want to modify.

2. Click the Attributes button.

   The Attributes dialog box appears. Notice that there is a special Attributes dialog box for modifying the attributes of a dimension feature.

3. Click the Dimension Style dropdown list and click the dimension style you want to assign to this feature. ▶

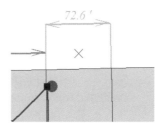

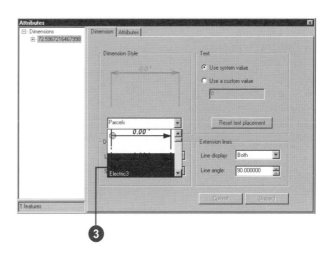

4. Click Commit.

   The dimension feature updates itself to reflect the new style.

5. Click the Close button to close the Attributes dialog box.

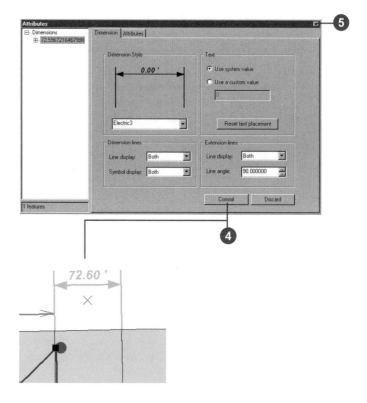

Working with a versioned geodatabase

15

With ArcGIS, multiple users can access geographic data in a geodatabase through *versioning*. Versioning lets users simultaneously create multiple, persistent representations of the database without data replication. Users can edit the same features or rows without explicitly applying locks to prohibit other users from modifying the same data.

An organization can use versioning to manage alternative engineering designs, solve complex what-if scenarios without impacting the corporate database, and create point-in-time representations of the database.

Primarily, versioning simplifies the editing experience. Multiple users can directly modify the database without having to extract data or lock features and rows before editing. If, by chance, the same features are modified, a conflict resolution dialog box guides the user through the process of determining the feature's correct representation and attributes.

Versioned databases may contain topologies. For more information on how versioning affects topologies, see *Building a Geodatabase*.

Versioned databases may also be the check-out databases for disconnected editors. For more on using a versioned database for disconnected editing, see *Building a Geodatabase*.

ArcInfo and ArcEditor

Integrating versioning with your organization's work flow

The geodatabase and versioning provide organizations with advanced data storage techniques that revolutionize the *work flow* process in many applications where spatial information is used. Engineers can generate design alternatives using the entire database. Spatial analysts can perform complex what-if scenarios without affecting the current representation of the database. Database administrators can create historical snapshots of the database for archiving or database recovery.

In the long run, an organization benefits from implementing a versioned database. The data is centrally located in one corporate database. There is never a need to extract units of the database to update, or lock, map sheets or individual features. These factors simplify the administrative process.

The work flow process

The evolution of the work flow process—how projects or *work orders* transpire over time—varies greatly from organization to organization and throughout each sector of the business community. Therefore, the geodatabase's versioning process has been designed to be flexible enough to accommodate the most basic of work flow processes as well as the most complex and to be sufficiently restrictive with or without additional application customization.

Common work flow processes usually progress in discrete stages. At each stage, different requirements or business rules may be enforced. Typically, during each stage of the process, the project or work order is associated by a named stage. For example, within the utility domain, common stages include working, proposed, accepted, under construction, and as built. The process is essentially cyclical. The work order is initially generated and assigned to an engineer and modified over time as it progresses from stage to stage, and finally the changes are posted, or applied, back to the corporate database.

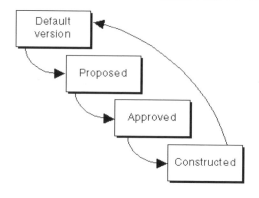

A common work flow process evolving through each stage of a project

This is one example of how versioning can help simplify the work flow process. Because the work flow process may span days, months, and even years, the corporate database requires continuous availability for daily operations. If a work order applied restrictive locks to the data involved in the process, other database users might not be able to perform their daily work assignments.

To implement your work flow in the geodatabase, versions can be created to correspond with each stage of the work flow process. Alternatively, you may want to create one version for each work order and modify the version's name to represent the current stage as the process proceeds through each step.

The current structure of your organization's work flow significantly influences how the geodatabase's versioning process is implemented to manage your spatial transactions. The flexibility and openness of the system allows you to determine the best solution to meet the requirements of your business processes.

The remaining sections of this chapter will help illustrate how to use ArcCatalog and ArcMap to perform various versioning tasks. In particular, the last section provides examples of how an organization can implement work flow processes using the geodatabase's versioning capabilities. For additional details on managing your organization's work flow with versions, read *Modeling Our World*.

ArcInfo and ArcEditor

Registering data as versioned

Before editing feature datasets, feature classes, and tables, you must first register the data as versioned in ArcCatalog.

Making a feature class or table multiversioned requires a unique integer field. Only the owner of the data may register or unregister the object as versioned.

When unregistering a dataset or feature class as versioned in ArcCatalog, a warning dialog box may appear informing you that outstanding edits still remain in existing versions. Therefore, unregistering the class as versioned will remove all the edits. To preserve the edits, you must compress the database.

Tip

Registering data as versioned

Registering a feature dataset as versioned registers all feature classes within the feature dataset as versioned.

1. In the ArcCatalog tree, right-click the feature dataset, feature class, or table you want to register as versioned.

2. Click Register As Versioned.

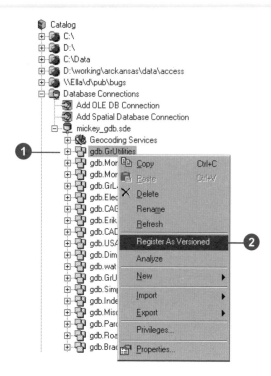

Creating and administering versions in ArcCatalog

ArcCatalog lets you create new versions, rename existing versions, delete versions, and modify version properties. These administrative tasks are accomplished using the Version Manager dialog box.

Initially, the database consists of one version named DEFAULT owned by the ArcSDE administrative user. The new versions that are created are always based on an existing version. When the new version is created, it is identical to the version from which it was derived. Over time, the versions will diverge as changes are made to the parent version and to the new version.

A version consists of several properties: an alphanumeric name, an owner, an optional description, the creation date, the last modified date, the parent version, and the version's permission. ▶

Creating a new version

1. Create a new connection to the database in ArcCatalog with the Add SDE Connection dialog box.

2. Right-click your database connection in the Catalog tree and click Versions. ▶

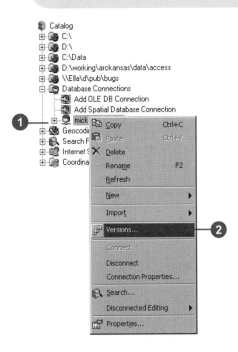

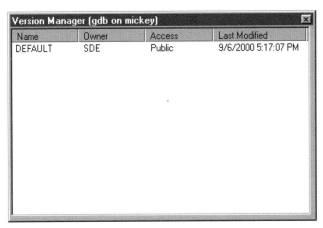

A version's permission can only be changed by its owner. The available permission settings are:

- Private—only the owner may view the version and modify available feature classes.

- Protected—any user may view the version, but only the owner may modify available feature classes.

- Public—any user may view the version and modify available feature classes.

Only the version's owner can rename, delete, or alter the version. A parent version cannot be deleted until all dependent child versions are first deleted.

To improve database performance, the database should be compressed periodically. Compressing the database removes all unreferenced database states and redundant rows. Only the ArcSDE administrator can perform this task. For additional details, see the 'Versioning scenarios' section at the end of this chapter. ▶

3. Right-click a version and click New.

4. Type the new version's name.

5. Type a description.

6. Click the appropriate permission type; the default is Private.

7. Click OK.

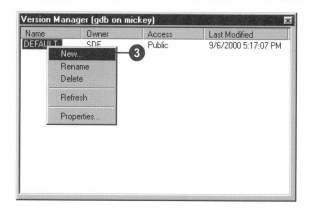

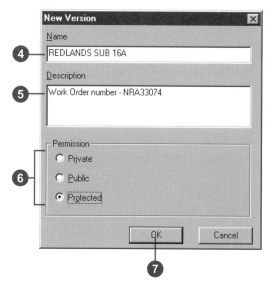

Finally, after compressing the database or editing the data, the Analyze command should be executed to update the database statistics for each dataset or feature class. This will help improve display and query performance.

Descriptions

Descriptions are useful for providing meaningful information regarding the version's purpose.

Sorting versions

In the Version Manager dialog box, you can sort versions by clicking a column heading.

Renaming a version

1. Right-click your database connection and click Versions.

2. Right-click the version you want to rename and click Rename.

3. Type a new name and press Enter.

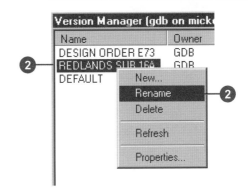

Deleting a version

1. Right-click your database connection and click Versions.

2. Right-click the version you want to delete.

3. Click Delete or press Delete on your keyboard.

ArcInfo and ArcEditor

Tip

Refresh

Use the Refresh command to update the properties of each version with current values.

Changing a version's properties

1. Right-click your database connection and click Versions.

2. Right-click a version.

3. Click Properties.

4. Type the new description.

5. Click the new permission type.

6. Click OK.

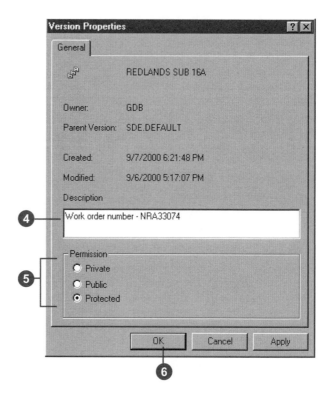

See Also

For more information on how to customize ArcCatalog, see Using ArcCatalog *and* Exploring ArcObjects.

Adding the Compress command to ArcCatalog

1. In ArcCatalog, click View, point to Toolbars, and click Customize.

2. Check Context Menus in the list of toolbars. ▶

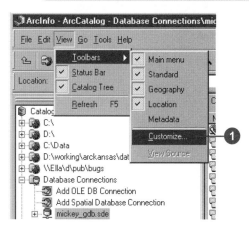

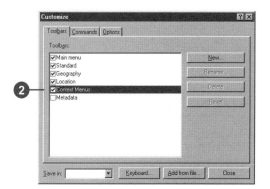

3. Click the Context Menus menu.

4. Click the arrow next to the Remote Database Context Menu.

   The Remote Database Context Menu submenu will remain open.

5. Click the Commands tab in the Customize dialog box.

6. Click Geodatabase tools.

7. Click and drag the Compress Database command from the Commands list and drop it on the Remote Database Context Menu submenu.

   The command appears in the context menu.

8. Click Close on the Customize dialog box.

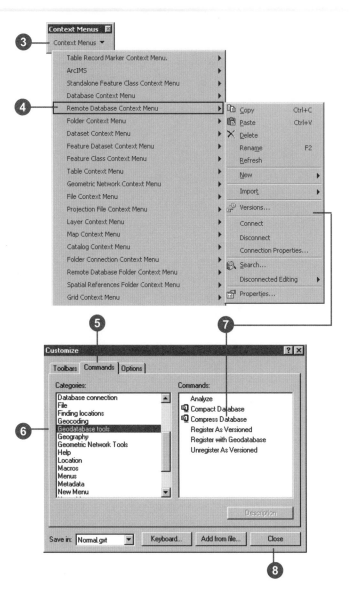

Compressing the database

1. In ArcCatalog, create a new database connection as the ArcSDE administrative user.

2. Right-click the new database connection and click Compress Database.

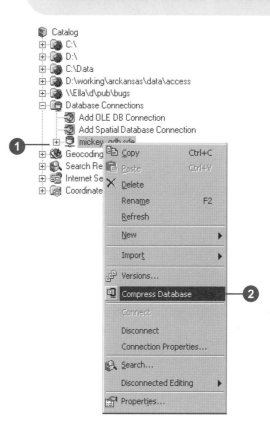

ArcInfo and ArcEditor

Working with versions in ArcMap

In ArcMap, you can view and work with multiple versions simultaneously, create new versions, and change the feature classes or tables from one version to another version. You can also use the version manager, refresh a version's *workspace* connection, and modify available feature classes in ArcMap.

To create a new version, at least one version must be present in the map. If multiple versions are present, you will need to specify the parent version. The newly created version will then be identical to the parent version.

Changing versions allows you to quickly navigate between two versions by changing the feature classes currently in the map. This simplifies the process of viewing the differences between feature classes or performing an analysis with two versions. ▶

Tip

Creating new versions
Create alternative versions as online backups to the original version.

Creating a new version in ArcMap

1. Add the Versioning toolbar to the map.

2. Click the Create New Version button. At least one version is required to be in ArcMap prior to the command becoming enabled.

3. Click the Parent Version dropdown arrow and click the parent version from which you want to create the new version.

4. Type the new version's name.

5. Optionally, type a description.

6. Click the appropriate permission type.

7. Optionally, if you are not currently editing, check the check box to switch the parent version to the new version.

8. Click OK.

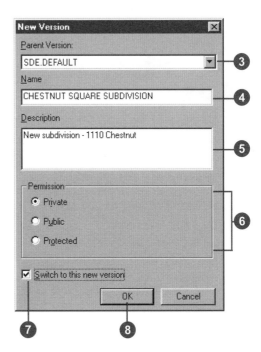

When a version workspace is changed to a different version, all feature classes present in the workspace will represent the target version.

Two methods are available in ArcMap for changing versions. You can change versions from the Versioning toolbar or in the table of contents.

When you work in a multiuser environment, the database may be modified by another user at the same time you're viewing the database. Therefore, the feature classes present in ArcMap may become outdated.

To update feature classes in ArcMap, you can refresh one or all of the version workspaces present by clicking the Refresh button on the Versioning toolbar. While you are editing, the Refresh button is unavailable.

You can have as many versions in the map as needed, but you can only edit one version per edit session.

Tip

The Change Version command

Use the Change Version command instead of adding multiple version workspaces to your map document.

Changing versions

1. Click the Source tab at the bottom of the ArcMap table of contents to list the workspaces in your map.

2. Right-click a version workspace.

3. Click Change Version.

4. Click the version to which you want to change.

5. Click OK.

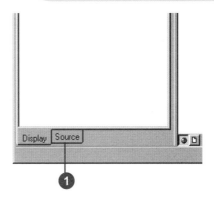

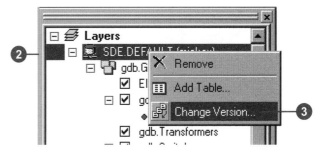

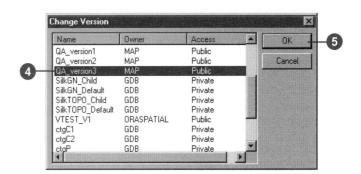

ArcInfo and ArcEditor

Tip

Preserving a version

If you need to preserve a current representation of the database, create a new version before refreshing.

Refreshing a workspace

1. Click the Refresh button on the Versioning toolbar.

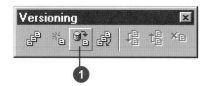

Editing and conflict resolution

The geodatabase is designed to efficiently manage and support long *transactions* using versions. The geodatabase also allows multiple users to edit the same version at the same time. Each edit session in ArcMap is its own representation of the version until you save. Saving the edit session applies your modifications to the version, making these changes immediately accessible in the database.

When multiple users simultaneously edit a version or *reconcile* two versions, *conflicts* can occur. Reconciling is the process of merging two versions. Conflicts occur when the same feature or topologically related features are edited by two or more users and the database is unclear about which representation is valid. Conflicts are rare but can occur when overlapping geographic areas in the database are edited. To ensure database integrity, the geodatabase detects when a feature has been edited in two versions and reports it as a conflict. ArcMap provides the necessary tools for conflict resolution, but your interaction is still required to make the final decision as to the feature's correct representation.

ArcMap provides tools to resolve conflicts and reconcile and *post* versions. The next sections explain these capabilities in more detail.

Reconcile

The Reconcile button in ArcMap merges all modifications between the current edit session and a target version you select. Any differences between the features in the target version and the features in the edit session are applied to the edit session. Differences can consist of newly inserted, deleted, or updated features. The reconcile process detects these differences and discovers any conflicts. If conflicts exist, a message is displayed followed by the conflict resolution dialog box. Reconciling happens before posting a version to a target version. A target

version is any version in the direct ancestry of the version, such as the parent version or the DEFAULT version.

In addition, the reconcile process requires that you are the only user currently editing the version and that you are the only user able to edit the version throughout the reconcile process until you save or post. If another user is simultaneously editing the version or attempts to start editing since you have reconciled, an error message will inform you that the version is currently in use.

The reconcile process requires that you have full permissions to all the feature classes that have been modified in the version being edited. If a feature class is modified in the version for which you do not have update privileges, an error message appears. You will not be able to reconcile the versions; a user with adequate permissions to perform the reconcile must do this for you.

For example, suppose you have completed your changes in a version and need to post the version to the DEFAULT version. You must first reconcile the version with a target version you select, resolve any conflicts if necessary, then post.

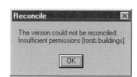

An error message appears when you do not have permissions to a feature class to reconcile versions.

Autoreconciliation

Suppose that since you started editing a version, another user has saved edits to the same version. Enabling or disabling autoreconciliation affects whether you are notified of the other user's edits when you save yours. If you want to be notified so you can review the results of the merge before saving your edits, disable autoreconciliation. If you do not want to be notified and want to save without reviewing the results of the merge, enable autoreconciliation. Regardless of how you set autoreconciliation, ArcMap will always notify you if there are conflicts when you save.

This message displays if you disable autoreconciliation and attempt to save after another user has saved.

Post

You can post a version after you have first performed a reconcile. Once the edit session has reconciled with a target version, clicking the Post button synchronizes the version with the reconciled version and performs a save. Posting cannot be undone, as you are applying changes to a version that you are not currently editing. If the reconciled version is modified between reconciling and posting, you will be notified to reconcile again before posting.

This message indicates that the target version has been modified since the reconciliation; reconcile again before posting.

Conflicts

Conflicts occur when the same feature, or topologically related features or relationship classes, is modified in two versions: the current version being edited and a target version. Conflict detection only occurs during the reconciliation process. If conflicts are detected, a message appears followed by the conflict resolution dialog box.

There are three types of conflicts that can occur when an edit version is reconciled with a target version: update–update, update–delete, and delete–update. An update–update conflict occurs when the same feature has been updated in each version. An update–delete conflict occurs when a feature has been updated in the edit version and deleted in the reconcile version. A delete–update conflict occurs when a feature has been deleted in the edit version and updated in the reconcile version.

When conflicts are detected, the parent version's feature representation takes precedence over the edit session's representation. Therefore, all conflicting features in the current edit session are replaced by their representation in the parent version. If multiple users are editing the same version and conflicts are detected, the feature that was first saved, the current version's representation, is preserved by replacing the edit session's feature representation. ArcMap ensures database integrity by forcing you to interactively inspect each conflict and resolve the conflict by replacing the feature in the current version with your edit session's representation.

Conflict resolution

Once conflicts are detected, a conflict resolution dialog box appears, containing all the conflict classes and their features or rows in conflict. The conflict resolution dialog box allows you to interactively resolve conflicts at the level of the feature class or individual feature. Resolving the conflict implies that you will make a decision as to the feature's correct representation; this could mean doing nothing at all if you are satisfied with the current feature's representation.

You can choose from three representations of the conflicting feature or row to resolve the conflict. The pre-edit version is the feature's representation when you initially started editing, before making any changes. The edit session version represents the feature as it existed before you performed the reconcile. The last representation is the conflict version, the feature's representation in the conflicting version.

Selecting a feature class or individual feature displays any of the three representations of the feature in the map. The pre-edit's version is displayed in yellow, the edit session's version is displayed in green, and the conflict's version is displayed in red. You can also optionally enable or disable the display settings for each version—pre-edit, edit session, and conflict—by clicking the Display command on the context menu and checking or unchecking the corresponding version.

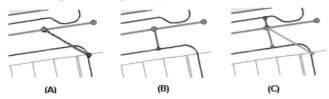

(A)   (B)   (C)

The lateral in blue as it existed prior to editing (A), the lateral after being modified (B), and the three representations during conflict resolution (C).

When you select a feature in the conflict resolution dialog box, each version's representation of the feature's or row's attributes is listed in the bottom half of the box. A red dot to the left of the field name identifies why the feature is a conflict. For example, if the feature's geometry was edited in each version, a red dot appears next to the shape field. The same principle holds true for

attribute conflicts. If a feature has been deleted in either version, <deleted> appears for that version's attribute value. Therefore, a red dot marks each column, signifying that each column is an update/delete or a delete/update conflict.

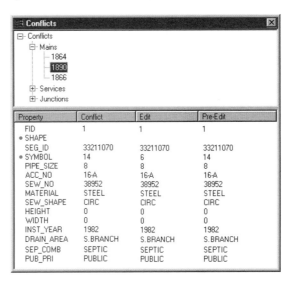

This conflict resolution dialog box shows three feature classes with conflicts and a feature with each of its version's attributes.

Resolving a conflict implies that you made a conscious decision about the feature's correct representation. You can select the feature in the conflict resolution dialog box and replace the current feature in the map with any of the three representations of the feature. This allows you to quickly update and replace conflicting features. If further modifications are required, you can simply use any of the ArcMap editing tools to update the feature.

Conflicts with geometric networks, feature-linked annotation, relationships, and topology

Resolving conflicts with features that are related to other features through geometric networks, feature-linked annotation, and relationship classes is different from resolving conflicts with simple feature classes. Because each of these feature classes has specific geodatabase behaviors that can impact other feature classes, resolving a feature conflict may impact related features.

When you edit network features, changes to the geometric network and to the logical network may create conflicts.

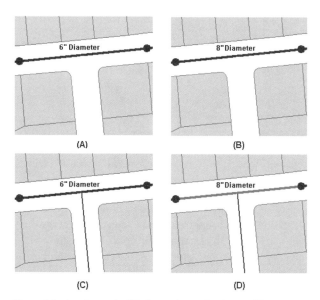

(A)

(B)

(C)

(D)

The original water main (A), the water main changed to an 8-inch diameter in the first edit session (B), a new service was inserted in the second edit session (C), and the water main in red is shown as a conflict (D).

For example, when you add a service to a main, the main will not be physically split in the geometric network but will be split in the logical network. Therefore, while you have not directly edited the main's geometry, it has been edited logically. If the target version you are reconciling has also modified the main, then the new service you inserted will create a conflict with the main.

Resolving a conflict involving geometric network feature classes requires understanding how the Replace With command in the conflict resolution dialog box will update the existing network topology present in the edit session.

In the previous example, two users modified the water main—one by changing an attribute and the other by connecting a new service. Resolving the conflict would merely require investigating the differences and seeing that the conflict is valid and no further resolution is required. Since the main contains the correct attribute for the diameter, the new service is correctly connected to the main. But there are cases when resolving conflicts involving a junction feature class will also update the connected network edge.

Working with feature-linked annotation requires remembering one rule: when replacing a feature that has feature-linked annotation, both the feature and the annotation are replaced with the new feature and annotation. You may have to further edit the new annotation. For example, you may encounter a conflict in which you have moved a feature and repositioned its annotation. The conflict version has performed the same edit, moving the feature and rotating the annotation. Your decision is to replace the feature with the conflict version's feature. This action deletes the existing feature-linked annotation, inserts the conflict feature, and creates a new annotation. You will then need to further edit the new annotation by moving and rotating it as necessary.

Relationships have similar dependencies to feature-linked annotation. Deleting a feature from an origin relationship class may trigger a message to delete a feature from the destination relationship class. Therefore, be aware of the ramifications of simply replacing conflicts involving feature classes that participate in relationship classes.

An example of when a conflict can arise between relationship classes is if you were to update the origin class primary field, breaking the relationship in version A. At the same time, in version B, the destination class-related feature is also updated. When you reconcile the versions, since the destination class is dependent on the origin class, a conflict is detected. A similar example is if you were to delete a pole that has a relationship to a transformer, the transformer is also deleted. But in the conflict version, the transformer's attributes are edited. An update–delete conflict would be detected when reconciled.

For more information on topologies, see Chapter 4, 'Editing topology', or *Building a Geodatabase*.

ArcInfo and ArcEditor

Editing a version

You use the versioning toolbar in ArcMap to reconcile versions, resolve conflicts, and post versions.

When you start editing, if multiple versions are present in the map, you will have to select one version. Starting an edit session on a version creates a new, unnamed, temporary version that exists until you save or end the edit session. You are the only user who can see your changes until you explicitly save.

When saving an edit session, you have an option to enable or disable autoreconciliation. If enabled, autoreconciliation will automatically reconcile your edit session with the version's current database state and save, making your changes available to others using the database. If autoreconciliation is not enabled, then when you save, your edit session will be reconciled with the version's current database state. A message will inform you that the edit session has been reconciled but has not been saved. This will only occur if a second user has also edited the version and saved since you started editing. You will need to save again to make your ▶

Enabling and disabling autoreconciliation

1. Click Editor and click Start Editing.

2. Click Editor and click Options.

3. Click the Versioning tab.

4. Check the box to enable or disable autoreconciliation.

5. Click OK.

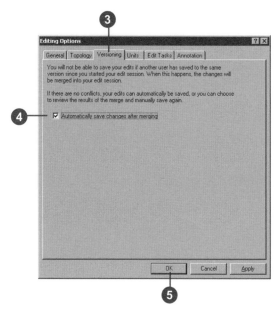

changes available to others using the database.

Based on your organization's work flow, you may eventually need to reconcile two versions. Reconciliation is the process of merging features from a target version into the current edit session. Reconciliation must be done before posting changes to another version.

During reconciliation, conflicts may be discovered. Conflicts arise when the same feature is updated in each version or updated in one and deleted in the other.

When conflicts arise, an interactive conflict resolution dialog box will provide the tools necessary to resolve the conflicts. For each conflict, you can choose whether to replace the feature in your edit session with the conflict version, the version from your edit session, or the version as it existed at the beginning of your edit session.

Once you have successfully completed the reconciliation, you can post the version. The post operation synchronizes your edit session with the target version. They are then identical.

Reconciling

1. Click the Reconcile button on the Versioning toolbar.
2. Click the target version.
3. Click OK.

Posting

1. Click the Post button on the Versioning toolbar.

ArcInfo and ArcEditor

Displaying conflicts

1. Click the Conflicts button on the Versioning toolbar.

2. Right-click Conflicts and click Display.

3. Check a box to display a conflict category.

4. Click OK.

5. Click the Close button to close the Conflicts dialog box.

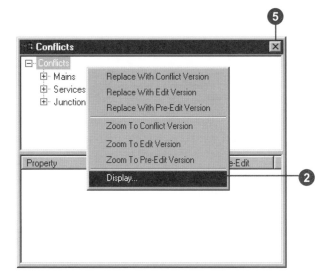

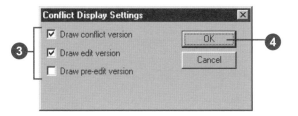

See Also

For information on typology and versioning, see Building a Geodatabase.

Resolving conflicts

1. Click the Conflicts button on the Versioning toolbar.

2. Click a feature class.

3. Click a feature and right-click to display the context menu.

4. Click the appropriate Replace With command to resolve the conflict.

5. Click the Close button to close the Conflicts dialog box.

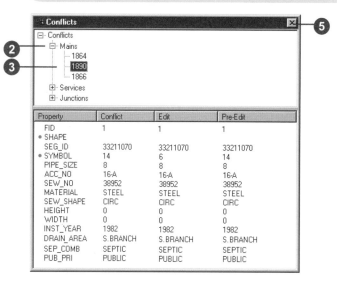

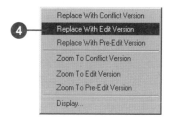

ArcInfo and ArcEditor

Versioning scenarios

The following scenarios show how an organization can implement its work flow process using a versioned database. These examples demonstrate several techniques available for performing long transactions in a multiuser environment. It is likely that organizations will, in some manner, use each of these techniques, depending on the task.

Scenario 1: Simple database modifications

Task: Multiple users are concurrently editing the database, performing common map sheet changes, such as inserting new features, updating attributes, and removing out-of-date facilities.

Solution: Users can simply connect to the DEFAULT version, simultaneously, start editing, and save their changes when their work is complete. Users do not have to create new versions to modify the database. If another user has edited the DEFAULT version since the current user has started editing, the user saving is notified that the version has been changed, and therefore, the version will need to be saved again. Users may bypass this warning message by enabling autoreconciliation in the ArcMap Options dialog box. In addition, if two users modify the same feature during their edit sessions, the second user to save encounters a conflict. The user then has to decide what the feature's correct representation is and save the edit session.

Scenario 2: Transactions spanning multiple days

Task: Update the database to incorporate new and updated facilities in the field, which will likely require multiple edit sessions and a couple of days to complete.

Solution: A user creates and switches to a new version derived from the DEFAULT version. The user starts editing the new version and begins modifying features and saving as required. The user can resume the edit session, as appropriate, the following day or possibly the following week. When the changes

are complete and ready to be posted to the DEFAULT version, the user must first click the Reconcile button on the Versioning toolbar. If conflicts are detected, the user can resolve the differences and complete the transaction by clicking the Post button. The posting process applies all the changes in the user's version to the DEFAULT version. The user can then delete the version.

Scenario 3: A work flow process

Task: Create individual versions for each step or stage of the work order and work flow process and post the work order to the database.

Solution: A user or supervisor creates a new version derived from the DEFAULT version. The user starts editing the new version and begins modifying features or creating a new design. When the user has completed the design or proposed modifications, the work order can be submitted to a supervisor for review. At this time, a new version can be created to ensure the preservation of the initial design. The new version can then be further modified or adjusted as required. Once the work order has been approved for construction, another version can be created. The purpose of this version is to reflect any changes that may occur while the work order is being constructed in the field. Finally, as the construction is completed and the new facilities are in service, the work order must be posted to the database. A user can then start editing the work order, perform a reconcile with the DEFAULT version, resolve any conflicts, if necessary, and post.

The solution allows the organization to create new versions of the work order for each step of the project—the initial design or proposed version, a working or accepted version, and a version for the construction phase. Each version is preserved and available to review for historical purposes. The final step is to post the constructed version to the database. The project completes a full circle from start to finish, creating individual versions at each step.

Scenario 4: Restricting permissions to the database

Task: The organization's supervisor has restricted write access to the DEFAULT version, requiring managerial review of each user's edits prior to posting the changes to the database.

Solution: To restrict write permissions to the database (the DEFAULT version), the ArcSDE administrative user can set the permission of the DEFAULT version to protected using the version manager. This allows users to continue to view the DEFAULT version but does not allow users to start editing the version. Therefore, users will need to create new versions for editing the database, similar to Scenario 2. When a user has completed and saved the edit session, the ArcSDE administrator can reconcile the version with the DEFAULT version. To accomplish this task, the manager who connects to the database as the ArcSDE administrator starts editing the user's version and clicks the Reconcile button. The process will merge all the changes in the user's version and the DEFAULT version. If conflicts are detected, the manager can resolve the conflicts and save the edit session. Once the edits are acceptable to the manager, the version is ready to be posted to the DEFAULT version. The ArcSDE administrative user can then start editing the version, perform a reconcile, and post the version. The user's version can then be deleted.

Scenario 5: Compressing the database

Task: The geodatabase has been edited for an extended time, and the number of database states and rows in each feature classes' delta tables has significantly increased. How do you improve performance by running the Compress command?

Solution: The *Compress* command will remove all database states that are no longer referenced by a version and move all the rows in the delta tables, which are common to all versions, to the base table. To achieve the maximum benefit when running the Compress command, you can optionally first reconcile, post, and delete each version with the DEFAULT version. Sometimes this may not be a reasonable option based on your organization's work flow. At minimum, to improve performance, simply reconcile each version with the DEFAULT version and save, then perform the compress. This will ensure that all the edits in the DEFAULT version will be compressed from the delta tables to the business table. Remember, the Compress command can still be executed without first reconciling, posting, and deleting each version, but the benefits may not be as noticeable.

Glossary

absolute mode

See digitizing mode.

active data frame

The data frame currently being worked on—for example, the data frame to which layers are being added. The active data frame is highlighted on the map, and its name is shown in bold text in the table of contents.

alias

An alternative name specified for fields, tables, and feature classes that is more descriptive and user-friendly than the actual name of these items. On computer networks, a single e-mail alias may refer to a group of e-mail addresses. In database management systems, aliases can contain characters, such as spaces, that can't be included in the actual names.

aligned dimension

A drafting symbol that runs parallel to the baseline and indicates the true distance between begin and end dimension points. ArcInfo supports aligned dimension and linear dimension.

annotation

Descriptive text used to label features on or around a map. Information stored for annotation includes a text string, a position at which it can be displayed, and display characteristics.

annotation construction methods

Procedures that dictate what type of annotation feature is created and the number of points required to create new annotation features. Construction methods include horizontal, straight, curved, leader line, and follow feature

annotation feature class

A geodatabase feature class that stores text or graphics that provide additional information about features or general areas of a map (annotation). An annotation feature class may be linked to another feature class, so that edits to the features are reflected in the annotation (feature-linked annotation). Annotation in a geodatabase is edited during an edit session, using the tools on the Annotation toolbar.

annotation target

In ArcMap, the annotation group or feature class in a map document where new annotation will be created when using the New Text tools on the Draw toolbar or when copy-pasting annotation. Annotation created with the Annotation Edit tools is created in the current Editing target, not in the annotation target.

ArcInfo workspace

A file-based collection of coverages, grids, triangulated irregular networks (TINs), or shapefiles stored as a directory of folders in the file system.

aspect

The compass direction in which a topographic slope faces, usually expressed in terms of degrees from the north. Aspect can be generated from continuous elevation surfaces. The aspect recorded for a TIN face is the steepest downslope direction of the face. The aspect of a cell in a raster is the steepest downslope direction of a plane defined by the cell and its eight surrounding neighbors.

asynchronous

Not synchronous; that is, not happening, existing, or arising at the same time. For example, in disconnected editing, modifying the properties of a check-out is an asynchronous operation; changes made to the check-out in a master geodatabase do not affect the associated check-out in a check-out geodatabase.

attribute

Information about a geographic feature in a GIS, generally stored in a table and linked to the feature by a unique identifier. For example, attributes of a river might include its name, length, and average depth.

attribute domain

In a geodatabase, a mechanism for enforcing data integrity. Attribute domains define what values are allowed in a field in a feature class or nonspatial attribute table. If the features or nonspatial objects have been grouped into subtypes, different attribute domains can be assigned to each of the subtypes.

attribute table

A database or tabular file containing information about a set of geographic features, usually arranged so that each row represents a feature and each column represents one feature attribute. In raster datasets, each row of an attribute table corresponds to a certain region of cells having the same value. In a GIS, attribute tables are often joined or related to spatial data layers, and the attribute values they contain can be used to find, query, and symbolize features or raster cells.

Attributes dialog box

In ArcMap, a dialog box that displays attributes of selected features for editing.

azimuth

The angle, measured in degrees, between a baseline drawn from a center point and another line drawn from the same point. Normally, the baseline points true north and the angle is measured clockwise from the baseline. Azimuth is often used to define an oblique cylindrical map projection or the angle of a geodesic between two points.

behavior

The way in which an object in a geodatabase functions or operates. Behavior rules define how geodatabase objects can be edited and drawn. Defined behaviors include, but are not limited to, validation rules, subtypes, default values, and relationships.

Bowditch rule

See compass rule.

buffer

A zone around a map feature measured in units of distance or time. A buffer is useful for proximity analysis.

CAD

A computer-based system for the design, drafting, and display of graphical information. Also known as computer-aided drafting, such systems are most commonly used to support engineering, planning, and illustrating activities.

CAD feature class

A read-only member of a CAD feature dataset, comprised of one of the following: polylines, points, polygons, multi-patch, or annotation. The feature attribute table of a CAD feature class is a virtual table comprised of select CAD graphic properties and any existing field attribute values.

centroid

The geometric center of a feature. Of a line, it is the midpoint; of a polygon, the center of area; of a three-dimensional figure, the center of volume.

check-in

The procedure that transfers a copy of data into a master geodatabase, overwriting the original copy of that data and reenabling it so it can be accessed and saved from that location.

check-out

A procedure that records the duplication of data from one geodatabase to another and disables the original data so both versions cannot be accessed or saved at the same time.

check-out geodatabase

A personal or ArcSDE geodatabase that contains data checked out from a master geodatabase.

check-out version

The data version created in a check-out geodatabase when data is checked out to that database. This version is created as copy of the synchronization version. Only the edits made to this check-out version can be checked back in to the master geodatabase. See also check-out geodatabase, master check-out version.

circle

A two-dimensional geometric shape for which the distance from the center to any point on the edge is equal; the closed plane curve defining such a shape or the surface bounded by such a curve.

circular arc

A line with two vertices, one situated at each endpoint, rather than a line composed of numerous vertices with line segments between them.

closure report

The summary of the difference between the endpoint coordinate of a traverse and the calculated endpoint.

cluster tolerance

In geodatabase feature classes, a definition for the minimum tolerated distance between vertices in the topology. Vertices that fall within the set cluster tolerance will be snapped together during the validate topology process.

clustering

A part of the topology validation process in which vertices that fall within the cluster tolerance are snapped together.

coded value domain

A type of attribute domain that defines a set of permissible values for an attribute in a geodatabase. Coded value domains consist of a code and its equivalent value. For example, for a road feature class, the numbers 1, 2 and 3 might correspond to three types of road surface: gravel, asphalt and concrete. Codes are stored in the geodatabase and corresponding values appear in the attribute table.

COGO

1. Coordinate geometry. A set of algorithms for converting survey data (bearings, distances and angles) into coordinate data.

2. Automated mapping software used in land surveying that calculates locations using distances and bearings from known reference points.

coincident

Occupying the same space. Coincident features or parts of features occupy the same space in the same plane. In geodatabase feature classes, vertices or boundaries that fall within the set cluster tolerance of one another are coincident; they are snapped together during the validate topology process.

column

The vertical dimension of a table. Each column stores the values of one type of attribute for all of the records, or rows, in the table. All the values in a given column are of the same data type; for example, number, string, BLOB, date.

compaction

See compression.

compass rule

1. Also known as the Bowditch rule, this widely used rule for adjusting a traverse assumes that the precision in angles or directions are equivalent to the precision in distances. This rule distributes the closure error in the whole traverse by changing the Northings and Eastings of each traverse point in proportion to the distance from the beginning of the traverse. More specifically, a correction factor is computed for each point as the sum of the distances along the traverse from the first point to the point in question, divided by the total length of the traverse. The correction factor at each point is multiplied by the overall closure error to get the amount of error correction distributed to the point's coordinates.

2. One of three adjustment methods available for adjusting closure error for a traverse computation. The other two methods are the transit rule and the Crandall rule.

composite relationship

A link or association between objects where the lifetime of one object controls the lifetime of its related objects. The association between highways and shield markers is a composite relationship, since shield markers can't exist without a highway.

compression

A reduction of file size for data handling and storage. Examples of such methods include quadtrees, run-length encoding, and wavelet.

computer-aided design

See CAD.

conflict

An opposing action of incompatibles that occurs when multiple users simultaneously edit a version or reconcile two versions. Conflicts occur when the same feature or topologically related features are edited in both the edit and reconciliation versions, and it is unclear in the database which representation is valid.

conflict resolution

The process of solving uncertainty within a database that occurs when two versions of the same data are edited at the same time. Conflicts can occur when multiple users simultaneously edit the same feature or topologically related features, or reconcile two versions of a dataset. Resolving a conflict requires that the user make a decision about the feature's correct representation and identify it in the Conflict Resolution dialog box.

connectivity

1. In a geodatabase, the state of edges and junctions in a logical network that controls flow, tracing, and pathfinding.

2. In a coverage, topological identification of connected arcs by recording the from-node and to-node for each arc. Arcs that share a common node are connected.

connectivity rule

A rule that constrains the type and number of network features that can be connected to one another in a geodatabase. There are two types of connectivity rules: edge–junction and edge–edge.

constraints

Limits imposed on a model to maintain data integrity. For example, in a water network model, an 8-inch pipe cannot connect to a 4-inch pipe.

construct features

In ArcMap, an edit command that takes selected features from one or more feature classes and creates new features in a target feature class. The Construct Features tool uses the input geometries of the selected features to construct polygons or lines following polygon boundaries, depending on the geometry of the target feature class.

context menu

List menus that pop up when the right mouse button is clicked in Windows applications. Some keyboards also have an application key that opens context menus.

control

In mapping, a system of points with established horizontal and vertical positions that are used as fixed references for known ground points or specific locations. The establishment of controls is one of the first steps involved in digitizing.

coordinate geometry

See COGO.

coordinate system

A fixed reference framework superimposed onto the surface of an area to designate the position of a point within it; a reference system consisting of a set of points, lines and/or surfaces, and a set of rules, used to define the positions of points in space in either two or three dimensions. The Cartesian coordinate system and the geographic coordinate system used on the earth's surface are common examples of coordinate systems.

coordinates

Values represented by x, y, and possibly z, that define a position in terms of a spatial reference framework. Coordinates are used to represent locations on the earth's surface relative to other locations.

coverage

A data model for storing geographic features using ArcInfo software. A coverage stores a set of thematically associated data considered to be a unit. It usually represents a single layer, such as soils, streams, roads, or land use. In a coverage, features are stored as both primary features (points, arcs, polygons) and secondary features (tics, links, annotation). Feature attributes are described and stored independently in feature attribute tables. Coverages cannot be edited in ArcGIS.

cracking

A part of the topology validation process in which vertices are created at the intersection of feature edges.

Crandall rule

1. A special-case, least-squares based method for adjusting the closure error in a traverse. It is most frequently used in a closed traverse that represents a parcel from a subdivision plan. This is because it ensures that tangency between courses remains intact as, for example, when applied to a tangent curve. It assumes that course directions and angles have no error, and therefore all error corrections are applied only to the distances. This method uses a least squares adjustment to distribute the closure error, and applies infinite weight to the angles or direction measurements to ensure that they are not adjusted. In some circumstances the results of this adjustment method may be unexpected, or the adjustment may not be possible. In these circumstances an alternative method is required.

2. One of three adjustment methods available for adjusting closure error for a traverse computation. The other two methods are the transit rule and the compass rule.

current task

During editing in ArcMap, a setting in the Current Task dropdown list that determines the task with which the sketch construction tools (Sketch, Arc, Distance–Distance, and Intersection) will work. The current task is set by clicking a task in the Current Task dropdown list.

custom behavior

A set of methods, functions or operations associated with a geodatabase object that has been specifically created or overridden by a developer.

custom feature

In geodatabases, a feature with specialized behavior instantiated in a class by a developer.

custom object

An object with custom behavior provided by a developer.

dangle

An endpoint of a line that is not connected to another line because the line features do not form closed loops. A dangle may be formed when the line extends too far past the line it is supposed to touch (an overshoot) or not quite far enough (an undershoot). A dangle is not always an error; for example, it can represent cul-de-sac or dead end street segments.

data

Any collection of related facts arranged in a particular format; often, the basic elements of information that are produced, stored, or processed by a computer.

data frame

A map element that defines a geographic extent, a page extent and a coordinate system, and other display properties for one or more layers in ArcMap. A dataset can be represented in one or more data frames. In data view, only one data frame is displayed at a time; in layout view, all a map's data frames are displayed at the same time. Many cartography texts use the term map body to refer to what ESRI calls a data frame.

data integrity

The degree to which the data in a database is accurate and consistent according to data model and data type. Data integrity is maintained through the creation of attribute domains and through mandatory conflict resolution between versions of a dataset.

data source

Any geographic data. Data sources may include coverages, shapefiles, rasters, or feature classes.

data type

The attribute of a variable, field, or column in a table that determines the kind of data it can store. Common data types include character, integer, decimal, single, double, and string.

data view

An all-purpose view in ArcMap and ArcReader™ for exploring, displaying, and querying geographic data. This view hides all map elements, such as titles, North arrows, and scalebars. See also layout view.

database

One or more structured sets of persistent data, managed and stored as a unit and generally associated with software to update and query the data. A simple database might be a single file with many records, each of which references the same set of fields. A GIS database includes data about the spatial locations and shapes of geographic features recorded as points, lines, areas, pixels, grid cells, or TINs, as well as their attributes.

dataset

Any organized collection of data with a common theme.

dataset precision

The mathematical exactness or detail with which a value is stored within the dataset, based on the number of significant digits that can be stored for each coordinate. In a geodatabase, the precision of the dataset is the number of internal storage units that are allocated to each of the linear units of a coordinate system.

decimal degrees

Values of latitude and longitude expressed in decimal format rather than in degrees, minutes, and seconds.

default junction type

In geometric networks, the user-established junction type which automatically connects two edge types in the absence of a current user choice, in cases where two edge types may be connectable through more than one junction type. An edge may also have a default end junction type, used for the free ends of new edges.

deflection

The creation of a segment at an angle relative to an existing segment.

degree

A unit of angular measure represented by the symbol °. The circumference of a circle contains 360 degrees, and fractions of a degree are represented as decimal values.

degrees/minutes/seconds (DMS)

A unit of measure for describing latitude and longitude. A degree is 1/360th of a circle. A degree is further divided into 60 minutes and a minute is divided into 60 seconds.

destination

The secondary object in a relationship. For example, a table containing attributes that are associated with features in a feature class.

digitizer

A device connected to a computer, consisting of a tablet and a handheld puck, that converts positions on the tablet surface as they are traced by an operator to digital x,y coordinates, yielding vector data consisting of points, lines, and polygons. See also puck.

digitizing

The process of converting the geographic features on an analog map into digital format using a digitizing tablet, or digitizer, which is connected to a computer. Features on a paper map are traced with a digitizer puck, a device similar to a mouse, and the x,y coordinates of these features are automatically recorded and stored as spatial data.

digitizing mode

One of the ways in which a digitizing tablet operates. In digitizing mode, locations on the tablet are mapped to specific locations on the screen. Moving the digitizer puck on the tablet surface causes the screen pointer to move to precisely the same position.

dimension construction methods

Procedures that dictate what type of dimension feature is created and the number of points required to complete the feature's geometry. Construction methods include simple aligned, aligned, linear, rotated linear, free aligned, and free linear.

dimension feature

A special kind of geodatabase annotation that shows specific lengths or distances on a map. A dimension feature may indicate the length of a side of a building or land parcel, or it may indicate the distance between two features such as a fire hydrant and the corner of a building. ArcInfo supports aligned dimensions and linear dimensions.

dimension feature class

A collection of spatial data in the geodatabase that shares the same dimension features. Like other feature classes in the geodatabase, all features in a dimension feature class have a geographic location and attributes and can either be inside or outside a feature dataset.

dimension style

Description of a dimension feature's symbology, what parts of it are drawn, and how it is drawn. Every time a new dimension feature is created, it is assigned a particular style according to its shared characteristics. A collection of dimension styles is associated with a dimension feature class. Styles for a dimension feature class are created, copied, and managed using ArcCatalog or the editing capabilities in ArcMap. Styles are then assigned to individual dimension features.

Dimensioning toolbar

A toolbar in ArcMap that facilitates the creation of dimension features.

direct connect

A two-tier configuration for connecting to a spatial database. Direct connect moves processing from the server to the client. It does not require the ArcSDE application server to connect to a spatial database. With direct connect, ArcSDE processing still occurs, but it primarily happens on the client side.

dirty areas

Regions surrounding features that have been altered after the initial topology validation process and require an additional topology validation to be performed to discover any errors.

disconnected editing

The process of copying data to another geodatabase, editing that data, then merging the changes with the data in the source or master geodatabase.

disk

A storage medium consisting of a round, flat, spinning plate coated with a magnetic material for recording digital information.

displacement link

A link created to define the source and destination coordinates for a spatial adjustment. Links are represented as arrows with the arrowhead pointing toward the destination location. Links can be created manually or loaded from a link file.

distance units

The units of length (for example, feet, miles, meters, or kilometers) that are used to report measurements, dimensions of shapes, and distance tolerances and offsets.

domain

See attribute domain.

double precision

The level of coordinate exactness based on the possible number of significant digits that can be stored for each coordinate. Datasets can be stored in either single or double precision. Double-precision geometries store up to 15 significant digits per coordinate (typically 13 to 14 significant digits), retaining the accuracy of much less than one meter at a global extent. See also single precision.

edge

1. A line between two nodes, points, or junctions that forms the boundary of one or more faces of a spatial entity. In an image, edges separate areas of different tones or colors. In topology, an edge defines lines or polygon boundaries; multiple features in one or more feature classes may share edges.

2. In a geometric network, a linear feature (for example, a pipeline in a sewer system). A network edge can be simple or complex. A simple edge is always connected to exactly two junction (point) features, one at each end. A complex edge is always connected to at least two junction features at its endpoints, but it can be connected to additional junction features along its length.

edge element

A line connecting nodes in the network through which a commodity, such as information, water, or electricity, presumably flows.

edge–edge rule

In geodatabases, a connectivity rule that establishes that an edge of type A may connect to an edge of type B through a junction of type C. Edge–edge rules always involve a junction type.

edge–junction cardinality

In a relationship between objects in a geodatabase, the number of edges of one type that may be associated with junctions of another type. Edge–junction cardinality defines a range of permissible connections that may occur in a one-to-many relationship between a single junction and many edges.

edge–junction rule

A connectivity rule in geodatabases establishing that an edge of type A may connect to a junction of type B.

edgematching

A spatial adjustment process that aligns features along the edge of one layer to features of an adjoining layer. The layer with the least accurate features is adjusted, and the adjoining layer is used as the control.

Edit Annotation tool

A tool on the Annotation toolbar that is used to manipulate geodatabase annotation. Text can be interactively moved, scaled, and rotated. Context menu options allow control of the position, orientation, symbology, content, size, and style of text.

edit cache

See map cache.

edit session

In ArcMap, the environment in which spatial and attribute editing take place. After starting an edit session, a user can modify feature locations, geometry, or attributes. Modifications are not saved unless the user explicitly chooses to save them.

Editor toolbar

In ArcMap, a set of tools that allows the creation and modification of features and their attributes.

ellipse

A geometric shape equivalent to a circle that is viewed obliquely. It is described mathematically as the collection of points whose distances from two given points add up to the same sum.

error

See topology error.

exception

An error that is an acceptable violation of a topology rule. In ArcMap, for example, a cul-de-sac is a legitimate exception to the Must Not Have Dangles rule.

explode

An editing process that separates a multipart feature into its component features, which become independent features.

extent

The coordinate pairs defining the minimum bounding rectangle (xmin, ymin and xmax, ymax) of a data source. All coordinates for the data source fall within this boundary.

feature

1. A group of spatial elements which together represent a real-world entity. A complex feature is made up of more than one group of spatial elements: for example, a set of line elements with the common theme of roads representing a road network.

2. A representation of a real-world object on a map. Features can be represented in a GIS as vector data (points, lines, or polygons) or as cells in a raster data format. To be displayed in a GIS, features must have geometry and locational information.

feature attribute table

See attribute table.

feature class

A collection of geographic features with the same geometry type (such as point, line, or polygon), the same attributes, and the same spatial reference. Feature classes can stand alone within a geodatabase, or they can be contained within shapefiles, coverages, or other feature datasets. Feature classes allow homogeneous features to be grouped into a single unit for data storage purposes. For example, highways, primary roads, and secondary roads can be grouped into a line feature class named "roads". In a geodatabase, feature classes can also store annotation and dimensions.

feature dataset

A collection of feature classes stored together that share the same spatial reference; that is, they have the same coordinate system and their features fall within a common geographic area. Feature classes with different geometry types may be stored in a feature dataset.

feature-linked annotation

Annotation that is stored in the geodatabase with links to features through a geodatabase relationship class. Feature-linked annotation reflects the current state of features in the geodatabase: it is automatically updated when features are moved, edited, or deleted.

field

1. A column in a table that stores the values for a single attribute.

2. The place in a database record, or in a graphical user interface, where data can be entered.

See also attribute, column.

fillet

A segment of a circle, or an arc, that may be used to connect two intersecting lines. Fillets are used to create smoothly curving connections between lines, such as edge of pavement lines at street intersections, or rounded corners on parcel features.

foreign key

A column or combination of columns in one table whose values match the primary key in another table. A value in the foreign key can only exist if there is a corresponding value in the primary key, unless the value is NULL. Foreign key—primary key relationships define a relational join.

formatted text tag

See text formatting tag.

geocoding

The process of assigning x,y coordinate values to street addresses or ZIP Codes so that they can be displayed as point features on a map. In a GIS, address geocoding requires a reference data set that contains address attributes for the area of interest.

geodatabase

An object-oriented data model introduced by ESRI that represents geographic features and attributes as objects and the relationships between objects, but is hosted inside a relational database management system. A geodatabase can store objects such as feature classes, feature datasets, nonspatial tables, and relationship classes.

geodatabase data model

A geographic data model that represents real-world geographic features as objects in an object-relational database. In the geodatabase data model, features are stored as rows in a table, and geometry is stored in a shape field. Objects in the geodatabase data model may have custom behavior.

geographic information system (GIS)

An arrangement of computer hardware, software, and geographic data that people interact with to integrate, analyze, and visualize the data; identify relationships, patterns, and trends; and find solutions to problems. The system is designed to capture, store, update, manipulate, analyze, and display the geographic information. A GIS is typically used to represent maps as data layers that can be studied and used to perform analyses.

geometric coincidence

The distance within which features in a geometric network are deemed to be coincident, and therefore, connected.

geometric network

Topologically connected edge and junction features that represent a linear network such as a road, utility, or hydrologic system.

georelational data model

A geographic data model that represents geographic features as an interrelated set of spatial and attribute data. The georelational model is the fundamental data model used in coverages.

GIS

See geographic information system (GIS).

global positioning system (GPS)

A constellation of 24 radio-emitting satellites deployed by the U.S. Department of Defense and used to determine location on the earth's surface. The orbiting satellites transmit signals that allow a GPS receiver anywhere on earth to calculate its own location through triangulation. The system is used in navigation, mapping, surveying, and other applications in which precise positioning is necessary.

gon

See gradian.

GPS

See global positioning system (GPS).

grade

See gradian.

gradian

A unit of angular measurement in which the angle of a full circle is 400 gradians and a right angle is 100 gradians.

heads-up digitizing

Manual digitization of features by tracing a mouse over features displayed on a computer monitor, often as a method of vectorizing raster data.

identity link

An anchor that prevents the movement of features during a rubber sheet spatial adjustment. See also rubber sheeting.

index

A data structure used to speed the search for records in a database or for spatial features in geographic datasets. In general, unique identifiers stored in a key field point to records or files holding more detailed information.

instance

See service.

intersect

A geometric integration of spatial datasets that preserves features or portions of features that fall within areas common to the input datasets. See also union.

IP address

Internet protocol address. The identification of each client or server computer on the Internet by a unique number. IP addresses allow data to travel between one computer and another via the Internet, and are commonly expressed as a dotted quad, with four sets of numerals separated by periods.

item

1. An element in the Catalog tree. Items include data sources such as shapefiles and geodatabases, and nonspatial elements such as folders.

2. A column of information in an INFO table.

See also field.

junction

A node joining two or more arcs.

junction element

In a linear network, a network feature that occurs at the intersection of two or more edges or at the endpoint of an edge that allows the transfer of flow between edges.

label

1. Text placed next to a feature on a map to describe or identify it.

2. To run the labeling process in ArcMap; to begin dynamically placing attribute-driven text for map features.

label class

A category of labels that represents features with the same labeling properties. For example, in a roads layer, label classes could be created to define information and style for each type of road: interstate, state highway, county road, and so on.

label expression

A statement that determines the label text. Label expressions typically concatenate or modify the contents of one or more fields, and may add additional text strings to create more informative labels. They can contain Visual Basic script or JScript to add logic, text processing, and formatting for the labels.

Label Manager

The tool used to display and set labeling properties for the currently active data frame. The Label Manager is accessible through the Labeling toolbar.

layer

1. A set of references to data sources such as a coverage, geodatabase feature class, raster, and so on that defines how the data should be displayed on a map. Layers can also define additional properties, such as which features from the data source are included. Layers can also be used as inputs to geoprocessing tools. Layers can be stored in map documents (.mxd) or saved individually as layer files (.lyr).

2. A standalone feature class in a geodatabase managed with SDE 3.

layout view

In ArcMap and ArcReader™, the view for laying out a map. Layout view shows the virtual page upon which geographic data and map elements, such as titles, legends, and scalebars, are placed and arranged for printing. See also data view.

linear dimension

A measurement of the horizontal or vertical dimension of a feature. Unlike aligned dimensions, linear dimensions do not represent the true distance between begin and end dimension points.

logical network

An abstract representation of a network. A logical network consists of edge, junction, and turn elements, and the connectivity between them. It does not contain information about the geometry or location of its elements.

magnifier window

A secondary window in ArcMap data view that shows a magnified view of a small area without changing the map extent. Moving the magnifier window around will not affect the current map display.

map

1. A graphic depiction on a flat surface of the physical features of the whole or a part of the earth or other body, or of the heavens, using shapes to represent objects, and symbols to describe their nature; at a scale whose representative fraction is less than 1:1. Maps generally use a specified projection and indicate the direction of orientation.

2. The document used in ArcMap to display and work with geographic data. In ArcMap, a map contains one or more layers of geographic data, contained in data frames, and various supporting map elements, such as a scalebar.

map cache

A setting used in ArcMap that allows temporary storage of features from a given map extent in the desktop computer's RAM, which may result in performance improvements in ArcMap for editing, feature rendering, and labeling.

map document

In ArcMap, the file that contains one map, its layout, and its associated layers, tables, charts, and reports. Map documents can be printed or embedded in other documents. Map document files have a .mxd extension.

map projection

See projection.

map topology

A temporary set of topological relationships between coincident parts of simple features on a map, used to edit shared parts of multiple features.

map units

The ground units—for example, feet, miles, meters, or kilometers—in which the coordinates of spatial data are stored.

master check-out version

The data version in the master geodatabase, created when data is checked out, that represents the state of the data at the time it was checked out. See also check-out version, master geodatabase.

master geodatabase

A geodatabase from which data has been checked out. See also check-out geodatabase.

merge policy

In geodatabases, rules that dictate what happens to the respective attributes of features that are merged together during editing in ArcMap. A merge policy can be set to assign a default value to the new attribute, summarize the values of the merged attributes, or create a weighted average from the merged attributes.

minimum bounding rectangle

A rectangle, oriented to the x and y axes, that bounds a geographic feature or a geographic dataset. It is specified by two coordinate pairs: xmin, ymin and xmax, ymax. For example, an extent can define a minimum bounding rectangle for a coverage.

mouse mode

One of the ways in which a digitizing tablet operates. In mouse mode, the digitizer puck behaves just like a mouse; there is no correlation between the position of the screen pointer and the surface of the digitizing tablet, but interface elements can be chosen with the pointer.

multipart feature

A feature that is composed of more than one physical part but only references one set of attributes in the database. For example, in a layer of states, the state of Hawaii could be considered a multipart feature. Although composed of many islands, it would be recorded in the database as one feature.

multipoint feature

A feature that consists of more than one point but only references one set of attributes in the database. For example, a system of oil wells might be considered a multipoint feature, since there is a single set of attributes for multiple well holes.

multiuser geodatabase

A geodatabase in an RDBMS served to client applications—for example, ArcMap—by ArcSDE. Multiuser geodatabases can be very large and support multiple concurrent editors. They are supported on a variety of commercial RDBMSs including Oracle®, Microsoft® SQL Server™, IBM® DB2®, and Informix®.

network

A set of edge, junction, and turn elements and the connectivity between them; also known as a logical network. In other words, an interconnected set of lines representing possible paths from one location to another. A city streets layer is an example of a network.

network feature

One of the topologically connected edge or junction features, representing a linear network, such as a road, utility, or hydrologic system, that compose a geometric network.

network trace

A function that follows connectivity in a geometric network. Specific kinds of network tracing include finding features that are connected, finding common ancestors, finding loops, tracing upstream, and tracing downstream. See also geometric network.

node

In a geodatabase, the point representing the beginning or ending point of an edge, topologically linked to all the edges that meet there.

null value

The absence of a recorded value for a geographic feature. A null value differs from a value of zero in that zero may represent the measure of an attribute, while a null value indicates that no measurement has been taken.

object

In GIS, a digital representation of a discrete spatial entity. An object may belong to an object class and will thus have attribute values and behavior in common with other defined elements.

object class

1. In a geodatabase, a collection of nonspatial data of the same type or theme. While spatial objects (features) are stored in feature classes in a geodatabase, nonspatial objects are stored in object classes.

2. A collection of objects in the geodatabase that have the same behavior and the same set of attributes. All objects in the geodatabase are stored in object classes.

origin

The primary object in a relationship. For example, a feature class containing points where measurements are taken; the measurements are stored in another table. See also relationship, destination.

overshoot

The portion of an arc digitized past its intersection with another arc.

overview window

A secondary window in ArcMap data view that shows the full extent of the data, without changing the map extent. A red box in the window represents the current map extent.

pan

To move an onscreen display window up, down, or across a map image without changing the viewing scale.

parametric curve

A curve that is defined mathematically rather than by a series of connected vertices. A parametric curve has only two vertices, one at each end.

password

A secret series of characters that enables a user to access a computer, data file, or program. The user must enter his or her password before the computer will respond to commands. The password helps ensure that unauthorized users do not access the computer, file, or program.

personal geodatabase

A geodatabase that stores data in a singleuser relational database management system (RDBMS). A personal geodatabase can be read simultaneously by several users, but only one user at a time can write data into it.

planarize

The process of creating multiple line features by splitting longer features at the places where they intersect other line features. This process can be useful when you have nontopological linework that has been spaghetti digitized or imported from a CAD drawing.

point

A zero-dimensional abstraction of an object; a single x,y coordinate pair that represents a geographic feature too small to be displayed as a line or area at that scale.

point mode digitizing

A method of digitizing in which a series of precise points, or vertices, are created. See also stream mode digitizing.

polygon

A closed, two-dimensional figure with at least three sides that represents an area. It is used in GIS to describe spatial elements with a discrete area, such as parcels, political districts, areas of homogeneous land use, and soil types.

polyline

A two-dimensional feature representing a line containing one or more line segments—that is, any line defined by two or more points. Line features such as boundaries, roads, streams, and power cables are usually polylines.

port number

The TCP/IP port number on which an ArcSDE geodatabase service is communicating.

post

During versioned geodatabase editing, the process of applying the current edit session to the reconciled target version.

precision (dataset)

See dataset precision.

primary key

A column or set of columns in a database that stores a unique value for each record. A primary key allows no duplicate values and cannot be NULL.

projection

A method by which the curved surface of the earth is portrayed on a flat surface. This generally requires a systematic mathematical transformation of the earth's graticule of lines of longitude and latitude onto a plane. It can be visualized as a transparent globe with a light bulb at its center casting lines of latitude and longitude onto a sheet of paper. Generally, the paper is either flat and placed tangent to the globe (a planar or azimuthal projection) or formed into a cone or cylinder and placed over the globe (cylindrical and conical projections). Every map projection distorts distance, area, shape, direction, or some combination thereof.

property

An attribute of an object defining one of its characteristics or an aspect of its behavior. For example, the Visible property affects whether a control can be seen at run time. You can set an item's properties using its Properties dialog box.

pseudonode

In a geodatabase topology or ArcInfo coverage, a node connecting only two edges or arcs, or the endpoint of an edge or arc that connects to itself (an island).

puck

The handheld device used with a digitizer to record positions from the tablet surface.

pull check-in

A check-in operation initiated from a master geodatabase.

push check-in

A check-in operation initiated from a check-out geodatabase.

query

A request that selects features or records from a database. A query is often written as a statement or logical expression.

radian

The angle subtended by an arc of a circle that is the same length as the radius of the circle, approximately 57 degrees, 17 minutes, and 44.6 seconds. A circle is 2(pi) radians.

range domain

A type of attribute domain that defines the range of permissible values for a numeric attribute. For example, the permissible range of values for a pipe diameter could be between 1 and 32 inches.

rank

A method of assigning an accuracy value to feature classes to avoid having vertices from a feature class collected with a high level of accuracy being snapped to vertices from a less accurate feature class. Vertices from higher ranking feature classes will not be moved when snapping with vertices with lower ranked feature

classes. The highest rank is 1; up to 50 different ranks can be assigned.

raster

A spatial data model that defines space as an array of equally sized cells arranged in rows and columns. Each cell contains an attribute value and location coordinates. Unlike a vector structure, which stores coordinates explicitly, raster coordinates are contained in the ordering of the matrix. Groups of cells that share the same value represent geographic features. See also vector.

RDBMS

Relational database management system. A type of database in which the data is organized across several tables. Tables are associated with each other through common fields. Data items can be recombined from different files. In contrast to other database structures, an RDBMS requires few assumptions about how data is related or how it will be extracted from the database.

reconcile

In version management, to merge all modified datasets, feature classes, and tables in the current edit session with a second target version. All features and rows that do not conflict are merged into the edit session, replacing the current features or rows. Features that are modified in more than one version are conflicts and require further resolution via the Conflict Resolution dialog box.

record

1. A set of related data fields, often a row in a database, containing all the attribute values for a single entity. For example, in an address database, the fields which together provide the address for a specific individual comprise one record. In SQL terms, a record is analogous to a tuple.

2. A row in a database or in an attribute table that contains all of the attribute values for a single feature.

reference scale

The scale at which symbols will appear on the page at their true size, specified in page units. As the extent is changed, the text and symbols will change scale along with the display. Without a reference scale, the symbols will look the same at all map scales. ArcGIS Desktop uses reference scales for annotation groups, geodatabase annotation feature classes, geodatabase dimension feature classes, and data frames.

relate

An operation that establishes a temporary connection between records in two tables using an item common to both.

relational database management system

See RDBMS.

relational join

An operation by which two data tables are related through a common field, known as a key.

relationship

An association or link between two objects in a geodatabase. Relationships can exist between spatial objects (features in feature classes), between nonspatial objects (rows in a table), or between spatial and nonspatial objects.

relationship class

An item in the geodatabase that stores information about a relationship. A relationship class is visible as an item in the ArcCatalog tree or contents view.

relative mode

See mouse mode.

row

1. A record in an attribute table.

2. The horizontal dimension of a table composed of a set of columns containing one data item each.

rubber banding

See rubber sheeting.

rubber sheeting

A procedure to adjust the coordinates of all the data points in a dataset to allow a more accurate match between known locations and a few data points within the dataset. Preserves the interconnectivity, or topology, between points and objects through stretching, shrinking, or reorienting their interconnecting lines.

scanning

The process of capturing data in raster format with a device called a scanner. Some scanners also use software to convert raster data to vector data.

schema

1. The structure or design of a database or database object such as a table. In a relational database, the schema defines the tables, the fields in each table, and the relationships between fields and tables. Schemas are generally stored in a data dictionary. In ArcCatalog, the schema can either be modeled in UML using a CASE tool or defined directly within ArcCatalog using wizards.

2. The organization and definitions of the feature classes, tables, and other items in a geodatabase. Creating or deleting items, or changing their definitions, modifies the schema. The schema does not include actual data, only its structure.

schema-only check-out

A type of check-out that creates the schema of the data being checked out in the check-out geodatabase but does not copy any data.

segment

A line that connects vertices. For example, in a sketch of a building, a segment might represent one wall.

select

To choose from a number or group of features or records; to create a separate set or subset.

selectable layers

Layers from which features can be selected in ArcMap with the interactive selection tools. Selectable layers can be chosen using the Set Selectable Layers command in the Selection menu, or on the optional Selection tab in the table of contents.

selected set

A subset of features in a layer or records in a table that is chosen by the user.

selection anchor

In an ArcMap editing session, a small "x" located in the center of selected features. The selection anchor is used in the snapping environment, or when rotating, moving, and scaling features.

server

A computer in a network that is used to provide services—such as access to files or e-mail routing—to other computers in the network. Servers may also be used to host Web sites or applications that can be accessed remotely.

service

A collection of persistent, server-side software processes that provides data or computing resources for client applications. Examples include ArcSDE application server and DBMS server.

shape

The characteristic appearance or visible form of a geographic object. Geographic objects can be represented on a map using one of three basic shapes: points, lines, or polygons.

shapefile

A vector data storage format for storing the location, shape, and attributes of geographic features. A shapefile is stored in a set of related files and contains one feature class.

shared boundary

A segment or boundary common to two features. For example, in a parcel database, adjacent parcels will share a boundary. Another example might be a parcel that shares a boundary on one side with a river. The segment of the river that coincides with the parcel boundary would share the same coordinates as the parcel boundary.

shared vertex

A vertex common to multiple features. For example, in a parcel database, adjacent parcels will share a vertex at the common corner.

shortcut key

A command's shortcut key executes the command directly without first having to open and navigate a menu. For example, Ctrl + C is a well-known shortcut for copying a file in Windows.

simple feature

A point, line, or polygon that is not part of a geometric network and is not an annotation feature, dimension feature, or custom object.

simple relationship

A link or association between data sources that exist independently of each other.

single precision

Refers to a level of coordinate exactness based on the number of significant digits that can be stored for each coordinate. Single precision numbers store up to seven significant digits for each coordinate, retaining a precision of ±5 meters in an extent of 1,000,000 meters. Datasets can be stored in either single or double precision coordinates. See also double precision.

sketch

In ArcMap, a shape that represents a feature's geometry. Every existing feature on a map has this alternate form, a sketch, that allows visualization of that feature's composition, with all vertices and segments of the feature visible. When features are edited in ArcMap, the sketch is modified, not the original feature. A sketch must be created in order to create a feature. Only line and polygon sketches can be created, since points have neither vertices nor segments.

sketch constraint

In ArcMap editing, an angle or length limitation that can be placed on segments created using the Sketch tool.

sketch operation

In ArcMap, an editing operation that is performed on an existing sketch. Examples are Insert Vertex, Delete Vertex, Flip, Trim, Delete Sketch, Finish Sketch, and Finish Part. All of these operations are available from the Sketch context menu.

Sketch tool

In ArcMap, a tool that adds points, vertices, or segments to create an edit sketch. Sketch points can be defined by heads-up digitizing, snapping, or manually entering coordinates.

snapping

An automatic editing operation in which points or features within a specified distance or tolerance of other points or features are moved to match or coincide exactly with each other's coordinates.

snapping environment

Settings in the ArcMap Snapping Environment window and Editing Options dialog box that define the conditions in which snapping will occur. These settings include snapping tolerance, snapping properties, and snapping priority.

snapping priority

The order in which snapping will occur by layer during an ArcMap editing session, set from the Snapping Environment window. See also snapping environment.

snapping properties

In ArcMap editing, a combination of a shape to snap to and a method for what part of the shape will be snapped to. Snapping properties can be set to have a feature snap to a vertex, edge, or endpoint of features in a specific layer. For example, a layer snapping property might allow snapping to the vertices of buildings. A more generic, sketch-specific snapping property might allow snapping to the vertices of a sketch being created.

snapping tolerance

In an ArcMap editing session, the distance within which the pointer or a feature will snap to another location. If the location being snapped to (vertex, boundary, midpoint, or connection) is within that distance, the pointer will automatically snap. Snapping tolerance can be measured using either map units or pixels.

SnapTip

In ArcMap, a user-assistance component that displays an onscreen description of the layer name or target being snapped to when the mouse pointer is paused over it. SnapTips only appear during an ArcMap edit session if they are enabled.

spatial adjustment

An ArcMap editing function that allows transformation, rubber sheeting, and edgematching of data, as well as attribute transfer.

spatial database

Any database that contains spatial data.

spatial domain

For a spatial dataset, the defined precision and allowable range for x and y coordinates and for m- and z-values, if present. The spatial domain must be specified by the user when creating a geodatabase feature dataset or standalone feature class.

spatial join

A type of table join operation in which fields from one layer's attribute table are appended to another layer's attribute table based on the relative locations of the features in the two layers.

spatial reference

The coordinate system used to store a spatial dataset. For feature classes and feature datasets within a geodatabase, the spatial reference also includes the spatial domain.

split policy

All attribute domains in geodatabases have a split policy associated with them. When a feature is split into two new features in ArcMap, the split policies dictate what happens to the value of the attribute with which the domain is associated. Standard split policies are duplicate, default value, and geometry ratio.

SQL

See Structured Query Language (SQL).

standard annotation

Annotation that is stored in the geodatabase, consisting of geographically placed text strings that are not associated with features in the geodatabase.

sticky move tolerance

When editing in ArcMap, a setting that defines the minimum number of pixels the pointer must move on the screen before a selected feature is moved.

stream mode digitizing

A method of digitizing in which points are recorded automatically at preset intervals of either distance or time. See also point mode digitizing.

stream tolerance

During stream digitizing, the minimum interval between vertices. Stream tolerance is measured in map units.

Structured Query Language (SQL)

A syntax for defining and manipulating data from a relational database. Developed by IBM in the 1970s, SQL has become an industry standard for query languages in most relational database management systems.

style

An organized collection of predefined colors, symbols, properties of symbols, and map elements. Styles promote standardization and consistency in mapping products.

subsumption

Within a geometric network, the replacement of an orphan junction by a non-orphan junction from a user-defined feature class. The original junction is deleted from the network, and the non-orphan junction assumes the connectivity of the subsumed orphan junction.

subtype

In geodatabases, a subset of features in a feature class or objects in a table that share the same attributes. For example, the streets in a streets feature class could be categorized into three subtypes: local streets, collector streets, and arterial streets. Creating subtypes can be more efficient than creating many feature classes or tables in a geodatabase—for example, a geodatabase with a dozen feature classes that have subtypes will perform better than a geodatabase with a hundred feature classes. Subtypes also make editing data faster and more accurate because default attribute values and domains can be set up. For example, a Local Street subtype could be created and defined so that whenever this type of street is added to the feature class, its speed limit attribute is automatically set to 35 miles per hour.

symbol

A graphic representation of a geographic feature or class of features that helps identify it and distinguish it from other features on a map. For example, line symbols represent arc features; marker symbols, points; shade symbols, polygons; and text symbols, annotation. Many characteristics define symbols including color, size, angle, and pattern.

symbology

The set of conventions, or rules, that define how geographic features are represented with symbols on a map. A characteristic of a feature may influence the size, color, and shape of the symbol used.

synchronization version

A data version created in a check-out geodatabase when data is checked out to that geodatabase. This version exists as a copy of the original data and represents the state of the data at the time of the check out. See also check-out version, master check-out version.

table

A set of data elements arranged in rows and columns. Each row represents an individual entity, record, or feature and each column represents a single field or attribute value. A table has a specified number of columns but can have any number of rows.

table of contents

A list of data frames and layers on a map that show how the data is symbolized.

tabular data

Descriptive information, usually alphanumeric, that is stored in rows and columns in a database and can be linked to map features. See also table.

tagged value

Used to set additional properties of UML elements. For example, you can set the maximum number of characters in a string field by using a tagged value.

target layer

In an ArcMap editing session, the layer to which edits will be applied. The target layer must be specified when creating new features and modifying existing features.

text formatting tag

Tags used with text in ArcGIS that allow formatting to be modified for a portion of a text string. This allows the creation of mixed-format text where, for example, one word in a sentence is underlined. Text formatting tags adhere to XML syntax rules, and can be used most places where both a text string and a text symbol can be specified. The tags are most commonly used with labels, annotation, and graphic text.

tic

A registration or geographic control point for a coverage representing a known location on the earth's surface. Tics allow all coverage features to be recorded in a common coordinate system such as Universal Transverse Mercator (UTM). Tics are used to register map sheets when they are mounted on a digitizer. They are also used to transform the coordinates of a coverage, for example, from digitizer units (inches) to the appropriate values for a coordinate system (meters for UTM).

tolerance

The minimum or maximum variation allowed when processing or editing a geographic feature's coordinates. For example, during editing, if a second point is placed within the snapping tolerance distance of an existing point, the second point will be snapped to the existing point.

topological association

The spatial relationship between features that share geometry such as boundaries and vertices. When a boundary or vertex shared by two or more features is edited using the topology tools in ArcMap, the shape of each of those features is updated.

topological feature

A feature that supports network connectivity that is established and maintained based on geometric coincidence.

topology

1. In geodatabases, a set of governing rules applied to feature classes that explicitly defines the spatial relationships that must exist between feature data.

2. In an ArcInfo coverage, the spatial relationships between connecting or adjacent features in a geographic data layer (for example, arcs, nodes, polygons, and points). Topological relationships are used for spatial modeling operations that do not require coordinate information.

3. The geometric relationships, determined mathematically, between connecting or adjacent features in a geographic dataset. Topology may include information about connectivity, direction, length, adjacency, and polygon definition. Topology makes most types of geographic analysis possible because it allows analysis of spatial relationships between features.

topology cache

A temporary collection of edges and nodes used in ArcMap to query and edit the topological coincidence between features. The cache is built for the current display extent and is stored in the computer's memory.

topology error

Violation of a topology rule detected during the topology validation process.

topology fix

In ArcMap, a predefined method for correcting topology errors. For example, predefined topology fixes for a dangling line include snapping, trimming, or extending to another line.

topology rule

An instruction to the geodatabase defining the permissible relationships of features within a given feature class or between features in two different feature classes.

tracing

The process of building a set of network features based on some procedure.

transaction

1. A group of atomic data operations that comprise a complete operational task, such as inserting a row into a table.

2. A logical unit of work as defined by a user. Transactions can be data definition (create an object), data manipulation (update an object), or data read (select from an object).

transformation

Converting the coordinates of a map or an image from one system to another, typically by shifting, rotating, scaling, skewing, or projecting them. Also known as rectification, the conversion process requires resampling of values.

transit rule

1. An infrequently used rule for adjusting the closure error in a traverse. This rule is used infrequently since it is only valid in cases where the measured lines are approximately parallel to the grid of the coordinate system in which the traverse is computed. Hence, modern literature does not recommend its use. It assumes that course directions are measured with a higher degree of precision than the distances. Compared to a compass adjustment, the transit rule will adjust course distances more and course directions less. This rule distributes the closure error by changing the Northings and Eastings of each traverse point in proportion to the Northing and Easting differences in each course. More specifically, a correction is computed for each Northing coordinate as the difference in the course's Northings divided by the sum of all the courses' Northing differences. Similarly, a correction is computed for each Easting coordinate using the Easting coordinate differences. The corrections are applied additively to each successive coordinate pair, until the final coordinate pair is adjusted by the whole closure error amount.

2. One of three adjustment methods available for adjusting closure error for a traverse computation. The other two methods are the Crandall rule and the compass rule.

traverse

1. A predefined path or route across or over a set of geometric coordinates.

2. A method of surveying in which lengths and directions of lines between points on the earth are obtained by or from field measurements across terrain or a digital elevation model.

traverse course

In ArcMap, a group of observed values that define a new coordinate. A traverse course starts from a preexisting coordinate, or a coordinate computed from the previous course.

true curve

See parametric curve.

two-tier connection

See direct connect.

undershoot

An arc that does not extend far enough to intersect another arc.

union

A topological overlay of two polygonal spatial datasets that preserve features that fall within the spatial extent of either input dataset; that is, all features from both coverages are retained. See also intersect.

username

The identification used for authentication when a user logs in to a geodatabase.

validate (topology)

The process of comparing the topology rules against the features in a dataset. When you validate a topology, features that violate the rules are marked as error features. Topology validation is typically performed after the initial topology rules have been defined, after the feature classes have been modified, or if additional feature classes or rules have been added to the map topology.

validation rule

A rule applied to objects in the geodatabase to ensure that their state is consistent with the system that the database is modeling. The geodatabase supports attribute, connectivity, relationship, and custom validation rules.

VBA

Visual Basic for Applications. The embedded programming environment for automating, customizing, and extending ESRI applications, such as ArcMap and ArcCatalog. It offers the same tools as Visual Basic (VB) in the context of an existing application. A VBA program operates on objects that represent the application, and can be used to create custom symbols, workspace extensions, commands, tools, dockable windows, and other objects that can be plugged into the ArcGIS framework.

vector

A coordinate-based data model that represents geographic features as points, lines, and polygons. Each point feature is represented as a single coordinate pair, while line and polygon features are represented as ordered lists of vertices. Attributes are associated with each feature, as opposed to a raster data model, which associates attributes with grid cells. See also raster.

vector data model

An abstraction of the real world in which spatial elements are represented in the form of points, lines, and polygons. These are geographically referenced to a coordinate system.

version

In geodatabases, an alternative representation of the database that has an owner, a description, a permission (private, protected, or public), and a parent version. Versions are not affected by changes occurring in other versions of the database.

vertex

One of a set of ordered x,y coordinate pairs that defines a line or polygon feature.

virtual page

The map page as seen in layout view in ArcMap

wizard

An interactive user interface that helps a user complete a task one step at a time. It is often implemented as a sequence of dialog boxes that the user can move through, filling in required details. A wizard is usually used for long, difficult, or complex tasks.

work flow

An organization's established processes for design, construction, and maintenance of facilities.

work order

One specific task that proceeds through each stage of an organization's work flow process, including design, acceptance, and construction in the field.

workspace

A container for geographic data. A workspace can be a folder that contains shapefiles, an ArcInfo workspace that contains coverages, a geodatabase or a feature dataset.

Index

D

Data 427, 428
  adding for editing 28
  editor
    mentioned 3
  field collected 89
  integrity
    defined 458
  loading from a geodatabase 28
  quality
    and topology 120
  source
    defined 459
  stopping the drawing of 28, 259, 260
Data frames
  defined 458
  editing a map with multiple 30
Data type
  defined 459
Data view
  defined 459
  editing in
    mentioned 4
Database 427, 428
  defined 459
Dataset
  defined 459
  precision
    defined 459
Decimal degrees
  defined 459
Default junctions
  described 328
  junction type
    defined 459
Default values
  editing in ArcMap 387
  mentioned 120
Deflection 69–70
  defined 459

Degrees
  defined 459
  described 111
Degrees Minutes Seconds
  defined 459
  described 111
  valid input formats 111
Deleting
  features 43
Delta X, Y 54
Destination
  defined 459
Digitizer
  aligning the map on 187
  attaching the map to 186–187
  configuring puck buttons
    for streaming 197
    using programming code 186, 194, 197
    using WinTab manager setup program 186
  creating features with 185
  defined 459
  installing driver software 186
  puck
    defined 469
  setting up 186
Digitizing
  a projected map 186
  creating a line or polygon 63
  creating a point or vertex 52
  defined 460
  described 185
  digitizer tab missing 189
  freehand 185
  heads-up
    defined 464
  in digitizing (absolute) mode 192, 193–194
  in mouse (relative) mode 192
  in point mode 192, 193–194
  in stream mode 192, 195–196, 197
  installing digitizer driver software 186
  mode
    defined 460

Digitizing (continued)
  preparing the map 186
  switching between digitizing and mouse
    modes 192
  switching between point and stream modes
    196
  using snapping 194
Digitizing tablet. *See* Digitizer
Dimension feature class
  and topology 144
  defined 460
Dimension features
  Attributes dialog box 396
  autodimension tools 392, 393
    baseline dimension 393, 419
    continue dimension 393, 417, 421
    dimension edge 393, 416
    mentioned 394, 398
  changing style 425
  construction methods
    aligned 393, 402
    defined 460
    described 392
    free aligned 393, 410
    free linear 393, 413
    linear 393, 404
    rotated aligned 393, 407
    simple aligned 391, 393, 399
  creating. *See* Dimension features: auto-
    dimension tools
  defined 460
  editing 392
  modifying 394, 396
    process described 423
  properties (table) 395, 397
Dimension styles
  baseline height 420
  defined 460
  described 394
Dimensioning toolbar 394, 398
  defined 460

Network trace
  defined 467
Nodes
  defined 467
  described 142
North Azimuth
  described 110
Null value
  defined 467

O

Object
  and relationships 302
  defined 467
Object class
  defined 467
Object Loader. *See also* Loading
Origin
  defined 467
Overshoot
  defined 467
Overview window
  defined 467

P

Pan
  defined 467
Parallel segments. *See* Segments: creating:
    parallel to existing
Parametric curve
  defined 467
Password
  defined 467
Pasting
  features. *See* Copying: and pasting features
Perpendicular segments. *See* Segments: creating:
    perpendicular to existing
Personal geodatabase
  defined 468

Placing points along a line 224
Planarize 183
  defined 468
  tool 181
    mentioned 140
Point
  defined 468
Point features
  creating 20, 47, 52–56, 65, 68
Point mode digitizing. *See also* Digitizing: in
    point mode
  defined 468
Polar angle
  described 110
Polygon
  defined 468
Polygon feature class
  creating from lines 139, 180
Polygon features
  creating 20–21, 63–67
  cutting a polygon shape out of 217
  reshaping. *See* Reshaping features
  splitting 214–215
  squaring 67–68
Polyline
  defined 468
Port number
  defined 468
Post 428, 441, 442, 446–447, 450
  defined 468
Precision
  setting 44
Primary display field 285
Primary key 302, 303
  defined 468
Privileges
  and versioning
    described 432, 441, 451
    private 432
    protected 432
    public 432

Projection
  defined 468
Projective transformation. *See also* Spatial
    adjustment
  spatial adjustment 247
Property
  changing for a sketch 235
  defined 468
Proportionally dividing a line 86–87
Pseudonodes
  defined 469
  described 142
  topology rules 128
Puck
  defined 469
Pull check-in
  defined 469
Push check-in
  defined 469

Q

Quadrant Bearing
  described 111
Query
  defined 469

R

Radians
  defined 469
  described 111
Range domain
  defined 469
Rank
  defined 469
  described 121
Raster
  defined 469

Reconcile 441, 446–447, 450
  defined 469
  described 441
Record
  defined 469
Reference scale
  defined 470
Registering a map
  adding additional control points 190
  described 188–189
  digitizing control points 188
  ensuring accuracy when 191
  entering ground coordinates 188
  error reporting 187, 189
  establishing control points 186
  for the first time 188
  removing ground coordinate records 190
  saving ground coordinates 188–189
  using existing tic files or saved coordinates 190–191
Relate
  defined 470
Related objects. *See also* Relationships
  deleting 320
Relational database management system
    (RDBMS)
  defined 469
Relational join
  defined 470
Relationship class
  and annotation 357
  and topology 144
  and versioning 442, 444
  composite 354
  defined 470
  destination class 354
  foreign key. *See* Foreign key
  origin class 354
  path labels
    editing in ArcMap
        307, 308, 310, 313, 314, 317, 319
    in ArcMap editing environment 320
  primary key. *See* Primary key

Relationships
  and versioning 444
  composite 321
  creating 301, 310
  creating and deleting 302
  creating new 303
  defined 470
  deleting 303, 314
  destination object 322, 354
  editing 307
  origin object 321, 354
  related object 314, 320, 321, 444
  rules
    in ArcMap editing environment 324
    mentioned 292
  splitting features 305
  validating 324
Relative mode. *See* Digitizing: in mouse (relative) mode
Reporting measurements. *See* Measurements: setting number of decimal places for reporting
Reshaping features
  by adding vertices 228–229
  by deleting vertices 228–229
  by moving vertices 230–233
  using a sketch you draw 226–227
Residual
  understanding 247
RMS error 187, 189. *See also* Digitizing
  equation 248
  understanding 247
Rod
  described 117
Root mean square error. *See* RMS error
Rotate
  a point's symbology 41
  annotation 373, 389. *See also* Annotation
    in rotate mode 374
  features 39, 41
Rotate mode 374. *See also* Annotation

Row. *See also* Object
  defined 470
Rubber sheeting 248. *See also* Spatial adjustment: rubber sheeting
  defined 470
Rule
  topology 121

S

Saving edits 29, 30
Scaling features 239
Scanning
  defined 470
Scenarios
  and versioning 450
Schema
  defined 470, 471
SDE. *See* ArcSDE
Segment Deflection. *See also* Editing: creating segments: using angles from existing segments
  command 72
Segments
  creating
    at an angle from the last segment 71
    by tracing features 81
    circular arcs 76–78
    parallel to existing 74
    perpendicular to existing 74
    using angles and lengths 69–70
    using angles from existing segments 72
  defined 471
  described 46
Select
  defined 471
Selectable layers
  defined 471
Selected set
  defined 471

Topology (continued)
  symbology 170
    layers 171
  toolbar
    adding 141
  tools
    Edit tool mentioned 122, 135
    Edit tool, moving nodes and edges with
      133
    editing and managing 5
    toolbar functionality 141
  validation 173
    defined 476
    selected area 173
    visible extent 173
    whole topology 173
Topology rules. *See* Rule: topology; Topology:
  rules
Trace tool. *See* Editing tools
Tracing. *See also* Editing tools
  defined 475
Transaction 441, 450–451
  defined 476
Transformation
  defined 476
Transit correction
  defined 476
  traverse adjustment 97
Traverse
  adding segment
    angle-distance 91
    curve 92
    direction-distance 90
    tangent curve 93
  adjusting
    compass correction 97
    Crandall correction 97
    process 98
    techniques 97
    transit correction 97
  closure report 96

Traverse (continued)
  convert angles and distances 114
  course
    defined 476
  defined 476
  loading 100
  modifying segment 95
  saving 99
  starting from known coordinate 89
  Traverse tool 89
Trimming line features 85, 218–220
True curve. *See also* Circular arcs
  defined 476

U

UML model
  setting tagged values 474
Undershoot
  defined 476
Union. *See also* Combining features: from
    different layers
  defined 476
Unplaced annotation 360, 362. *See also*
    Annotation
Unstacking
  annotation 384
Username
  defined 476

V

Valid feature 325
Validation
  geometric network 350
  topology 173
    defined 476
Validation rules. *See also* Attribute
    domains; Connectivity
    rules; Relationships: rules; Topology:
    validation

Validation rules (continued)
  defined 477
  mentioned 120
  validation order 292
VBA
  configuring digitizer puck buttons using
    186, 194
  defined 477
Vector datasets
  comparing the structure of 17
  defined 477
  vector data model
    defined 477
Version
  administering
    in ArcCatalog 431
  and annotation 390
  and ArcMap 438–439
  and editing 441–445
  autoreconciliation 441
    enabling and disabling 446
  changing 439
    Change Version command 439
  conflict. *See also* Conflict
    displaying 448
    resolution 441
    resolving 449
  creating
    in ArcCatalog 431
    in ArcMap 438
  defined 427, 477
  described 428–429
  descriptions 433
  editing 446–447
  in ArcMap 438–439
  modifying
    changing properties 434
    compressing 437
    deleting 433
    renaming 433
  permissions 432

Version (continued)
   post. *See also* Post
      process 447
   reconcile. *See also* Reconcile
      process 447
   refresh 434, 439
   registering data 430
   scenarios 450
   transaction. *See* Transaction
Vertices
   adding 21, 228, 236
      to annotation baseline sketches 382
   and annotation features 382
   and dimension features 394
   creating 52–56, 387
   defined 477
   deleting 21, 64, 194, 228
      from annotation baseline sketches 382
   deleting multiple while streaming with a
         digitizer 196
   described 46
   moving
      by dragging 230
      by specifying x,y coordinates 231–232
      relative to the current location 233–234
   undoing and redoing 55, 65
Virtual page
   defined 477
Visual Basic for Applications. *See* VBA

W

Wizard
   defined 477
Work flow 428
   defined 477
Work order 428
   defined 477
Workspace 438
   defined 477
   refreshing (versioning) 440

Y

Yard
   described 117

Z

Z-values
   editing 238
   using the current control 238